BEAUTY&
ATROCITY

BEAUTY& ATROCITY

PEOPLE, POLITICS AND IRELAND'S FIGHT FOR PEACE

JOSHUA LEVINE

Collins

First published in 2010 by Collins

HarperCollins Publishers
77–85 Fulham Palace Road
London W6 8JB

www.harpercollins.co.uk

13 12 11 10 09
9 8 7 6 5 4 3 2 1

A catalogue record for this book is
available from the British Library

ISBN 978 0 00 730947 4

Printed and bound in Great Britain by
Clays Ltd, St Ives plc

Mixed Sources
Product group from well-managed
forests and other controlled sources
www.fsc.org Cert no. SW-COC-001806
© 1996 Forest Stewardship Council

FSC is a non-profit international organisation established to promote the
responsible management of the world's forests. Products carrying the FSC
label are independently certified to assure consumers that they come
from forests that are managed to meet the social, economic and
ecological needs of present and future generations.

Find out more about HarperCollins and the environment at
www.harpercollins.co.uk/green

CONTENTS

1

THE STRANGER

In the autumn of 2008 I flew into Belfast to begin a journey. I had little idea where it would take me, although I knew that its first night would be spent in the Madison Hotel on Botanic Avenue. As I stood at the airport baggage carousel, I was nervous. I had never been to Northern Ireland before, and I decided that I ought to have a first impression, so I began to pay deliberate attention to everything around me. In the end I needn't have worried because my first actual impression almost overwhelmed me. The taxi driver taking me into town asked my name and, within a beat of my reply, asked whether I was 'a Jew'. I said I was. 'My son's name is Reuben,' he said. 'He sounds like more of a Jew than you.' I had absolutely no idea what to say. 'The Catholics are anti-Semitic, they support the PLO,' he continued, 'but I'm a Presbyterian and *we like you*.' He assured me that I had nothing to worry about because, when Christ comes again, the Jews are going straight to heaven. If I wanted to understand more, then I should visit an Orange Lodge. On he went, as though sent by the Tourist Board to give me an unforgettable first impression. Eventually, with a smile and a handshake, he dropped me outside the hotel.

I was in Belfast to try to discover what the Troubles had been about. I wanted to find out the history behind them, and in order to do that I wanted to meet the people who had lived through them, those who had suffered, and those who had caused the suffering. I wanted to know why people had behaved as they did, how representative they had been, and whether they now try to justify their actions. And I wanted a sense of the future, of whether Northern Ireland is moving beyond the Troubles. And so here I was, ten minutes into my journey, with lots of questions, and a place in heaven to look forward to.

I have a particular memory of the Troubles. Bombs and bullets did not affect me in any real way, but it is a memory worth recounting because it mirrors the experience of many who lived in London during the Seventies and Eighties, for whom the Troubles were always in the background. On a summer's afternoon in 1982 I was at home, wearing a green football shirt and gloves. I cleared some space on the floor, took down a picture, and started throwing a ball against the wall, diving to save it as it came back. I would play like that for hours, but on this particular day I was interrupted by a loud noise. Half a mile away, in the Inner Circle of Regents Park, a bomb planted underneath a bandstand blew up. In that moment seven people were torn to pieces.

I knew the bandstand very well. My father would take my sister and me to sit in deckchairs by the lake, where we would listen to brass bands playing funny mixes of military marches and West End show tunes. And now the masked bogeymen of the Provisional Irish Republican Army had decided to kill the performers – who had been in the middle of a medley from *Oliver!* – in front of people like us who'd come along to listen. According to a member of the audience, 'Suddenly there was this tremendous whoosh and I saw a leg fly past me. The bandstand seemed to lift off and I could see bandsmen flying through the air. For a moment I could not believe it.' I had not witnessed the bomb, but I can remember the bleakness and confusion that it conjured up. Who in the name of God had done this and why?

As the years went by, I, like almost every other English person, became very familiar with reports of the Troubles in the papers and on the news. But the sensible questions never seemed to be asked. The reports all blended into one another, leaving me with a tired stream of images so clichéd they sometimes bordered on the comic. I got to know men in bowler hats marching down streets, men in balaclavas firing over coffins and men with dubbed voices defending the latest outrage, but I had no context for these people, no real sense of them. I never noticed any genuine discussion about what they were fighting for, or how the situation might be resolved. Bombs and death just seemed to be things that happened over there and sometimes over here. The media seemed to want us to believe that Northern Ireland was populated by two kinds of people: bigots and psychopaths. If the real attitudes and beliefs of the people of Northern Ireland were ever reported – as they must have been – they certainly never filtered through to me. I cannot have been the only person in Britain to have been left in the dark about a subject that was never out of the news. Now I wanted to find out more.

As I was to discover, I had not been alone in my ignorance. The British government had very little sense of historical context when it sent its troops into Northern Ireland in August 1969. The arrival of its soldiers, in response to escalating violence, marked the start of the government's active participation in the Troubles, and represented an unusually vigorous British reaction to an old problem. For the first fifty years of Northern Ireland's existence, the British government had kept the province at arm's length. Northern Ireland was given its own parliament at Stormont, to set policy on internal matters, allowing Whitehall and Westminster to remain in the background. One little Home Office unit might cast an occasional glance towards Ulster, but the unit's importance can be gauged by the fact that it was also responsible for the Channel Islands, the Isle of Man, and the state licensing system in Carlisle. According to Ken

Bloomfield, the retired head of the Northern Ireland Civil Service, there were times when the government was less in touch with what was happening in its own province 'than it was with what was happening in Gambia or Outer Mongolia'.

In 1970 Reginald Maudling, the British Home Secretary, boarded a plane bringing him home from Northern Ireland with the words, 'For God's sake, someone bring me a large scotch. What a bloody awful country …' He gasped for a drink because he simply did not know what do about the essential problem of Northern Ireland, a problem that still exists today: the province is populated by two distinct groups. The overwhelmingly Protestant unionists consider themselves British and want the north to remain part of the United Kingdom. The overwhelmingly Catholic nationalists consider themselves Irish and want the north to become part of a united Ireland. A unionist might speak of 'Northern Ireland', a loyal province of the United Kingdom, and a nationalist might speak of the 'six counties', an arbitrarily displaced chunk of the Irish nation; but they are both referring to the same piece of land of 5,452 square miles, roughly half the size of Wales.

Back in the Seventies and Eighties I would probably not have heard the terms 'unionist' and 'nationalist' as often as the terms 'loyalist' and 'republican'. Broadly speaking – because these definitions are subjective – republicans are those who have supported the use of force to create a single independent Irish republic, while loyalists are grass-roots unionists, many of whom have supported the use of force to maintain the union with Britain.

When I arrived in Belfast the Good Friday Agreement was a decade old and the Troubles appeared to be over. But several months later Northern Ireland was reminded of what it had been missing. On the evening of Saturday, 7 March 2009 two pizza delivery men arrived at the Massereene army base in the town of Antrim. Four soldiers came out to the main gate to meet them. As the pizzas were handed over, gunmen in a nearby car opened fire with semi-automatic rifles, leaving all six men lying on the ground. The gunmen stepped out of their car, moved forward and opened fire again, before driving away. Two of the soldiers were killed. The other two soldiers and the delivery men, both Polish immigrants, were wounded. 'For the last ten years,' said Ian Paisley Jr. of the Democratic Unionist Party (DUP), 'people believed things like this happened in foreign countries, places like Basra. Unfortunately, it has returned to our doorstep.' Responsibility for the attack was claimed by the Real IRA, a group of dissident republicans who had broken away from the Provisional IRA in 1997. Shortly after the murders at the Massereene barracks a policeman was shot dead in Craigavon by the Continuity IRA, another dissident organization which had broken away from the Provisional IRA, back in 1986. These attacks were intended to provoke a reaction from loyalist para-militaries, to reignite the tit-for-tat killings that characterized thirty years of the Troubles, to force the British to bring soldiers back onto the streets of Northern Ireland, and to reawaken the war. The overwhelming majority of people in the north, including most of those for whom violence was once a way of life, are keen to see that the dissident republicans do not get their wish.

Northern Ireland has changed a great deal since the days of violence – but Belfast remains a city with a grim reputation to overcome. Paul Theroux, writing in 1983, was not seduced: 'I had never imagined Europe could look so threadbare – such empty trains, such blackened buildings, such recent ruins. And bellicose religion, and dirt, and poverty, and narrow-minded-ness, and sneaky defiance, trickery and murder, and little brick terraces, and drink shops, and empty stores, and barricades, and boarded windows, and starved dogs, and dirty-faced children – it looked like the past in an old picture.'

And if this is how it was to visit, how much worse to live in the place? A local man told me of a drive south along the Ormeau

Road in the late Seventies. He passed a building standing on its own, while those on either side lay in ruins. 'Look at that!' he remembers saying to his wife, 'How has that building escaped the bombs?' When he drove back up the road a few hours later, it was gone. Yet even during the bad times, when the evenings saw the city's streets empty, pubs deserted, and restaurants closed, there were visitors to Belfast who could see beyond the obvious. 'It's a charming port, one of the world's great deep water harbours, cupped in rolling downs on the bight of Belfast Lough,' wrote the often acerbic P. J. O'Rourke in 1988. He admired the buildings too: 'The city is built in the best and earliest period of Victorian architecture with delicate brickwork on every humble warehouse and factory. Even the mill hand tenement houses have Palladio's proportions in a miniature way.'

The port, the linen mills, the rope works, tea-drying, whisky and tobacco manufacture: these were the foundations of Belfast's once great civic pride. Walking around the city today, that pride hangs on in the self-conscious grandeur of the neo-classical buildings, the immensity of the Laganside cranes, the self-assurance of Queen's University, the extravagance of the Grand Opera House, and the dignity of the figures that stand in front of City Hall, embodying hard work and learning. Modern Belfast may not be a beautiful city, but it has nothing at all in common with the war-torn nightmare that sent Theroux scurrying on to his next port of call. While it may mourn the loss of its industrial strength, it has welcomed peace, and it is trying to create an identity for itself. It is busy and vibrant, a collection of areas rather than a unified whole, not yet sure whether it will be a city built around its specifics, or an urban mess of shopping malls and car parks. Its restaurants, clubs, hotels, and cafés are unselfconsciously appreciated. People in Belfast speak to you, they are friendly, city dwellers without the sneer. Perhaps that's because in Belfast you can exist in two worlds at once, staring out over Cave Hill as you wait for a bus in the centre of town. It does not take long to escape into the hills, where generations of Belfast children have played at being soldiers.

It doesn't do, however, to overstate the affability. While I found people from Belfast (Belfasters? Belfastians?) friendly and keen to talk entertainingly on all manner of subjects, I encountered wariness too. Of course I did. I was writing a book. I was a busybody, and an English busybody at that. Northern Ireland people have had every reason to be wary over the last few decades. As Seamus Heaney warned in the title of his 1975 poem 'Whatever You Say Say Nothing', saying the wrong thing to the wrong person could have dangerous consequences. As I settled into my journey, befriending strangers and begging interviews, encounters that began warmly could sometimes chill, as though I had stepped across an invisible line. A lot of the time that line should have been perfectly obvious. Once, standing about with a group of republicans, all of them friendly and chattering away, I asked a question about a particular man. I asked whether he had ever come under suspicion as an informer. It was a foolish, foolish question. For all I knew, he could have been a personal friend of everybody in the room. For all I knew, he could have been in the room. Everyone stopped speaking, and my legs gave way a fraction. 'Be very careful …' said one man, before repeating the warning twice. It was a lesson in Northern Ireland etiquette.

On another occasion somebody said of me, 'He knows more than he's letting on.' I'm still not entirely sure what the man meant, but I suppose he was suggesting that I might be working for the secret services. Once I was actually told by a republican that I'd been 'vetted' but it was all right, because I wasn't a 'spook'. When I asked him how he could be so sure, he smiled. The fact is that Belfast is a complicated but friendly place. Hospitable too. I was bought many drinks and cooked many meals by people who weren't flush with money. And if there was suspicion based on my English accent, or the level of interest I was taking, well, how could it be any other way in a place where informers are still reporting back to handlers? In the wake of the March 2009 killings the authorities were quick to reassure the public that the dissident groups were well infiltrated. And people have not forgotten about men like Robert Nairac, an undercover army officer who was killed in South Armagh in 1977 while pretending to be a Belfast republican. He raised suspicions by asking questions in a pub. An English stranger asking questions can still raise suspicions.

Belfast may have an impressive industrial heritage (after all, its yards built the *Titanic* and the *Olympic*), it may be strikingly situated, and it may be friendly, but these things are not what the city is known for today. It is known for its Troubles, its murals of gunmen and hunger strikers, and the great iron curtain that separates its communities, euphemistically described as the 'Peace Walls'. And no matter how much a visitor has read about this peculiar divide, it still comes as a shock to find the Catholics of the Falls Road and the Protestants of the Shankill Road living mutually exclusive lives, so close to one another.

It is difficult not to encounter striking images in the city. Walking around the 'interface' area of Ardoyne in north Belfast, I looked into a Catholic back garden backing onto a Peace Wall. The wall consists of ten feet of concrete, ten feet of steel, and thirty feet of wire-mesh fence on top. And there, in this cramped garden at the base of the wall, sits a well-used child's trampoline and a tiny washing line. If, in years to come, a museum of the Troubles is opened, the curators could do worse than to recreate this tableau in the entrance hall. On the other side of the wall lies a similar garden and a similar house, in a different world. Re-reading this paragraph, I see that it contains the phrase 'a Catholic back garden'. In Belfast a square of paving can have a religion.

But just as things that would be normal to a local person strike a visitor as odd, so the opposite is true. Taking a bus tour of the city, the guide pointed out the Royal Victoria Hospital, where, he gushed, 'Not only do Catholic and Protestant doctors work together, but for years they have treated Catholic and Protestant patients *side by side*.' In a world where segregated housing and education still exist, an integrated hospital passes for a tourist attraction.

To visit the interface areas of Belfast is to enter a world of frontier-like alertness. These were the paramilitaries' breeding grounds. I went to the Shankill Estate, a collection of grey, two-storey, postwar terraced houses, set around a grassy central area. I was taken there by a Catholic taxi driver who fidgeted nervously as we walked around. A few years ago, he said, he would never have dared come here, as we would have been challenged within seconds of our arrival. But things have changed. The Shankill Estate is now on the visitor's map. This is partly because of its edgy association with violence, but mainly because of its murals. They are painted on the gable ends of the terraces, and they represent scenes and individuals from mythology, history, and the very recent past. There are the paramilitary crests of the UVF (Ulster Volunteer Force) and the UDA (Ulster Defence Association), Union flags, and masked gunmen pointing their rifles directly at the tourist. There are men in sashes and bowler hats, demanding the right to march. There is the face of Oliver Cromwell, with, in capitals, a quote attributed to him: 'Catholicism is more than a religion. It is a political power therefore I'm led to believe that there will be no peace in Ireland until the Catholic Church is crushed.'

There is a massive photograph, transposed onto a wall, of 'Military Commander Stevie "Top Gun" McKeag, 1970–2000', who wears a backwards-facing baseball cap, an earring, and a thick gold chain. Stephen McKeag was a young man responsible for the killing of Philomena Hanna, a Catholic woman serving behind the counter of a pharmacy on the nearby Springfield Road. McKeag entered her shop, fired at her until she fell, and then fired into her head as she lay on the ground. Today, according to the mural, McKeag is 'sleeping where no shadows fall'.

One of the murals particularly caught my eye. It depicts a rock by the sea, on which sits a severed hand, oozing blood. In the background a hairy warrior stands on the prow of a ship, one hand in the air, as though he has just thrown something. Where his other hand should be is a bloody stump. The painting represents the story of the Red Hand of Ulster, of which there are several versions. In one, there is no rightful heir to the throne of Ulster, so the High King of Ireland suggests a boat race across Strangford Lough and whoever reaches the far shoreline first will be crowned king of Ulster. The race begins and one man, O'Neill, falls behind, but he has an idea. As his rival is about to reach the shore, he hacks off his own hand and hurls it onto the land. He wins the race and becomes king. In another version of the story the handless man isn't Irish at all; he is a Scot named MacDonnell. So the legend of the Red Hand has been used to support contrasting claims to the province. It has been present on loyalist paramilitary crests and on the official Ulster flag, but it has also appeared on the uniforms of the republican Irish Citizen Army, founded in 1913, and on badges of the Gaelic Athletic Association. It is now predominantly associated with unionism and loyalism, but it is an emotive symbol that has crossed the divide. Which is interesting – because the story of the Red Hand represents a state of mind that spans the divide. It is the story of a man who wants Ulster so badly that he is willing to cripple himself in order to lay his claim.

The confrontational style of the Shankill murals reflects the attitudes of the Shankill people. The area has the nervous energy of a pioneer post. Protestants may be in the majority in Northern Ireland, but they have always been a minority on the island of Ireland, and their 400-year fight for survival is the key to their identity. A British army officer, serving in Belfast in the early Seventies, told me of walking past a statue of William III with the slogan 'This we will maintain' carved on its base. He stopped a Protestant man and asked him, '*What* will you maintain?' and was told, 'I don't know – but we'll maintain it.' Nowadays, wandering around the city centre, the visitor might feel a sense of faded unionist pride, but on the Shankill this comes into sharper focus. These people fear they are losing their industrious province, and they refuse to stand for it. In this enclave they behave like frontiersmen, wagons drawn in a circle. Shankill people have long represented the most staunch elements of loyalism, the proud British identity which celebrates empire, the royal family, and the Battle of the Somme. If you want to destroy Ulster, it has been said, you start with the Shankill.

For all the talk of the divide, as an outsider walking through the centre of Belfast I cannot begin to tell who is a Protestant and who is a Catholic. But then neither can they. The Shankill Butchers, a gang of loyalist killers who sliced Catholics to death with kitchen knives in the mid-Seventies, searched for clues and even then killed some of their own by mistake. There are no distinct physical characteristics and the accents are more or less indistinguishable – although it is often said that a Catholic will pronounce the letter 'h' in isolation as 'haitch' and a Protestant will pronounce it 'aitch'. But in a province where allegiance counts for so much, and where people are quick to categorize one another – rather as my taxi driver could hardly wait until the meter was running to start probing – there are questions commonly asked to uncover allegiance. The answers given to 'Where do you live?', 'Where did you go to school?' and 'How many brothers and sisters do you have?' are good indicators. These are the sort of questions that were once asked at job interviews to gauge an applicant's suitability. But since these people look the same and talk the same, it amazes an outsider that they need walls to separate them.

The divide is very real, though. It is geographical, economic, political – and of course religious. It is a hoary old question whether the Troubles have been religious in nature, so I felt I ought to ask it as soon as I arrived in Belfast. One man told me that it would be simplistic to blame the Troubles on religion. Nobody has ever been shot dead in the name of transubstantiation. The majority of members of the IRA, INLA (Irish National Liberation Army), UVF and UDA (to account for both sides of the divide) were not religious; they were thinking of their people and their grievances, not God, when engaged in the struggle. On the other hand, without God, Catholicism, and Protestantism there would have been no struggle in the first place. Protestants would not have been sent to settle a Catholic country, there would have been no geographical split, no political discrimination, and no present-day labels to decide who stands on which side of the divide. Catholicism and Protestantism may be little more than symbols nowadays – but the effect of belonging to one or the other religion is much more than symbolic. Only 6 per cent of schools are integrated, the majority of people (more than before the Troubles) live in segregated communities, huge numbers of Catholics know no Protestants, and vice versa. The problem may often be spoken of as cultural rather than religious, but it seems rather simplistic not to allow religion some share of the blame. As Conor Cruise O'Brien almost said, if religion is a red herring, it's a red herring the size of a whale.

But if it is wrong to speak in terms of a religious conflict, it is surely also wrong to place too much stress on cultural divisions. One Protestant told me sadly about the Catholic man he works with in Derry. 'He thinks exactly the same way as me,' he said, 'there's just no difference between us. But the pubs in the city are all one or the other, and if I went to one of his pubs, his friends might recognize me.' A nurse from Belfast agreed: 'If people had got together, they'd have realized they had so much in common. The Falls and the Shankill houses were much the same, and the people were much the same. When they get away abroad they talk to each other as though they've known each other all their lives, and then when they get home they don't know each other.' Indeed a 1968 survey found that 81 per cent of northern Catholics and 67 per cent of northern Protestants felt that those of the other community were culturally 'the same as themselves'. So, while the sides clearly have different political cultures, perhaps it is reasonable to suggest that wherever their political bonds lie, their cultural bonds rest much closer.

Rather than seeing the Ulster divide in religious or cultural terms, it makes more sense to view it in terms of identities that have been created by perceptions of history, by economic and political relations, and by a rejection of the other side's identity: whatever they are, we are not. Protestants in areas such as the Shankill might have lived lives culturally similar to – and as economically deprived as – their Catholic neighbours, but members of the opposing communities have very rarely worked together towards shared goals. Their tribal identities have not allowed it.

From the Shankill, my taxi driver and I drove across the divide onto the Falls. The atmosphere here is slightly less intense, but the sense of republican identity is as strong as its equivalent on the other side. Just as the Shankill grew up on the old route between the Protestant counties of Down and Antrim, so the Falls grew up on the route out to the Catholic west, and it was populated by workers in the many mills that were built nearby. The Falls saw a great deal of street fighting in the early days of the Troubles, becoming a rallying point for republican resistance to the state. In the words of Provisional IRA hero Brendan Hughes, it was where the belief arose, in 1970, that 'We can beat these fuckers.' On that occasion, as so often, the 'fuckers' were the British army, who had raided the Falls in an attempt to remove a cache of weapons.

A visit to the Irish Republican History Museum, in Conway Mill, just off the Falls Road, is a memorable experience. At first sight it is a frightening place, full of guns, rubber bullets, prison doors, and clothes worn by the Provisional IRA. It feels like a sinister chapel, Armalite rifles and prison-carved harps in place of crucifixes and stained-glass windows. I have rarely been so self-conscious as I was in my first few minutes in this place; I felt as though I was wearing a Union Jack waistcoat as I wandered about, peering at artefacts and nodding at people who were drinking tea at a small table. I looked around the well-stocked library, then I walked into a recreated cell from Armagh Prison. After a while the place began to seem less like a shrine to violence and more like a focal point for the community. Its custodian is a friendly man, happy to explain the local perspective, and it became clear that the museum's intention is not to intimidate or to glory in brutality. Just as one side feels at the mercy of its enemies, so can the other, and this place reflects the fear and pride of a beleaguered people. In the end it is an interesting and well-run local museum with little chance of government funding.

When I first visited the Republican Museum, the Real IRA killings at Massereene barracks had not yet occurred. When I returned months later, with a peaceful future looking less certain, the place unnerved me a little once more. It had not changed and its custodian was as thoughtful and generous with his time as he had been on my first visit. But much else had changed, including my attitude to my work. What had begun as a history project, its subject matter more or less packaged, now felt like current affairs muddled with uncertainties. The guns were no longer just museum exhibits. The past and the present were blurring.

Seventy years ago Harold Nicolson wrote, 'The Irish themselves have no sense of the past; for them, the present began on 17 October 1171, when Henry II landed at Waterford. For them, history is always contemporaneous and current events are always history.' Walking around parts of Belfast, glancing at the murals and graffiti, it can seem as though the rebels of 1916 have only just risen, and the Somme is still being fought. Sometimes, in ordinary conversation, history comes tumbling out of people. The partition of Ireland or the Siege of Derry can appear as relevant to someone's state of mind as something that happened that morning. But the versions of the past that you will hear are unlikely to coincide. Identities do not allow it.

There is a Northern Ireland neologism, 'Whataboutery', that is used to describe the bouts of accusation-slinging that characterize local politics. When a politician from one side charges the other side with some wrongdoing, the matter will rarely be discussed rationally. Instead it will be answered with a corresponding accusation: 'What about such and such injustice?' Whataboutery is symptomatic of the chasm in the interpretation of history that exists between the communities. In Northern Ireland, it has been said, there is no one history. Indeed the Tower Museum in Derry makes the point graphically – it displays the story of the period between 1800 and 1921 along two parallel walls, one from the unionist-loyalist perspective, the other from the nationalist-republican perspective. You can walk down the middle and take your pick. By the same logic, the actions of the dissident republicans ought to be sending the politicians scurrying to their entrenched positions, from where they can interpret events accordingly. But that has not been happening. In the aftermath of the 2009 killings, the politicians have appeared united. The Reverend Ian Paisley, a man often blamed for kindling the fire that led to the Troubles, announced, 'There is grieving, there is despair, but beyond the despair there is being born a spirit of unity that we have never seen before.' If he is right – and the very fact that *he* is saying it suggests that he might be – perhaps this spirit of unity could create a single history in Northern Ireland, a single wall in the Tower Museum. The past might be consigned to the past. If that were to happen, then I would love to revisit the Shankill murals and the Irish

Republican History Museum, emotive reminders of a shared turbulent story.

It will take a lot to create just one history, however. The sense and depth of history arises out of continuity, out of a firm linkage of people to place. In parts of Northern Ireland surnames have remained constant for many hundreds of years, and this has created a society where family and community count for a great deal. As one nationalist put it, 'When we want to get something done here, we phone a cousin.' In the north, four hundred people can show up to a funeral, and when somebody is shot dead the lives of hundreds can be directly affected. With this continuity comes a sense of history and identity that is rarely questioned.

One Belfast man, whom I met early on in my travels, gave me a warning: 'All that everyone will say to you here – no matter how much of it seems to be foregrounded on fact – it's all subjective experience. None of it is true. There is no truth in this place. Anyone who gives you the true version, well, you know immediately not to trust them.' He had offered me a liar's paradox: if a Northern Ireland man tells me that in Northern Ireland people don't tell the truth, how can I believe him? Riddles aside, I was to hear many 'true versions' over the coming months, from the senior politician who cheerfully informed me that Catholics cannot be considered Christians, to the ex-IRA man who was certain that the British government retains a strong strategic interest in Northern Ireland. A lot of the time, however, these 'true versions' would consist of interpretations that sounded plausible until somebody else said something just as plausible but wholly contradictory. I was to find myself deluged by such declarations of identity. At times I would listen with interest, at other times with weariness – and sometimes with something close to jealousy. Louis MacNeice wrote of his native Northern Ireland:

We envy men of action
Who sleep and wake, murder and intrigue
Without being doubtful, without being haunted.
And I envy the intransigence of my own
Countrymen who shoot to kill and never
See the victim's face become their own
Or find his motive sabotage their motives.

It is quite possible for an outsider to feel envy in the province, a place seemingly free from doubt. My own world of moral equivalence, where one is not encouraged to pass judgement on the beliefs of others, can seem, by comparison, to be a place without conviction. How fortifying it must be to have something always to believe in, and somebody always to react against. Is this what Dominic Behan wrote about in his lovely song, 'The Patriot Game': 'For the love of one's country is a terrible thing, it banishes fear with the speed of a flame, and it makes us all part of the Patriot Game'?

Now flip the coin. Perhaps Northern Ireland is a place where judgement is too readily passed. It has produced people prepared to die, prepared to cut off a hand for the cause, but not prepared to make lesser compromises. A weaker identity might produce a stronger society. One Belfast republican told me of time spent, many years previously, in Coventry. There he became friendly with a local Labour Party activist, but he could never understand how someone could be politically active in a 'twilight city' where nothing ever happened, where the construction of a zebra crossing was held up as a political achievement. For many in Northern Ireland, politics is not about the mundane or the consensual, it is about the struggle of identities: them and us. Why give a damn about helping kids across a road when there is an identity to preserve?

Alongside intensity of belief can sit self-importance. When a great deal of time is spent gazing inwards, it is possible to lose –

or fail to gain – perspective on one's position in the world. MacNeice again, this time seething with indignation:

I hate your grandiose airs,
Your sob stuff, your laugh and your swagger,
Your assumption that everyone cares
Who is the king of your castle.

In a speech to the House of Commons in 1922, Winston Churchill (a member of the Liberal government team that negotiated the Anglo-Irish treaty with Michael Collins, and, according to his bodyguard, the subject of an attempted assassination by the IRA the previous year) noted that while the First World War might have overturned great empires, and altered ways of thinking across the globe, it had not changed attitudes everywhere: 'As the deluge subsides and the waters fall short, we see the dreary steeples of Fermanagh and Tyrone emerging once again. The integrity of their quarrel is one of the few institutions that has been unaltered in the cataclysm which has swept the world.' Churchill's speech has often been quoted to underline the unchanging nature of Northern Irish politics. Yet it is his perception of people so unaffected by world events, so in thrall to their own reflections, that is most striking.

Seventy-nine years later Northern Ireland *would* gain a perspective of its position in the world. On 11 September 2001, as Al Qaeda mounted a raw and shocking attack on New York City, the Troubles were suddenly made to seem stale, predictable and petty. Blinkers fell away as all parties were forced to look beyond themselves, and to accept that men with stronger senses of identity were now commanding the world's attention. Fewer people – in particular fewer Americans – now cared who was the king of *their* castle. September 11 was an attack on all that the world understood, and it shook some of the certainty and self-importance out of Northern Ireland. In its aftermath the move towards peace accelerated.

Not long after I arrived in Belfast, I met a man who told me a story. He had been sitting at home with his wife and small daughter, watching the film *Schindler's List*. During a brutal camp scene the man's wife leant across to him and whispered, 'Is that what *your* prison was like?' The man, a former member of the IRA who had planted bombs, shot at British soldiers, and served time in jail, explained that however hard prison had been for him, however brutal the screws, his treatment could not be compared to that of concentration-camp inmates. The next day, as he drove his daughter to school, the little girl asked him whether he'd really been in prison. 'Yes.' 'But aren't prisons for bad people?' 'Not always. You saw the film last night? Those prisoners weren't bad people. They were put in prison by bad people. Sometimes the bad people aren't the prisoners.'

These are the words of a father explaining his past to his daughter, but they could easily be addressed to the world at large. Over the course of this book we will encounter people who have done things that most would consider unacceptable. Some have placed morality to one side more readily than others, but how many of them now consider what they did to be wrong? Some may see their acts as having been politically motivated, in defiance of an unjust system, or in defence of their communities. These may not have been the only – or sometimes even the primary – reasons for their behaviour; they could be handy rationalizations, cynical assaults on a morally sustainable position. But they could also be sincere responses to a complex history, and they may explain why one likeable man feels able to compare his captive status, if not his actual treatment, to that of a Holocaust victim. So how should we approach men who used violence – other than with great care? Is it wrong to judge people in terms of absolutes? While a man may have committed terrible acts *in certain situations*, in all other areas of life he may have behaved in an entirely moral fashion. If he believes that he had right on his side, can we take him at his own estimation of himself?

We will meet those who suffered the direct consequences of these terrible acts. One man, an ex-police officer – who was himself injured in a bomb attack – told me of arriving at the scene of an explosion to find a friend and colleague lying dead. His reaction had not been one of anger or vengeance, but sadness and a sense of futility. He told me how he would have loved to bring the people responsible down to the scene, where he could ask them exactly what uniting Ireland was *about*.

We will meet those who never used and sometimes never endorsed violence, but who are entrenched in traditional ways of thinking: people from the Protestant tradition who consider themselves *British* at a time when *Britishness* is losing its meaning and relevance for the English, Welsh and Scots; people from Catholic backgrounds whose lives have been devoted to reuniting with the Irish Republic despite its lack of interest in reuniting with them. Slighted by their chosen partners, many of these uneasy neighbours now stand together under the umbrella of the Good Friday Agreement. What divides them unites them.

It is important to remember that the overwhelming majority of people in Northern Ireland, whether Orange or Green, did not participate in, or support, the violence of the Troubles. Yet many of them were affected by it. In 1999 researchers from the University of Ulster published the 'Cost of the Troubles Study', for which they had interviewed 3,000 men and women across Northern Ireland to gauge the effects of the Troubles on ordinary people. Of those interviewed, a quarter had seen people killed or injured, a fifth had experienced a deterioration in their health which they attributed to a Troubles-related trauma, and almost one in twenty had been injured in a bomb explosion or a shooting. As well as recording a large increase in alcohol consumption and the taking of medication, the study found a high level of fear of straying from one's own area and an acute wariness of outsiders.

The 'Cost of the Troubles Study' opens up a vista on a world beyond belief and self-importance. It is a world with few spokesmen, but plenty of inhabitants. These are the people whose voices were rarely heard in the reports that filled the English newspapers. One man told me of sitting in a bar on the Falls Road, listening to some old-time republicans boasting of the length of time they'd spent in prison. After a while another man tired of what he was hearing. 'Fucking lucky for you!' he shouted. 'You done twenty years sitting in a safe wee cell? And your family provided for? What about the poor man who had to go out to work every morning, risking fucking death? You were in a fucking sanctuary!'

At the junction between the two worlds, an act of common kindness could attract recrimination. A Catholic man from Claudy told me how he had once tended a policeman who had been shot in the street. He put a tourniquet around the policeman's leg and sat with him until an ambulance arrived. A while later, at his holiday home across the border in Donegal, an IRA man on the run approached him and asked why he had helped the policeman. He replied that he would have helped a dog if he had needed it. 'In fact,' he added, 'I might even have helped you.' Days later he was threatened: 'We're very worried for you and your family so long as you stay here …' I asked him how republicans in one town had known of an incident that occurred in another. 'Kick one of them,' he said, 'and they all limp.'

One man who spoke for the citizens of the stifled world was Seamus Heaney. Heaney, a Catholic from Derry, was once asked by Sinn Féin director of publicity Danny Morrison, 'Why don't you write something for us?' 'No,' replied Heaney, 'I write for myself.' His poem 'Whatever You Say Say Nothing' gives voice to a passive people, too cowed to speak out against 'bigotry and sham'. According to Heaney, 'smoke signals are loud-mouthed compared with us'. The poem ends:

> *Is there a life before death? That's chalked up*
> *In Ballymurphy. Competence with pain,*
> *Coherent miseries, a bit and sup,*
> *We hug our little destiny again.*

A 'little destiny' is not much of a thing to hug. It is hardly surprising that so many of the people of Northern Ireland, once denied a life before death, now fear a return to the Troubles; nor is it surprising that tens of thousands of these people gathered in Belfast, Derry, Newry, Lisburn, and Downpatrick to rally for peace in March 2009 in the wake of the dissident killings.

And yet 'The Grauballe Man', another of Heaney's poems from the same collection, includes the words 'hung in the scales with beauty and atrocity'. Echoing W. B. Yeats, who spoke of 'a terrible beauty' born of the 1916 Easter Rising, Heaney is daring to hint at a beauty to the modern Troubles. While giving a voice to those silenced by the violence in one poem, he is suggesting a nobility to that violence in another.

Northern Ireland is built on such contradictions. It was created as a political compromise to bring an end to conflict, but conflict has flourished within it. It goes by the name of 'Northern Ireland', but its northernmost point lies to the south of part of the Irish Republic. Its people are divided by religion, but their quarrel is not religious. And while they *are* divided, they are also united. As a man once said, 'If you understand Northern Ireland, you don't understand Northern Ireland.'

As I eased my way into this world of divided, united people, I made my first base just outside the pretty town of Killyleagh, on the banks of Strangford Lough in County Down. I was staying with the Lindsays, a warm and generous family who had never met me before yet welcomed me like an old friend. Katie, their daughter, is a talented artist who works with patients at the Mater Hospital in Belfast. Their lives were a world away from my own in London, but I quickly became very adept at lighting a wood fire, and sitting by it with a glass of whisky. Through the Lindsays I had the fortune to meet Bobbie Hanvey, a photographer, writer, broadcaster, and one-time nurse in Downshire mental hospital, a man described by J. P. Donleavy as 'Ireland's most super sane man'.

Bobbie hosts a programme, *The Ramblin' Man*, every Sunday night on Downtown Radio, in which he interviews local personalities. His easy-going charm allows him to get away with asking some very awkward questions. He prised several seconds of rare silence from Ian Paisley by asking him whether, had he been born a Catholic, he could have been a member of the IRA. It cannot be easy for Paisley to accept that God could have made him a Catholic, never mind that he could have been a member of the IRA. The eventual answer was, 'No, I don't think so,' followed by an unprovoked denial that he had ever supported loyalist violence. A Hanvey trademark is the undercutting of a serious subject with a flash of mischief. He interrupted the ex-leader of the UVF, in mid flow on the subject of large booby traps, with the observation that the biggest booby trap he'd encountered was a brassiere. He also advised a Chief Constable of the Royal Ulster Constabulary (RUC), who had once worked in vice, to write a memoir with the title *Pros 'n' Cons*. Nonplussed, his guest thanked him for 'that very impressive suggestion'.

But Bobbie's irreverence cannot mask a keen intellect and a shrewd understanding of the complexities of Northern Ireland, from which he seems to stand aloof, friendly with men and women of all sides. I would become very grateful for his insights, and even more grateful for the chance to quote from his interviews in this book. One of my abiding memories of my time in Northern Ireland is of an evening spent upstairs in his Downpatrick house, listening to recordings of interviews. As I wondered where I could get something to eat, I heard footsteps coming up the stairs and Bobbie appeared in the doorway, his Marty Feldman hair silhouetted against the light. He walked in and plonked a plate down in front of me, on which sat two foil-wrapped chocolate marshmallows. 'I've got to tell you,' he said, 'I'm not much of a cook.'

Maybe not, but he was a very helpful ally in this strange and familiar place. He phoned me recently, asking me to find him a couple of Chasidic Jews to photograph. As though I'd have them around the house. That's fair enough, though. He's brought me his people. He can have a pair of mine.

2

THE SETTLERS

Samuel Johnson once told James Boswell that the Giant's Causeway was worth seeing, but not worth going to see. Early on in my journey I visited it with a guide who was even less enthusiastic. Just before it came into view, he turned to me and said, 'You're going to find this place disappointing.' Luckily I was able to set both verdicts aside, especially the one from the man being paid to promote Northern Ireland. On an early summer's day, with a stiff breeze blowing, the hexagonal black and gold columns seemed eerie and romantic. The Causeway was a bit smaller than I'd expected, and there were a lot of people around, but it didn't matter; I was in a good mood, and my expectations had been set very low. Standing on a stone crop, staring out to sea, I was joined by the guide who took me into his confidence. All this, he assured me, wasn't made by molten rock, forced up through the ground. It couldn't be. The columns are perfect. They've got to be man-made. They must have been built by Stone Age people. *Stone Age Irish people.*

There is a legend concerning the Giant's Causeway that it was actually built by Finn McCool (Fionn MacCumhaill in Irish), the leader of a band of great warriors, as a land bridge between Ireland and Scotland. McCool and a Scottish giant had been shouting insults across the sea at each other, but McCool wanted to be able to confront his rival in person. Constructing such a mighty land bridge proved hard work, however, and McCool fell asleep as soon as he had finished. While he slept the Scottish giant thundered down the Causeway towards him, but McCool woke up and spotted him. Perturbed by the size of his opponent, McCool – thinking extremely laterally – built a huge crib and lay down inside it, pretending to be a massive baby. The giant arrived, looked inside the crib, saw this grotesque infant, and panicked. If this was the size of McCool's baby, how enormous must McCool be? The giant ran back to Scotland, tearing up the Causeway as he went, leaving only the remains that Dr Johnson did not consider worth going to see. Whether it was actually built by Finn McCool, a figure who came to inspire the republican movement, or by Stone Age nationalists laying claim to Irish territory, the Causeway, like so much else in Northern Ireland, has been used to service contemporary claims.

Perhaps the greatest character in Irish mythology is Cuchulainn, the Irish Achilles, who is supposed to have defended Ulster single-handedly against the warriors of Queen Medb of Connaught. Cuchulainn, fearless, earthy, and principled, is a character with whom many have wanted to be associated. Mortally wounded, he is said to have bound himself to a pillar so that he might die standing up, and this scene is recorded on a bronze statue inside Dublin's General Post Office, erected in memory of the 1916 republican rising. But Cuchulainn is also claimed by unionists and loyalists; a huge mural on the Shankill Estate shows him waving his sword in defiance at those who would threaten Ulster. When I asked a leading unionist politician about the legend of Cuchulainn, he reacted crossly to the word 'legend'. Cuchulainn's defence of Ulster is not a legend, he made it clear; it is history.

I found an interesting version of history in a 1982 play, co-written by Andy Tyrie, then leader of the Ulster Defence Association, a loyalist paramilitary organization. *This Is It!* is a sharply observed piece of drama that tells the story of a young working-class Protestant who grows disillusioned with unionism's lack of political ambition. It particularly caught my eye for the views of one of its characters, Sam, who gives an account of Ulster's early history from a Protestant perspective. Sam argues that the people of Ulster, Protestant and Catholic alike, share a common ancestry that predates the coming of the Celts in the centuries before Christ; in those days, Sam claims, Ulster and Scotland were populated by the same race, called the Picts in Scotland and the Cruthin in Ulster. When the Celts invaded Ulster, they carried out a long and cruel extermination, forcing the Cruthin to move to Scotland. So, says Sam, 'You could even suppose that some of those who came over here for the Plantation [Ulster's colonization by English and Scottish Protestants four centuries ago] were *in effect* coming home *again*.' This reading of history allows Sam to argue that Ulster is the Protestant homeland: 'Our roots are here! Ulster people – Catholic and Protestant – both have a common ancestry and a common right to be here.'

Fascinated by this, I spoke to a respected university professor who prefers not to be named. Evidently the subject is rather controversial. The professor told me that the pre-Christian period of Irish history is very dark. The Picts were present in parts of Scotland, and there is indeed a tradition of a Cruthin people in East Ulster. But while these people might well have communicated with each other across the sea, and there may even have been an exchange of population, it is impossible to say that the Picts and the Cruthin were the same race. With regard to the Celts, the professor says that although there is a tradition that they arrived in Ireland in the years just before the birth of Christ, no archaeological evidence exists for a mass arrival or for an invasion, and there is no evidence at all that they carried out a long and cruel extermination of indigenous people. There is a tradition of a migration of people from Ireland to western Scotland at the time of the Roman invasion of Britain, but it is no more than a tradition. So far as the idea of settlers 'coming home' to Ulster at the time of the plantations is concerned, the professor says that the seventeenth-century Scottish settlers came primarily from Scotland's border with England. These settlers were not Gaelic speakers, and it would be wrong to consider them the same people as those who *may* once have left Ulster. It would, the professor says, be very difficult to identify an 'Ulster people'. I am left with the strong caveat that I should be careful of historical interpretations which carry an underlying political motivation.

'Throughout history,' declares Sinn Féin's website, 'the island of Ireland has been regarded as a single national unit. Prior to the Norman invasion from England in 1169, the Irish had their own system of law, culture, and language, and their own political and social structures.' While it makes political sense for Sinn Féin to describe pre-1169 Ireland as a 'single national unit', it makes less historical sense. During this period the island was a patchwork of independent chiefdoms, often at war with one another, and ready to make alliances to achieve greater power. One such alliance led to the arrival of the English in Ireland. It was struck between Dermot MacMurrough, deposed King of Leinster, and Henry II, King of England, and its legacy has dominated the story of Ireland for the past eight hundred years. Henry granted MacMurrough the services of Anglo-Norman barons to help him to regain his lost kingship. One of these barons, the Earl of Pembroke, known as 'Strongbow', overran Waterford and Dublin, and defeated the High King of Ireland in battle. Fearing the emergence of a rival Norman kingdom across the sea, Henry landed an army at Waterford in 1171, with which to confront the ambitious Earl. Strongbow quickly pledged obedience to Henry and promised him the lands that he had conquered. As Henry proceeded through Ireland, the native Irish kings swore fealty to him in turn – all except the rulers of Ulster.

This story of England's first intervention in Ireland is told by the Welsh-Norman chronicler Giraldus Cambrensis, who describes a meeting at Armagh called by the Irish clergy 'concerning the arrival of the foreigners in the island'. The clergy's opinion was that God was allowing the English to 'enslave' the Irish, 'because it had been formerly been their [the Irish people's] habit to purchase Englishmen indiscriminately from merchants as well as from robbers and pirates, and to make slaves of them'. As a result they decreed that 'throughout the island, Englishmen should be freed from the bonds of slavery'. Unfortunately for the churchmen, this decree did not result in an English withdrawal. Giraldus proceeds to declare proudly, 'Let the envious and thoughtless end their vociferous complaints that the kings of England hold Ireland unlawfully. Let them learn, moreover, that they support their claims by a right of ownership resting on five different counts …' Three of these counts rest on legends, one being the claim that the kings of Ireland once paid tribute to King Arthur, 'that famous king of Britain'. The fourth count is that English rule had the authority of the Pope. The fifth is that 'the princes of Ireland freely bound themselves in submission to Henry II, king of England, by the firm bonds of their pledged word and oath'. And so, from this casual intervention many hundreds of years ago, described by a highly partial observer, Anglo-Irish relations came to assume their familiar antipathy and bloodshed.

A problem for the English kings who came after Henry II, attempting to assert their authority on Ireland, was the tendency of their representatives to assimilate. The lords who were meant to be cementing English rule began instead to adopt Irish customs, language, and laws, and became difficult to distinguish from the existing Irish chieftains. By the end of the fifteenth century the English Crown's authority covered only a small area around Dublin, known as 'the Pale'. The area outside of English influence was therefore considered 'beyond the Pale', and

remained subject to an anarchy of tribal conflict. Henry VIII attempted to re-anglicize the 'Old English' lords; he forced them to drop their Irish titles, and he re-granted them their lands under English feudal law, but his authority was not noticeably strengthened as a result. Henry's daughter, Elizabeth I, faced six rebellions from the Old English and the Irish. She put these down ruthlessly, and appointed officials with little sympathy for the local people. One of these officials was the poet Edmund Spenser, author of the tender couplet 'Such is the power of love in gentle mind, that it can alter all the course of kind.' But Spenser's gentle mind did not extend to the Irish people, whom he considered 'vile catiff wretches, ragged, rude, deformed'. As England became wealthier and more powerful, Ireland became a country to be suppressed and civilized. By the end of Elizabeth's reign a centralized English administration was in place, as was a bitterly confirmed resentment of English rule.

By this time the issue of religion had also emerged. The Reformation of the Church had taken hold in England, but it had failed to do so in Ireland. It was proving difficult enough to impose an English administration on a resistant, widely scattered population, and utterly impossible to impose the Protestant religion. So a new policy was adopted: the colonization of the province by loyal Protestants. In 1606 Sir John Davies, the Irish attorney general, described Ulster as 'the most rude and unreformed part of Ireland' and he hoped that 'that the next generation will in tongue and heart and every way else become English'. What better way to achieve this, and to deter the French and Spanish from creating an Irish bridgehead from which to invade England, than by settling Ulster with English and Scottish Protestants? A good part of the existing Irish population was forced from its land by these 'plantations', and the repercussions have been felt down the centuries. The Northern Ireland government of much of the twentieth century would be run by, and for, the descendants of Protestants who were brought to the province in the first half of the seventeenth century.

Lessons learnt in Ulster were immediately put to use by the English in their next effort at colonization by plantation, across the Atlantic in Virginia and New England. The Ulster plantation was the forerunner of the foundation of America. In the New World the native population was all but extinguished by slaughter and Old World diseases, leaving the settlers to thrive and give thanks every November. In Ulster, where the natives did not die off, a population with split allegiances and long memories was created.

Early in my travels I met a man named John Beresford-Ash. He lives just outside Derry with his beautiful French wife, Agnès, in a lovely late-seventeenth-century house, Ashbrook, that benefits from looking and feeling its age. John is a wonderfully old-fashioned character, impeccably mannered, entertaining, honest, and indiscreet. His family can be traced back over four centuries to the earliest Protestants to arrive in Ulster, and I had been told that he would be an interesting man to speak to, so I telephoned him and was immediately invited to lunch the following day. I showed up and sat with John and Agnès, intending to interview him after the meal, but the food was good, the wine kept coming, and the conversation bubbled along, taking in subjects as various as Lord Lucan (an old friend of John's who is *indisputably* dead) and the Nuremberg Trials (another old friend was the junior British counsel). I finally rolled out of Ashbrook, virtually incapable, with the promise of an interview the following day. The promise was warmly kept.

Ashbrook was originally granted to Beresford-Ash's ancestor, General Thomas Ash, by Elizabeth I in recognition of his loyal service to the Crown. Another ancestor was Tristram Beresford, the first land agent for the merchants of the City of London. Beresford was evidently a pragmatist. According to his descendant: 'The Spanish were very short of oak trees to build their warships and one day some Spanish galleons turned up in the River Foyle. There were a lot of lovely oak trees here in Derry, *doire* being the Irish for oak grove, and though Elizabeth was a marvellous queen, she was awfully tight-fisted and she hadn't paid her troops. My ancestor practically had a mutiny on his hands because his troops hadn't been paid, and the Spanish had an awful lot of gold, so he said to the Spaniards, "If you can pay, I will give you the oak trees of Derry," which he did – and thus committed high treason. He was had up by the court of the Star Chamber, but fortunately for him – and indeed most fortunately for me – he was a great friend of Walter Raleigh, who interceded on his behalf, so he didn't get his neck stretched.'

Many of the plantations in Ulster were undertaken privately, the settlers being Presbyterian Scots whose independence of spirit has shaped the history of the province. In Derry, however, the settlement was funded by the livery companies of the City of London and many of the original settlers were Londoners. According to a 1609 privy council document, 'It [the settlement] might ease [London] of an insupportable burthen of persons, which it might conveniently spare.' In 1613 the London Companies were granted land by a royal charter, and the name Derry was changed to Londonderry because, according to John Beresford-Ash, 'The London companies were keen on the fact that it was their money and their expertise that was being used. And it encouraged the people who came to live here, who were being harassed by the native population. The native population naturally resented these invaders coming – but whether they were invaders or not depends on your point of view.'

Invaders or not, the Protestant settlers lived apprehensive lives, surrounded by Irish Catholics who resented them for taking their land and repressing their religion. In 1641 the Irish rebelled, launching attacks on the settlements. A near-contemporary Protestant account describes the attacks, and blames them on the influence of the Catholic church:

'The Priests gave the Sacrament unto divers of the Irish, upon condition that they should neither spare man, woman, nor child of the Protestants … One Joan Addis they stabbed, and then put her child of a quarter year old to her breast, and bid it to suck English Bastard, and so left it to perish … They brake the backbone of a youth, and left him in the fields, some days after he was found, having eaten the grass round about him; neither then would they kill him outright, but removed him to better pasture … At Portadown Bridge, there were one thousand men, women, and children, carried in several companies, and all unmercifully drowned in the river … Elizabeth Price testified upon oath, that she and other women, whose husbands and children were drowned in that place, went hither one evening, at which time they saw one like a woman rise out of the river breast-high, her hair hanging down, which with her skin, was as white as snow, often crying out, Revenge, Revenge, Revenge.'

It is estimated that about 12,000 Protestants were killed during the rebellion and, however exaggerated contemporary accounts might have been, they helped to condition attitudes that survive to this day. In the following years Oliver Cromwell came to Ireland and took the revenge called for by the snow-white apparition. In the wake of a massacre at Drogheda where as many as 3,500 soldiers, civilians and clergymen were killed by his troops, Cromwell wrote, 'It is right that God alone should have all the glory.' An Irish Catholic tract composed in 1662 begins presciently, 'It is a sad and severe position, that this contention between the two parties in Ireland will never have an end.' The author's solution is plain: 'The country must at length give denomination to all that inhabit it: and the posterity of those that proclaim loudly the English interest, must within an age, admit themselves to be called Irish as well as descendants from the first Colony of English planted in Ireland.' Almost 350 years later John Beresford-Ash describes his identity to me: 'I'm entirely English. My family came from

England and we were there before the Norman conquest. We can prove it.'

An Account of the Publick Affairs in Ireland, published in 1678, lays out English strategy in Ireland: 'The principal and present security of the Kingdom consists of balancing the numbers of Irish with a superiority of strength, and leaving them naked, and the English in Arms.' In 1685, however, the policy threatened to unravel. In that year the Catholic King James II came to the English throne. His succession brought hope to Irish Catholics, and he proceeded to grant them patronage, but three years later his Dutch Protestant son-in-law, William of Orange, landed in England with an army. He came at the invitation of Protestant nobles who sought to save England from Catholicism. James chose to escape to France rather than fight his rival in England, and in James's absence Parliament declared that he had abdicated his throne. William was crowned King of England in April 1689, by which time James had gathered an army and landed at Kinsale, on the south coast of Ireland, intending to use that country as a base to reclaim his throne. He marched to Dublin in triumph and continued north. It appeared as though he would take Ireland with ease; only the Protestants of Ulster would resist him. Protestants from across the province flocked to Derry with its strong defences, and James's army besieged the city. 'We were in our small house,' says John Beresford-Ash, 'and King James came over headed by the French, and all the Protestants emigrated within the walls of Derry. Ashbrook was burnt by James's troops, and it was rebuilt after the siege. Thomas Ash was the senior member of the family, his father was dead, and he was in the yeomanry. He was obviously a fairly decent character.'

Thomas Ash kept a journal chronicling the siege. 'Apart from eating rats,' says his descendant, 'I don't suppose there was much else to do.' At the start of his diary, written while King James was still on the throne, Ash stresses the insecurity felt by Ulster Protestants: 'We had been alarmed by reports that the Roman

Catholics intended to rise in arms against us, and to act over the tragedy of 1641.' These reports coincided with news reaching Derry that a Catholic army garrison was on its way to the city to relieve the existing Protestant garrison. The Protestants of the city did not know what course to take. To refuse entry to the king's garrison was treasonable, but they feared that the garrison was being sent to massacre them. Ash wrote: 'While we were in this confused hesitation, on 7th December 1688, a few resolute Apprentice Boys determined for us: these ran to the Gates and shut them, drew up the bridge, and seized the Magazine. This, like magic, roused an unanimous spirit of defence, we determine to maintain the city at all hazards.'

The true siege began four months later, once William had become king and James had arrived in Ireland to try to win back his throne. On 15 April 1689 Ash writes of his suspicion that the man in charge of the city's army garrison, Robert Lundy, was a traitor. Days later he records, 'Colonel Lundy deserted our garrison, and went in disguise to Scotland, and by this, proved the justness of our former suspicions.' To this day a traitor to the Protestant cause is known as a 'Lundy', and the man has become the Ulster Protestant equivalent of Guy Fawkes: his effigy is burned every December in the centre of Derry. Ash's journal records a steady rain of 'bombs' and 'mortars' falling on the city from Jacobite guns, killing and injuring his acquaintances. On 10 July he records that inside one bomb there was no gunpowder but rather a 'written paper' offering James's terms for surrender. 'Be not obstinate against your Prince,' read the paper, 'expose yourselves no longer to the miseries you undergo …' The cannonball that once contained this note is now on display in the vestibule of St Columb's, Derry's Anglican cathedral.

By 26 July the miseries of the besieged men, women and children had grown so bitter that 'an experiment was tried on a cow at Shipquay. She was tied, and smeared with tar, and tow stuck to it, which was set on fire to make her roar, thinking that the enemy's cows which were grazing in the orchard would come to her.' The experiment was not a success. The following day Ash writes, 'God knows, we never stood in so much need of a supply; for now there is not one week's provision in the garrison: of necessity we must surrender the City, and make the best terms we can for ourselves. Next Wednesday is our last, if relief does not arrive before it.' The entry also states that horses' blood was changing hands within the city for two pence per quart, and it ends: 'There is not a dog to be seen, they are all killed and eaten.'

His entry for the next day begins: 'A day to be remembered with thanksgiving by the besieged in Derry as long as they live, for on this day we were delivered from famine and slavery.' Two ships laden with supplies had burst through the boom placed across the river, and sailed into the quay below the city walls, while a third engaged the enemy's guns. The siege was broken. The captain of the leading ship, the *Mountjoy*, was Michael Browning, the brother-in-law of Thomas Ash. According to John Beresford-Ash, 'It was always said that Captain Browning was fanatically Presbyterian and anti-Catholic, but he simply wanted to rescue his wife who was inside the walls, so he persuaded the admiralty to allow him to take a ship up the Foyle. Tragically, he was shot before he got to relieve his wife – who remarried and had a baby about a year later. Pragmatic lady.' He showed me a delicate tie pin, presented to the family by King William IV almost a hundred and fifty years after the siege, on which miniatures of the three ships are painted, with the words 'To the memory of the gallant Captain Browning 1689'. Towards the end of his journal Thomas Ash writes: 'The Lord who has preserved this city from the enemy I hope will always keep it to the Protestants.'

The city's refusal to surrender ensured that James's army did not take Ireland, and was not able to mount an attack on England. In June 1690 William landed at Carrickfergus and on 12 July his army defeated James's troops at the Boyne. The triumph of the Protestants was complete, and the siege of Derry has symbolized Protestant defiance ever since. When men of the 36th (Ulster) Division went over the top at the Somme on 1 July 1916, their cries of 'No surrender' surprised members of a neighbouring battalion. Why shout about surrender at the start of a major push? But the cries were not referring to the current battle, but to a siege long gone, and to a state of mind ever present.

Walking through John Beresford-Ash's house, with its portraits and its treasured jumble collected down the centuries, gave me a vivid sense of the family's continuity. But his story is interesting in its own right. He came back to Northern Ireland in 1959, after school at Eton and a spell in the Irish Guards. 'I became the first member of either the Beresford family or the Ash family to employ Catholics. Of course, they had had Roman Catholic tenants, but they had never employed them in the house, or on the farm, or as coachmen. I did it because I thought it was the most sensible thing to do.'

Beresford-Ash says that he could see the political situation deteriorating in the Sixties: 'It was entirely the intransigence of the Proddies. The problem was not just the virulent speeches of people like Paisley, but also the blind stupidity of the so-called posh Protestants who ran everything. Roman Catholics in the Creggan and the Bogside had no vote at all. It was just so thick and stupid. And the British government took no interest in the situation. They couldn't give a damn. I joined what was then the Unionist and Conservative party, and I had ideas. I said, "You're riding for a fall!" I said the business about voting and gerrymandering has to end, but I was told that I was a new boy, and that I knew absolutely bugger-all about anything. Those were the things that kept us free, as they put it. Up in the Creggan, the roads were one-track because it was said the Roman Catholics would never have enough money to buy cars, so there was no need for cars to be able to pass each other. All this went on until the mid-Sixties. Most extraordinary blinkered situation among the Proddies over here.'

He remembers the reaction of other Protestant landowners to the fact that he was employing Catholics:

'Oh, they thought I was beyond the pale. I was "one of them". But my employees got on perfectly well with each other. There was no way they would be allowed to fight – or I would just sack the lot of them. I was the first member of our family to go to the Catholic church on Beech Hill, to a funeral. Paddy Gormley, our stack man, had died. I put on tails and a top hat, and I went inside the church, and none of them had ever seen that before. It impressed them that I would bother to do that, but I didn't expect my Presbyterian men to go inside the church. They were willing to stand outside, and go to the grave – and none of them had ever done that before.'

In 1970 he met Cardinal Conway, the Catholic Primate of All Ireland:

'The Cardinal had been asked to St Columb's by the Dean, but nobody would talk to him at the Diocesan tea party afterwards. So I said to Agnès, "For God's sake, go and get a table, and I'll bring him over." We started talking about life – not about Northern Ireland – and he realized that Agnès was French, and he said, "Whereabouts are you from?" and she said her father lived in Bar-le-Duc, and he said, "I remember coming back from Rome once, we stopped there when I was a young priest, and we went to the barber. We were talking among ourselves in Gaelic, and the barber said to us, in French, 'What the hell language is that?' and I said it was Gaelic. The barber looked at me and said, '*Mon père, vous êtes préhistorique!*'" But nobody else would talk to Conway at this tea party, and Agnès said that the thing to do was not to treat him as a bloody pariah. Agnès can do that, and so can I, and that's how you make friends.'

For all that he recognized the political tension in Northern Ireland forty years ago, Beresford-Ash did not foresee the Troubles. 'I don't think anybody did,' he says. He and Agnès were married in Paris in the spring of 1968, at the time of the student riots: 'It's so funny, I remember all the people at the reception after the service, saying it was wonderful that I was taking Agnès away to this lovely place from the ghastly city of Paris. Then, the next forty years ...'

In 1971 Beresford-Ash almost lost his life, during an encounter with a local figure: 'I was listening to the ten o'clock news one evening, and I realized I'd run out of cigarettes. I got in the car – Agnès was away in Paris – and I went to Guild-hall Square. But the cigarette machine had been vandalized, so I went to Fiorentini's café. There were two girls sitting in the café, and they asked me if I could give them a lift home. I thought to myself, well now, two young girls, my wife's away. What about it? So I said yes, and asked where they lived. They said in a very subdued whisper, "The Creggan." I thought about it – my God! This really is an opportunity. The Creggan was a no-go area, I could say that I've been there, and nobody else has. So I said OK, and I finished my cup of coffee, and Mr Fiorentini gave me two packets of cigarettes. We got in the car, and went up into the Lecky Road, and there were armed IRA men all over the place. The girls said some password to them, and we were let through. Then we were let through a second one by Free Derry Corner. Just after that there was a third one – and all hell broke loose. The car was surrounded. I was pulled out and forced onto the ground, and the girls were taken away.

'Now, I looked and sounded like a British officer; I was about 30, and spoke the Queen's English, so somebody must have assumed that I was a British officer, or that I was trying to spy on the IRA. My car was taken away, and I was bundled into the back of another car, and I was sat on by about five heavy young men – which was a most horrid thing. I was given a few kicks – not in the balls – but around the back and arms, and I was manhandled across a bit of green in front of the modern Catholic cathedral, into a place where I was sat in a chair, with a lightbulb above me, just like interrogations in films. A couple of fellows were behind me with old-fashioned Sterling machine guns, pointing at the back of my head, and then the most extraordinary sight. A crocodile of about a dozen men entered, all in balaclavas, a pretty shambolic-looking lot. Then an extraordinary character came in, who had the air of a deserter from the army. He was clean, fair-haired and much younger than me.' (This man would one day rise to political prominence in the republican movement.)

'The man took position behind my head, drew a pistol from his belt, and asked me various questions – which were pretty banal. Since I wasn't in the army, and I wasn't in the Ulster Defence Regiment, he couldn't get any information out of me. He said, "Your car's been seen going out of Ebrington Barracks on many occasions, so you must be a spy!" I said to him, "My dear fellow, you're completely and absolutely crazy! These are my friends. These people were at school with me. Of course I'm going to go and see them and have them to my house. Do you think they're going to tell me secrets about you? You'd have to be joking – they just don't do that sort of thing!" Eventually he got fed up talking to me, and I stayed with these fellows guarding me for several hours. There was absolutely no brutality whatsoever, no question.

'Eventually somebody else came in, and said, "OK, you. We'll give you back your car" and I was led outside, and there was the car, engine running. The man who had been interrogating me was in an absolute fury. His eyes were just full of fury. He drew his pistol, cocked it, put it beside my head, and this other fellow said, "Oh no! Don't kill him! We've checked him out with the boys in Ardmore, and he and his family have always been decent to people like us. He's OK." I remember those words very well; one tends to listen if you think you're about to be killed. The man was absolutely livid. He put his pistol back in his belt and said, "Fuck off!" So I got in the car and drove away. But I had to ask, "Could you please show me the way out? I've never been here before." And they did – they got into another car and they drove in front of me! They also pinched my cigarettes, which I really objected to. I still didn't have any cigarettes after the whole bloody night.'

Many years later Beresford-Ash came across his interrogator again. 'We were in a pizza restaurant one day, eating our nice pizzas, and as I walked through to have a pee, I walked past him. His table had a screen in front, with a bit of ivy on it, and as I went past, I put my fist through the screen, just to annoy him. I don't know if he saw my face, but he could have seen my fist, all right.'

Thirty years after his experience in the Creggan, Beresford-Ash was again fortunate to escape with his life; between August 1997 and June 1998 his house was fire-bombed three times. He explains, 'On the feast of the Assumption in August – the "Catholic Twelfth" as it's called over here – they have a bonfire. People from the local council estate cut down an awful lot of our trees to make the bonfire, and this particularly annoyed me because there is so much dead wood lying about in our woods, all you've got to do is go and pick it up. I'd actually help them pick it up and make their bonfire with them – not a hope – they must go and cut down young trees instead. I got fed up with this, and I remonstrated with them.' He was told, 'We'll get you for this!'

One night shortly afterwards Beresford-Ash and his wife were asleep in bed, when 'there was a crash. It was the hall windows coming in, and petrol bombs landing. I was a damn sight fitter in those days, and I was down in a few seconds. My daughter also came down and, between us, we put the fires out.'

Six months later the house was attacked again. 'This time it was much more dangerous, because they bust a hole through a window, and put a can of petrol on the window seat. They sprayed paraffin all round it, and set it alight; the idea was that when I came down to put the fire out, it would explode and blow me up, and the house as well. But someone – "the man upstairs" – was looking after me because the petrol can leaked. So when I came downstairs I saw a terrific ball of fire. There were fumes, and smoke, and flames, but I could see the white faces of my ancestors on the walls, and I remember saying to them, "It's all right, chaps! I'll save you!" And by God, I bloody well did! I still get quite emotional about that. I went over to pick up the water fire-extinguisher, and my bloody hip dislocated. Agnès was ringing up the fire brigade in the kitchen, and she heard me yelping, and she thought I'd caught fire, so she came in with a bucket of water. "Darling, don't throw it over me," I said, "throw it on the fire!" Then the fire brigade arrived, and they were absolutely superb.'

A few months later Beresford-Ash had a sixtieth-birthday party. 'The local paper took a picture of Agnès, myself, and our three daughters outside the house, which they published, and we had a nice birthday lunch. Very soon after that, there was a hell of a thumping on the windows. By this stage we'd got bullet-proof security windows, so they couldn't fire-bomb the house. Instead they lit five fires on the gravel at the front, which represented myself, my wife, and our three children being burned.'

Beresford-Ash is convinced that he knows the identity of the chief culprit: 'It was all done by the same people, led by the same man, and everybody knew it, the police knew it, it was the joke of the local pub.' He later met a barrister, and told him the whole story: 'I said, "For you, in the legal profession, how do you feel about this?" He said, "We know, and our judges know, who has done these things over the years, who these people have killed, and when and how they killed them." I said, "Look, mate, point of it is, you're prepared to say that, but then you're prepared to go back on Monday morning and draw the old pay?" And he said, "Yes. Why not? Because if I didn't, somebody else worse than me certainly would." What can you say to that?'

I asked Beresford-Ash whether he considered moving away from Ashbrook after the attacks. 'What? Leave here? Good God no! My dear Josh! This house has woodworm and dry rot, but, my God, I'm fond of it, and nobody's going to kick me out of here! My daughter summed it up: after the second petrol bombing, Agnès was fed up and said we ought to go, but my daughter said, "Come on, Mum! We were here before these people, and we'll be here after them!"'

Beresford-Ash is a man of great charm, who has made efforts over the years to foster good local relations, and this fact probably saved his life in the Creggan. Nevertheless, his attitude hardens as he discusses the peace process. 'When the process started, I would wake up in the morning and listen to the news on Radio 4, and think to myself, thank God another soldier or policeman hasn't been killed. But that has been the only real benefit. Otherwise I consider it the most disgraceful and despicable surrender by the British politicians, the judiciary, the legal profession, and it should have been stopped immediately it started. Because the Queen's enemies were attacking the Crown forces. They should still be hanged – they've done it. And that's my instinct.'

In Killyleagh I met another man whose family arrived in Ulster four centuries ago. Denys Rowan Hamilton is a man of precise military bearing beneath which lies a charming streak of mischief who, after coming to live in Northern Ireland in 1967, quickly became infuriated by much of what he saw. Born and raised in Scotland, Rowan Hamilton spent his childhood holidays in Ireland, and on leaving the army in his late forties he moved to County Down. He became the master of Killyleagh Castle, a fairy-tale fortress of towers and dogtooth walls that stands above the town. The first castle on the site was built by the Normans shortly their arrival. In 1604 the castle was taken over by Sir James Hamilton, an Anglican from Ayrshire, who was granted extensive lands in Ulster during the first plantation. It has remained in the family ever since. In 2000 Rowan Hamilton passed it on to his son and now lives in a house outside the town, where I kept him from his lunch, urging him to tell of his experiences.

'When I made up my mind to come here,' he says, 'I was wondering what the hell I was going to do. I was going to start a new life. It's quite a thing to do at 47.' He was immediately fêted by well-to-do society: 'They were saying, "We've got to have him!" and it was because I was the young Hamilton of Killyleagh. It really makes me laugh. They didn't know me at all. I might have been the most ghastly shit.'

Killyleagh Castle, into which the 'young Hamilton' was moving, had been requisitioned by the army during the war, and had suffered from years of neglect: 'My great uncle was clever, he wrote Latin poems and that sort of thing, but he was a useless fellow, and never did a stroke of work. Not much happened when he was in the castle. He sold a farm a year to pay his servants. When I finally took over, there were only twenty-seven acres left out of an estate that once ran up to Bangor. If we hadn't come along, the castle would never have survived. Now it's in better nick than it's been for 150 years. And my son, the first Hamilton in four hundred years to make a penny, has redecorated it very nicely.'

On arriving in Northern Ireland, Denys Rowan Hamilton took an interest in more than just his castle, however. He had entered a world that was quite alien to him: 'I had arrived from a sane society. *This place wasn't a democracy*!' He remembers meeting a clerk of the works at the council: 'He would wring his flat cap in humility, asking if I had any jobs for him to do, and then he would start talking about all the dreadful murders of Protestants throughout history. He knew them all. He'd been taught at his mother's knee how dreadful the Catholics were.' Rowan Hamilton was furious at much of what he saw and heard, and he freely expressed his views. His stance, he believes, reflected his family's values: 'My family had always been moderate and liberal in their views. When Catholics had wanted their own church, the Hamiltons provided them with a place to hold their services.'

Rowan Hamilton was asked to stand as a reforming unionist candidate in the 1969 General Election. 'I said I would stand. It was totally on principle. I wasn't a politician, but I couldn't believe that people could not try to get on with the other side. As soon as it was announced that I would stand, two staunch, bigoted unionists arrived at the castle. They demanded that I stood down. These were "respectable" people, masters of the stag hounds, and they marched towards me, yelling "No Surrender!" I pleaded my case to them, but they were pretty threatening. They told me that my mother would never speak to me again. I wouldn't have come here if I'd known it would be like this! It was disruptive of the peaceful life that I'd wanted!'

Rowan Hamilton lost the election heavily, but it is a measure of his principle and determination that in a later election he agreed to stand for the Alliance Party, which seeks to bridge the gap between Catholics and Protestants. 'In the run-up to that election,' he says, 'the person who invited me to stand, declined to come out in public and support me. He was frightened and didn't have the guts to stand up for his views. I would say that I was socially ostracized for my stance.' This foray into politics placed him in unlikely situations: 'I found myself taking part in a roadblock for half an hour near Seaforde, at a junction of some importance. I was compelled to do it for political reasons, but I was rather embarrassed. It wasn't really my thing.'

Rowan Hamilton is not the first member of his family to take a controversial political stance. His great-great-great grandfather, Archibald Hamilton Rowan, had been a prominent member of the Society of United Irishmen. The Society, formed in 1791 in Ulster, was a secret organization, intent on creating a single Irish nation, independent of Britain, that would unite Catholics and Protestants. Catholics were subjected to repressive Penal Laws by the British authorities, but the United Irishmen were not

Catholics; the original members were Protestants, mostly Presbyterians (known as 'dissenters') who were also subjected to
discriminatory measures. Many tens of thousands of Presbyterians had left Ulster during the eighteenth century to begin new
lives in the American colonies, where they contributed to the
revolutionary fervour of the War of Independence. The democratic ideas of Tom Paine that inspired the American revolution-
aries also stirred the United Irishmen. It would not be true to say
that the bulk of the Ulster Presbyterians were sympathetic to
Catholic grievances; the vast majority were sectarian in outlook.
Nevertheless, there were those who were keen to sever links with
Britain, and a few who were motivated by a desire for government by election and representation. While the Provisional IRA
would one day be made up almost exclusively of Catholics, the
leaders of the first republican movement to fight for an independent Ireland were Protestants.

Archibald Hamilton Rowan was an Anglican, born and raised
in England, and educated at Westminster School, where he
displayed 'animal spirits and love of bustle'. His Cambridge tutor
was John Jebb, an Irish radical who influenced his thinking, and
an acquaintance was Lord Sandwich, with whom he ate an
unusual meal of 'thin slices of bread and butter with cold meat
between each'. As a young man he went to live in France, where,
during the American War of Independence, he displayed an early
radical streak by introducing Benjamin Franklin, the American
representative in Paris, to two Englishmen who wanted to enlist
in the American forces. He came to Ireland in 1783 and became
known as a defender of the rights of the oppressed after he
espoused the case of a 12-year-old girl, Mary Neal, who had been
abducted by the owner of a bawdy house. He became a member
of the United Irishmen in November 1791 and wrote of the need
for 'reformation of the present state of the representation of the
people'. He took to wandering around Dublin in a green uniform
and standing up in theatres and shouting when 'God Save the

King' was played. In 1794 he was convicted of distributing inflammatory material – a pamphlet entitled 'Citizens to Arms!' – and sentenced to two years' imprisonment.

While in prison he was regularly visited by a close associate, Theobald Wolfe Tone, an Anglican lawyer from Belfast, who is nowadays the most celebrated of the United Irishmen. Hamilton Rowan asked Wolfe Tone to draft a memorandum to send to revolutionary France, encouraging the French to send an invasion force to Ireland. Wolfe Tone composed the memorandum, which assured the French that they would receive support from 'the great bulk of the people': 900,000 Presbyterians 'from reason and reflection' and 3,150,000 Catholics 'from hatred of the English name'. Hamilton Rowan made copies of the memorandum in his own hand – and one of these copies fell into the possession of the British authorities. Realizing that he would be convicted of high treason and executed, he conceived, aided by his wife, a plan to escape from prison. He persuaded his gaoler that he would have to return home briefly in order to sign papers relating to the sale of a property. For a £100 bribe the gaoler agreed to accompany him to the house and escort him back to prison. This, at least, is the official version; Denys Rowan Hamilton said that his ancestor 'bribed his gaoler to let him out of prison to screw his wife'. Either way Hamilton Rowan describes in his autobiography what happened next: 'I then descended from the window by a knotted rope, which was made fast to the bedpost and reached down to the garden. I went to the stable, took my horse, and rode to the head of Sackville Street, where Mat Dowling had appointed to meet me … Some of my friends advised my taking my pistols with me; but I had made up my mind not to be taken alive, so I only put a razor in my pocket.'

Hamilton Rowan was taken first to the seaside house of a United Irishman, and then onto a boat owned by smugglers. As the little vessel passed the west coast of England, it caught sight of the British fleet, but Hamilton Rowan arrived safely in revolutionary France. But his troubles were not at an end. Expecting to be welcomed by the French as a republican hero and an enemy of Britain, he found himself imprisoned by the local authorities on suspicion of being a British spy. He was only released when his plight came to the attention of a prominent official who happened to be Irish.

Once his identity had been verified, Hamilton Rowan was presented to Robespierre, the driving force behind the reign of terror that was gripping France. He set about convincing the French to mount an invasion of Ireland, with the aim of securing its independence. His plan was that he himself would lead the invasion; the official who placed the plan before Robespierre's Committee of Public Safety described Rowan Hamilton as 'the most striking patriot in Ireland'. It must have looked to Rowan Hamilton as though he was destined to become Ireland's great revolutionary leader, but the plan came to nothing. Robespierre and the Jacobins were overthrown, and Hamilton Rowan became 'much discontented with the distracted state of Paris, where they were too busy with their own intestine divisions to think of assisting Ireland'. He hurriedly left France for a slightly more established beacon of liberty – America.

The experience of living in Paris during the bloody reign of terror, and perhaps also the disappointment of watching his heroic destiny fail to materialize, seems to have dulled Hamilton Rowan's revolutionary zeal. From Philadelphia he wrote to his wife: 'I owe to you candidly, when it is of no avail, that my ideas of reform, and of another word which begins with the same letter, are very much altered by living for twelve months in France; and that I never wish to see the one or the other procured by force.' Nevertheless, within months he had been joined in Philadelphia by Wolfe Tone, whom he offered to introduce to the French Minister to the United States. For a while Wolfe Tone settled down to live as a farmer in Princeton, but he did not admire the attitudes he encountered, describing Americans as 'a selfish, churlish, unsocial race, totally absorbed in making money'. While Hamilton Rowan remained in America, eking out a living as a farmer, dyer, and brewer, Wolfe Tone sailed to France, where he resumed his efforts on behalf of the Irish people 'to break the connection with England, the never failing source of all our political evils'. Wolfe Tone achieved what Hamilton Rowan had not: he persuaded the French to mount an invasion of Ireland in 1796, which might have succeeded had the thirty-five expeditionary ships, laden with thousands of French troops, not been prevented by bad weather from landing in Bantry Bay in County Cork.

Wolfe Tone was on board a French ship during the failed Bantry Bay expedition, and he persuaded Napoleon Bonaparte to launch another invasion fleet in 1798. The United Irishmen attempted to stir up an internal rebellion to coincide with the French invasion, but the government's network of informers was effective, and the insurrection was ruthlessly put down in most areas. Only in County Wexford did a band of Catholic rebels mount a serious challenge to the army, but their indiscipline and lack of strategy eventually ensured their defeat. A small French fleet landed in County Mayo, but its troops surrendered to government forces when they could find no internal rebellion with which to join.

Wolfe Tone himself arrived with a subsequent French expedition, which was defeated by a British fleet in Lough Swilly. He was arrested and taken to Dublin, where he was sentenced to hang. While in custody he slit his throat with a penknife and a week later he died of his wounds. The rebellion of the United Irishmen was at an end, but republicans still gather at Wolfe Tone's grave in Bodenstown every year to honour the man they revere as the father of republicanism.

While Wolfe Tone was attempting to bring revolution to Ireland, Archibald Hamilton Rowan was living a quiet life of near penury in America. At home in Ireland, his wife was attempting to restore his reputation in the hope that he might be allowed to return. He was eventually given permission to come back, first to Europe, then to England, and finally to Ireland. He became the master of Killyleagh Castle in 1806, where he retained his liberal beliefs to the end of his life. He was known as a benevolent land-lord who reduced his tenants' rents during times of economic distress. He also expressed a strong disapproval of slavery; a story in his autobiography recalls an encounter with a slave in New York State in 1799: 'I lost one of my gloves, and having searched back the road for it in vain, I continued my route. Overtaking a Negro, I threw him the other, saying that "I had lost the fellow on that hill somewhere; that perhaps he might find it, and he never was possessed of such a pair in his life." The fellow smiled. "No, Master, you not lost it; here it is;" and he took the fellow out of his bosom and gave them both to me. And this man was a slave, whose portion was stripes, and *black dog* his appellation from a whey-faced Christian!'

Hamilton Rowan died in 1834 at the age of 84. His last public appearance was at a meeting of the Friends of Civil and Reli-gious Liberty, from which he was borne aloft by a triumphal crowd. Looking back on Hamilton Rowan's life, William Lecky, the nineteenth-century Irish historian, described him as 'fool-ish and impulsive, but also brave, honourable, energetic and charitable'.

Archibald Hamilton Rowan's son reversed the order of the family name, turning Hamilton Rowan into Rowan Hamilton. According to his great-great-grandson Denys, he did this partly to emphasize the Hamilton side of the family and partly to disas-sociate himself from his radical and embarrassing father. When Denys was at prep school, two American brothers with the surname Hamilton Rowan entered the school, and Denys has little doubt that they are relatives. 'To me it is quite obvious that Archibald Hamilton Rowan took a common-law wife while he was in America, and started a family, but when I said to the American Hamilton Rowans, "You're all from the wrong side of the blanket," they didn't like it much. Americans can be *churchy*.'

However fruitful his American legacy, the extent of Archibald Hamilton Rowan's Irish legacy – or at least the legacy of the United Irishmen – is considerable. Until the 1800 Act of Union, Britain and Ireland were legally distinct kingdoms with separate Parliaments. The Act brought the kingdoms together to create a 'United Kingdom'. *Some* Protestants objected to the Act of Union because it removed any prospect of an independent Ireland. And *some* Catholics welcomed the Act of Union because it offered the possibility of a more tolerant administration. Over time, however, attitudes migrated into those with which we are familiar today; Protestants came to believe that the union with Britain would guarantee them their ascendancy, and Catholics came to believe that their condition could only be improved by a repeal of the union. These beliefs lie at the very heart of the two communities' modern identities.

Republican movements arose in the years after the United Irishmen's failed rebellion; the forerunner of the modern IRA was the Fenian Brotherhood, named after Cuchulainn's band of warriors, the Fianna. Formed in the aftermath of the Irish famine of 1845–51, during which the population of Ireland fell by as many as two million, the Fenians planted a bomb in a wheelbarrow outside Clerkenwell Prison in London in 1867. The bomb killed six people and injured hundreds of others. Rumours spread through London of further planned Fenian attacks, sparking widespread panic. When, six years later, a bridge over Regent's Canal was destroyed by an explosion of gunpowder on a barge, it was immediately believed – wrongly – to be the work of Fenians: troops based at the nearby Albany Street barracks were mobilized to counteract the supposed Irish threat. Such fears would return a century later, when the Provisional IRA started planting bombs in England. And to this day 'Fenian' is a derogatory term used by Protestants to describe a Catholic.

In 1886 the Liberal Party in Westminster, led by William Gladstone, introduced a bill attempting to grant Home Rule to Ireland. Home Rule would have amounted to limited self-government, an early form of devolution. Gladstone's bill failed and Ulster unionists proceeded to do everything they could to prevent another bill from succeeding. The Presbyterians and Anglicans of Ulster had come to consider themselves defenders of the British empire, fearful for their prosperity and heritage in a Catholic-dominated Ireland. As another Home Rule bill passed through the House of Commons in 1913, a quarter of a million Protestant Ulstermen signed a covenant – some in their own blood – pledging to resist it. An Ulster Volunteer Force of 100,000 men was created, armed with weapons smuggled in from Germany, ready to fight for Ulster's future. But as the prospect of civil war loomed, the attention of all parties was diverted by the outbreak of a bigger conflict – the First World War. The implementation of Home Rule was delayed until after the end of the war, and young men from both sides of the Irish divide joined the British army; unionists in order to prove their loyalty to the King, nationalists in order to earn the right to have Home Rule implemented once the Great War was over.

On 24 April 1916, at the very height of the war, an event took place in Dublin which had a profound effect on the Irish people, whose attitudes were, to quote Yeats, 'changed utterly'. A small number of rebels, led by Patrick Pearse – a poet and schoolmaster who once wrote: 'There are many things more horrible than bloodshed; slavery is one of them' – seized public buildings in Dublin and proclaimed the formation of 'the Provisional Government of Ireland'. The rebellion was put down, and its leaders, including Pearse, were executed as traitors. The almost mystical influence that Pearse has come to exert on the modern republican movement was brought home to me by one republican, who told me this story. 'Patrick Pearse had no republican background. His father was an Englishman. But when he walked down the street he saw the kids in their bare feet on the cobble-stones, and their feet hacked with darkened blood. And the kids were playing, and singing about the Grand Old Duke of York, a bastard who had them shoeless and poverty-stricken in their own country. And he went up the stairs, and his brother Willie followed him up and said, "What's wrong, Patrick?" He said, "I've seen a terrible thing. Children, not fed properly, with their feet hacked, glorifying the Grand Old Duke of York." Pearse was a sensitive man, and an educated human being, and he was choked up, and the two men hugged, and swore that they would never desist until English rule in Ireland had ceased. It was the last straw. And the last straw wasn't theological or cultural. It was as simple as that.'

Following the executions of Pearse and the other rebels, Irish expectations changed. No longer was Home Rule considered a sufficient ambition. The national objective became full inde-pendence. For two years, between 1919 and 1921, a war (known by one side as the Anglo-Irish War and by the other as the War of Independence) was fought between the British government and the guerrilla IRA, until a truce was called. A treaty was signed which created the Irish Free State, a dominion state, similar in status to Canada, but not the republic for which the IRA had been fighting. Michael Collins, who negotiated the treaty on behalf of the republicans, argued that the treaty gave the Irish 'the freedom to win freedom'. Other republicans took the view that it repre-sented a betrayal of their principles. A bitter rift developed which gave way to a bloody civil war between recent brothers-in-arms. Yet as republicans argued about the constitutional status of the Free State, they barely questioned another result of the treaty: the formation of a northern state for the Protestants of Ulster.

The new state of Northern Ireland consisted of only six of the nine counties of the old province of Ulster, carefully chosen by unionists to ensure that the new state was large enough to be politically and economically viable, but small enough to embrace a large Protestant majority. Northern Ireland was granted its own Parliament, meaning that it was no longer subject to direct rule from Westminster – and so, with a certain irony, the province that had vowed to take up arms to resist Home Rule became the only part of Ireland actually to receive Home Rule.

The lack of vocal objection from republicans to the creation of Northern Ireland may have been because they expected a forthcoming Boundary Commission to reduce its size to an unviable four counties, forcing it to reintegrate with the Free State. But in the event the Boundary Commission merely ratified the existing border. More than one present-day republican would tell me, with great regret, that had Michael Collins suspected that the border would remain unchanged, he would never have signed the treaty.

Once in place, the government of Northern Ireland became, in the words of its first Prime Minister, Sir James Craig, 'a Protestant government for a Protestant people'. It viewed itself as an answer to the Free State's Catholic government. The British Prime Minister, David Lloyd George, sincerely believed that the partition of Ireland would finally solve the 'Irish problem', but hundreds of years of antipathy were not to be cancelled out by the stroke of a Boundary Commissioner's pen. Throughout the Troubles, republicans in Northern Ireland considered the results of the 1918 General Election and the 1920 Local Government Elections – the very last *all-Ireland* elections – as their mandate for a unified, independent Ireland. In those elections supporters of Irish independence won a majority of votes across the entire island. As a result, say republicans, the subsequent partition of the country was unlawful, and successive IRA campaigns aimed at reversing partition have been legitimate. Yet in the 1918 election unionist candidates won twenty-two out of twenty-nine constituencies in the north-eastern counties. Does this then confer on unionists the right to live in Ulster under British rule? The traditional republican view is that unionists are Irish men and women who will one day wake up to their true Irish identity, just as the United Irishmen once did. Unionists have little time for such an analysis. So far as they are concerned, they are loyal subjects living in a legitimate state, with a right to choose their own sovereignty.

There has been a long tradition of settlers arriving in Ulster, and that tradition has continued to the present day. Andy Park is a Presbyterian, born and raised in Glasgow, who decided to come to live in Northern Ireland in the early Seventies because 'I was a loyalist, and I felt that my country was under threat. I felt that my culture and heritage was disappearing here.' I went to visit Park at his smart home on a newly built estate in Lisburn. I arrived much later than I had intended, after setting off late and then being held up by a series of police roadblocks, but Park and his wife, Mary, could not have been friendlier. Park has a very cheeky, boyish manner, and I felt relaxed talking to him, but whenever I challenged him, he would stand his ground with a vehemence that made me wonder whether I was offending him. I don't think I was, but his is the passion of a man who has devoted his life to a cause, and that passion is not easily switched off, even over tea and KitKats, while a cat snoozes on his lap.

Park had a 'straight type of Scottish Presbyterian upbringing' in Glasgow. 'As a young teenager my Sunday consisted of Boys' Brigade Bible class between ten and eleven. Then I went to church. After that I had the Church Youth Fellowship, and then I had Sunday School. I came home from Sunday School, had something to eat, and then me and a couple of my friends went to a wee Apostolic church Sunday School from three to four. At half past six I went back to the Fellowship, and that was my Sunday. And we weren't allowed out to play. We had very clear guidelines on what was right and what was wrong.' Members of his family had moved from Ulster to Scotland over the previous century, and Park was enlisted in the 'Cradle Roll' of the Orange Order before he was even born. He became a member of the junior Orange Order when he was about seven, and later joined an Orange flute band: 'I learnt to read and appreciate music. I would never have got that at school.' His father left the Order because of the friendships he had made with Catholics during the war, when he was fighting in Italy with an Irish regiment. 'But,' says Park, 'he was still supportive, and he'd go to the Orange parades.'

Park began work in the shipyard in Clydebank, like his father before him, but the shipyards began to close and he found himself out of work, so he joined the Royal Engineers. 'When the Troubles started, there were people in the army who held republican views, and I felt challenged, so I put photographs from the *Belfast Telegraph* over my bed on 12 July [the anniversary of the Battle of the Boyne] and I was told to take them down.' He was sent to Northern Ireland with the Royal Engineers: 'I did three tours. The second tour was an interesting one because I was stationed in Lurgan, and I let it be known locally that I was an Orangeman, and I was invited to an Orange meeting that nobody knew about. I would have been in trouble if the army had found out.' Soldiers were supposed to be impartial; their role was to keep the peace between the sides. Active participation in the Orange Order hardly constituted impartiality.

When he left the army, Park moved to Northern Ireland because he felt his country was under threat. I asked him what he means when he says 'my country'. He explained, 'I'm British and I will defend my right to be British. I believe in the British way of life, I believe in the sense of justice and fairness that British society gives me. It's not religious, it's not sectarian, and it's not racist. It gives me my whole value system, the whole being and identity of who I am.' Later in our talk Park was to describe his membership of the Orange Order in almost identical terms:

'Orangeism is what gave me my value system, who I am today, gave me my roots, gave me my identity, my morals. It's a camaraderie, a fellowship.'

The key words here are 'camaraderie' and 'fellowship'. National identity is a very nebulous concept; Park's sense of sharing values with others who describe themselves as British may to be enough to give him a British identity, just as sharing values with those who describe themselves as Orangemen gives him an Orange identity. But I wanted to dig a little deeper. If people across the United Kingdom nowadays describe themselves as Scottish, as Welsh, as Londoners, but rarely as British, does it occur to him that the unionists of Northern Ireland are becoming isolated in stressing this identity? 'Yes, I've questioned this myself,' he says, 'Sometimes I feel more British than what the English do. I accept that. I think that's because we felt under threat for the last hundred years, so we said, "This is who we are, and what we are, and you're not taking it away from me!"' Britishness in this context could be construed as a negative: as a way of saying that, whatever we are, we are *not* Irish. But Park is adamant that his Britishness is far from negative: 'Britishness is about openness, it's about giving freedom to all. That's what William of Orange stood for – freedom for all faiths. It's not just a bland "I'm British" and it's not a white Anglo-Saxon thing either.'

When I asked Park how Scottish he feels, and how Northern Irish, he answered, 'Being British doesn't divorce me from my Scottishness, and it doesn't divorce me from my thirty-seven years in Northern Ireland.' He tells me the story of a loyalist politician who travelled to the United States several years earlier, where he was challenged by an Irish American on the subject of his identity. The politician said, 'You identify yourself as an Irish American when you're three or four generations down the line, and yet you say it's wrong for me to call myself British! Why can I not identify myself as British Irish?'.

I asked Park if he remembered what was in his head was when he settled in Northern Ireland in 1972. 'I wanted to come over and fight the war. If I had any skills, I wanted to bring them over to Northern Ireland. There was no use me sitting in a pub in Glasgow, talking about it.' What does he mean by 'fight the war'? 'I believed that the British army, for various reasons, wasn't defending Protestant people, either by government restraints or in personal restraints. Some of the squaddies were, in my eyes, republican sympathizers. That challenged me very much, so I came over.' He tells me that he did not join a paramilitary organization. Given that he had spoken of the need to 'fight the war', I asked him why not, and he told me, 'You're trying to make a distinction between being a member and not being a member. There's maybe no distinction. I maybe have given tacit support – and maybe more than tacit support – without being a member. So don't assume because I wasn't a member that I wasn't doing things.'

Park calls himself a loyalist. I asked him what this means. 'A loyalist is somebody who wants to maintain the union with Britain and will go to lengths to maintain that union.' What lengths? 'Defending the community. Because we felt under daily threat.' Park describes his politics as left-of-centre, and in recent years he has been an influential member of the Progressive Unionist Party (PUP), which once represented the paramilitary Ulster Volunteer Force but has proved forward-thinking in its policies. The PUP has strongly supported the peace process and attempted to forge links between working-class Protestants and Catholics. Its ideal is an inclusive socialist United Kingdom. I asked Park whether there was a contradiction between his loyalism – which would seem to have conservative overtones – and socialism. 'Most of the victims and perpetrators of this dirty war came from the working classes. Not too many middle-class people got their hands dirty. I'm not part of any Protestant ascendancy! As a working-class Prod, where's my ascendancy? I don't own a big house! And my daughter can't be Queen of England because she's a Presbyterian! I'm a dissenter! I started off in a worse place than the Roman Catholics did – at least they had a title! Presbyterianism is the core in Northern Ireland.'

In January 1976 Park was badly injured in an explosion in the Klondyke Bar in Belfast. He tells the story: 'People came from the IRA to bomb a pub in Sandy Row. The Klondyke was next to the bridge, and it was an opportunity for them because there were no visible guards, and they placed the bomb inside the door. I was standing just the other side of the door with my two mates when the bomb went off. I remember a flash; there was one of these gas fires in the pub and I had a vague thought something had happened with the fire. Up until a few years ago, I had a picture in my head of flying through the air – but I spoke to an ambulance driver who said, "Andy, it didn't happen that way. We dug you out. The roof caved in and the bar came on top of you." I've never read about the bomb, and I never saw a picture of it until recently.'

Park was in the Royal Victoria Hospital for almost a year. He lost part of his thighs and one hip, and had steel callipers on both legs for eight years. The initial medical view was that one leg would have to be amputated, but the leg was saved. Park was bedridden for three months. 'When I started putting my legs over the bed, just to sit – the blood rushing down was the worst pain I've ever felt.' He remembers incidents from his time in hospital. 'Just after the bomb, there was a guy next to me who was dying, and his sister was a nun. They were sitting there going through the rosary beads, and oh! Can you understand the anger, resentment, hatred I had for all things Roman Catholic? I couldn't distinguish between Roman Catholicism and the IRA. They were all the same. It was so hard. And then I remember the two night nurses. One night a bomb went off right outside the hospital and one of the nurses sat with me the whole night, did not move from my bed, comforted me, talked to me. I was …

Jesus … I was almost hanging from the ceiling. I later learnt that it was an IRA bomb and the bomber had blown himself up. I'm sorry to say, when I found that out it gave me a sense of satisfaction.'

Park's wife Mary would come to visit him twice a day in hospital, even while she was pregnant with their son. 'I'd give her a tongue-lashing if she was late. She brought me pieces of chicken and steak, and I wasn't grateful at all. The nurses would give me a bottle of Guinness to build me up, and my wife used to bring me a half-bottle of whisky or vodka, so I was drinking when I was still in hospital on medication. The only reason I wasn't falling about drunk because I was already lying down.'

Two of Park's friends died as a result of the explosion. One, John Smiley, was killed at the time; the other, Jackie Bullock, lost both of his legs, and drank himself to death over the next two years. Once he was out of hospital, Park began drinking several bottles of vodka a day. He describes his state of mind: 'Turmoil, hatred, anger. I hated them all. Hated them with a vengeance. I lay in bed at night, planning how I was going to get my revenge. I went through scenario after scenario, finding out where they lived, how I was going to visit them. Revenge, total revenge. And I became an alcoholic. It killed the pain. And the uselessness. I felt useless. Worthless. Even when I started on the road to physical recovery, I wasn't achieving what I set out to do, and it was hard for the wife and the family. I'll be straight with you – if the roles were reversed, I don't think I'd have been around to take the abuse. I wasn't physical, but I was sarcastic, cutting to the bone with a remark. I wasn't grateful at all to be alive. When I stopped drinking in 1984, I was six and a half stone.'

He explains how he managed to stop drinking: 'One time I was in hospital for about ten days, I'd burnt the gullet of my stomach lining with alcohol. The doctor was absolutely brilliant. She turned around to me and she said, "Andy, would you like to see someone who deals with alcohol-related illnesses?" She didn't say to me I was drinking too much, didn't say I was an alcoholic, and the upshot of that was I went into a mental home in Down-patrick, and I was there for nearly four months drying out and detoxing and things like that. And through that I joined Alco-holics Anonymous. It told me to get a sponsor, somebody you can identify and talk with, and the strange thing was that my first and only sponsor in AA was a Roman Catholic, a high member in the Gaelic Athletic Association – and I was sharing secrets with him that I hadn't shared with any person in my life. That was changing for me, and I became a twelve-step carer, I did prison visits, and I was also very heavy into politics.'

Park might have been sorting out his own chaos, but North-ern Ireland remained a chaotic place to live. 'Everything became normal. That's the crazy thing. You'd just think, there's a bomb over there, I'll cut down this way instead. Near the end of the Troubles my little sister came over to visit me from Scotland, and she brought a friend. One day there was a soldier lying in my garden, and I brought them home, and we had to step over the soldier to open the front door. The wee friend started getting in hysterics, saying, "There's a man lying in your garden with a gun!" I goes, "Aye, it's a soldier. It's all right.' It wasn't until later on that I saw that this wasn't normal. We never ventured outside of our own immediate areas. That wee geographical circle became your world. You wouldn't go into town after five o'clock, and there were no buses on. Being aware of where you could go, and where you couldn't go, became a natural instinct. You didn't even think about it. It's why I say that everybody in Northern Ireland has been a victim of this war.'

When Park travelled across to Scotland, he took his Belfast habits with him. 'I went out shopping in Glasgow, and when I came back to the car, I was down on my hands and knees check-ing underneath the car. Mum said, "What are you doing?" so I pretended I'd seen a flat tyre. Once when I went to get a drink with my dad, a car backfired, and I assumed the position down on my right knee. My dad didn't say anything.'

Park became the chairman of the Ulster Clubs movement. The movement was intended to unite loyalist groups against government moves to increase links between Northern Ireland and the Irish Republic, and to provide an association for loyalists unwilling to join a paramilitary group. In September 1988 the movement's treasurer, Colin Abernethy, a close friend of Park, was shot dead by the IRA on a commuter train. 'Colin was travelling to his work, and as the train drew in at Lambeg station, two guys dressed as postmen got up and shot him in the head. The statement came out that they'd killed the leader of the Ulster Clubs movement, but that was *me*. My son Andrew and Colin were very close. During that week Colin had come up with two fish tanks and all the equipment, said he'd be up next week to bring the fish. Andrew and Colin were both into tropical fish. Andrew took it quite badly at the time. The visual impact was that he lost all interest in tropical fish, and didn't set up the tank. He was spending more and more time in the house, you know, we thought it was him just growing up, his adolescence. I was getting heavily involved in the loyalist movement in my politics, and there were threats to my life, but I was trying to keep that away from him.'

One day Park received a message from his son's school. 'We went up to the school, and the teacher said, "Are you aware that Andrew is taking on your security?" He was getting up at seven o'clock in the morning, looking underneath the car, and on the nights I wasn't in he was sitting at the window waiting for me to come back. Mary was working as a nurse in Musgrave Park Hospital, and Andrew said to her, "Would you not give up that job, Mum? Because if anything happened to Daddy I wouldn't know what to do." I mean that came as a big, big blow to me because I thought I was keeping that side of my life away from the family.'

Years later, in 1996, when a bomb in Canary Wharf in London broke the IRA ceasefire, Andrew reacted badly: 'I was going up the stairs, and Andrew was coming down when we heard the news. Andrew would have been 20, a big, strapping lad, six foot one, and he wrapped his arms around me and started crying, and he said, "No, it's not starting again, Daddy, is it?" and I had to assure him that everything was all right. That's the scars that people don't see. At that time I was doing peace work, and it was risky, and if my own community was to find out who I was talking to, it would have been pretty bad. It started to edge out that I was doing these sorts of things, and we had a family conference and Andrew turned around and said, "Dad, how can you talk to these bastards? They blew you up, they killed your mates!" And that came as a shock to me because here was me, I was moving from one end of the sphere to the other, and trying to look at dialogue and mediation, and here was my son stuck with my pain, my anger. For our children, they've seen the aftermath of it, and we need to keep a cycle going where their children don't see physical force or violence.'

When I asked Park how his experiences have affected his loyalism, he told me, 'I'm still a loyalist, but now we can look at how we can achieve our aspirations in a different way. We don't need to kill and maim and blow each other up for it. There's a lot of scars out there, I mean I'm still living with the scars, I have post-traumatic stress disorder, I get into depressions, I shut myself away for days at end, but at the end of the day it's people like me and other people who do this work, it's the only way forward. If I relate it to how I felt in 1972, it was important for me to come over and fight the war for my culture, and I think it's also incumbent on me to fight for peace.'

I asked him whether genuine politics has come to Northern Ireland. 'We need to move into normal politics,' he replied. 'We're only starting – we're learners at the political game. We've got to learn what democracy is. We need to get involved in civic responsibility. I think working-class Prods have been disenfran-chised from civic society. My party, the Progressive Unionist Party, is a social-justice party. Left-of-centre politics: we try to look at bread-and-butter issues. We believe in maintaining the union of Great Britain and Northern Ireland, but we believe that's done and dusted. We try to be broad-based, and we stress the importance of health and education and real issues.'

Does he feel threatened by the possibility that Northern Ireland might one day become part of a united Ireland? 'Where are we going to be in fifty years politically? If the present circum-stances were to still exist, then yes, possibly I would feel threat-ened, and maybe wanting to take up arms again. But life changes. Everything's up for grabs within politics, and the onus is on republicanism to persuade me that I'd be better off. One thing I've not heard in all the talk of a united Ireland is what will they do about the northern Prods? Do they think northern Prods are going to roll over, have our bellies rubbed, and we'll be all right? I want to know where I am in this republican vision.'

Park fears a united Ireland in which unionists and loyalists would have little significance. He tells me of a recent attempt to mount an Orange parade in Dublin. 'Remember our head-quarters was once in Dawson Street in Dublin. So nowadays we'd get a wee corner of the road where we're not significant? That's not how I want to practise my culture, my heritage, my beliefs. We'll get a wee corner, with another corner for the Moslems, and another corner for the Jews. That's not what I want. I want my kids to be proud of who they are and what they are.' So is he frightened of becoming a minority in his own land? 'No, I'm not saying that. I am a minority in a certain sense. If Catholics and republicans want to be the majority, are they going to do the same things that the majority did to them, or they perceive the majority did to them?'

Despite his obvious concerns for the future, Park echoes the view of Ian Paisley about society coming together: 'I see an "usness" creeping in. I see a "we" instead of an "us" and "them". Maybe I'm being optimistic. But life's made me pragmatic. If I think too much about the past, I get hurt and pain. Now the future is what's important. I want to make sure that nobody else goes through that hurt and pain.'

As I say goodbye to him, Park tells me that there is stuff in his past that he will never divulge. 'I'll take it to my maker, and that includes people that I've talked to, and influence that I've had.' Andy Park, with his enthusiasm for life, his sudden bouts of intensity, his simultaneous openness and secrecy, his desire for tolerance and understanding within an unrepentant ideological framework, has been a good introduction to the Northern Ireland state of mind. Six decades before the Troubles began, G. K. Chesterton wrote:

> *The Great Gaels of Ireland,*
> *The men that God made mad*
> *For all their wars were merry,*
> *And all their songs were sad.*

I thought about this ditty as I drove away from Lisburn. Chesterton may not have had the Troubles in mind when he wrote it but, still, having spoken to Andy Park, it bothered me. Park's injuries, the deaths of his friends, and his part – whatever it may have been – in 'fighting the war' did not strike me as very merry. And no matter what God made the people of Northern Ireland, and no matter what the newspaper reports would have had us believe, it was surely not going to be possible to waive an airy hand, and dismiss them as 'mad'. Passionate, prejudiced, charming, conditioned, self-important, victimized, stubborn, self-righteous. But mad?

3

THE STATE

The Wild Birds Protection Act, passed by the Northern Ireland Parliament in 1931, was a significant piece of legislation – for birds and for nationalists. For birds it created designated sanctuaries. For nationalists it was the only bill sponsored by their political party to become law between the creation of the state of Northern Ireland and the suspension of its Parliament in 1972. Northern Ireland was a strange democratic anomaly for the first fifty years of its existence, demonstrating more concern for the welfare of curlews than Catholics.

Throughout that half-century Northern Ireland was governed by a single party – the Ulster Unionist Party (UUP). For almost all of that time the UUP had complete freedom to implement its policies. The Nationalist Party refused to participate in the 1921 Parliamentary election, believing the state to be illegitimate. This effectively left Catholics unrepresented, although four years later the party changed its policy and won a number of seats. Nevertheless, the Nationalist Party provided only slight opposition. It was disunited and ineffective, overwhelmed by the sheer determination of unionism to mould a state in its own image. As Britain looked the other way, unionists set about creating a democracy unlike any other in western Europe.

Fierce determination was not surprising among a Protestant people who had watched the extent of their authority steadily diminish on the island of Ireland. Brought up on folk memories of the siege of Derry and the Battle of the Boyne, events in which their ancestors had resisted Catholic challenges to their authority, they had lately watched their dominion shrink to just six of the nine counties of Ulster, while the Catholics received a Free State to the south.

In the first year and a half of its existence Northern Ireland was rocked by a level of bloodshed not to be repeated until the modern Troubles. Hundreds of people were killed, some by IRA incursions over the border, most by internal sectarian violence. The disorder added to unionists' insecurities and hardened their attitudes. At political meetings they carried placards bearing such legends as 'What We Have We Hold!' and 'No Surrender!' They feared the Catholics in their midst, and they mistrusted the British government, which they believed would only act half-heartedly – if at all – to ensure their survival. In their suspicion and cautious aggression they were probably not very different from their ancestors who, hundreds of years earlier, had arrived in Ulster to stake their claim in the midst of a resentful enemy.

To ensure their survival, unionists introduced their own security measures. The mixed Royal Ulster Constabulary and the exclusively Protestant 'B Special' reserve were created to defend against insurrection, and the Civil Authorities (Special Powers) Act, 1922, was passed, giving the right to intern suspects without trial and allowing juryless courts to order the flogging of a prisoner. Over and above these powers, however, that Act – which remained in force until 1973 – gave the Home Affairs Minister the right to 'make any regulation at all necessary to preserve law and order'. These were desperate measures introduced by desperate people.

When the Ulster Unionist Party leader David Trimble accepted his Nobel Prize for peace in 1998, he made a speech offering an insight into unionist thinking over the previous eighty years. 'Ulster Unionists, fearful of being isolated on the island, built a solid house,' he said, 'but it was a cold house for Catholics. And northern nationalists, although they had a roof over their heads, seemed to us as if they meant to burn the house down.' It does not take much imagination to see why Protestants would have been happy to keep the house cold, even if some unionists still deny that the temperature was ever turned down. In his maiden speech to the House of Commons in 2001, Gregory Campbell, the Democratic Unionist Party member for Londonderry, said that 'the acceptance of that premise has done untold harm in the past 30 years'.

Yet the Northern Ireland government *did* employ some very brazen political strategies to retain its mastery. In 1923 the system of proportional representation, which had been introduced by the British government throughout Ireland to safeguard the interests of minority communities, was abolished for local elections. Nationalists were swiftly relieved of their majorities in over half of the councils over which they had control. Unionists were so pleased with this outcome that proportional representation was subsequently abolished for Parliamentary elections as well.

One factor that helped the unionist cause was the fact that only the owners or tenants of a house had the right to vote in local elections. Sub-tenants, lodgers, and others did not. Not only that, but for every additional £10-a-year valuation of a house after the initial £10, additional voters could be appointed up to a maximum of six. This meant two things: first, that poorer people could not vote at all, and second, that wealthier people could vote several times. And of course the poorer people tended to be Catholic while the wealthier tended to be Protestant.

Another rotten measure was the system of gerrymandering in areas where unionists were outnumbered. This involved the reorganization of boundaries within districts. The most famous example of gerrymandering in Northern Ireland – although by no means the only one – occurred in Derry, where a predomi-

nantly Catholic populace would consistently find itself returning a Protestant-dominated council. In the build-up to the 1938
elections, the number of council wards in Derry was reduced
from five to three. Almost the entire Catholic population of
9,500 voters found itself crammed into the South ward, which
returned eight councillors, while 7,500 Protestant voters were
divided between the North ward and the Waterside ward, which
between them returned twelve councillors. At a 1936 public
inquiry into the arrangement – whose findings were ultimately
ignored by the Northern Ireland government – the Catholic
barrister Cyril Nicholson asked the unionist councillor James
Welch how the arrangement looked to him. 'It looks a bit slightly
out of proportion,' Welch admitted.

Not only was gerrymandering a bit slightly out of proportion,
but it laid the ground for future trouble. It encouraged the
development of further segregation and all the disharmony this
entailed. It also meant that when opportunities arose to build
houses for Catholics within the 'wrong' ward, these opportunities were rejected, however badly the housing was needed. The
need to maintain political control would always trump the desire
to improve the conditions of 'the other lot'.

So it was that unionism remained solid – even as trouble was
being stored up. But it would be wrong to think that the standard of living of most unionists was good. For the gentry and the
professional classes it might have been, but, for the working
classes of both traditions, poverty was a reality. Unemployment
was high, incomes were considerable lower than those in Britain,
and the standard of housing and public amenities was poor.
Many country farmhouses and town terrace houses had no
mains water or provision for gas lighting until well into the
twentieth century. Protestants, you might say, were second-class
citizens, while Catholics were a class below that.

With regards to employment, though, it was better to be
second- than third-class. Many firms employed almost exclusively

Protestant workforces. An Englishman who came to Northern Ireland in the late Fifties to work as a personnel manager relates how a Ministry of Labour official taught him to distinguish Protestant names from Catholic names, and then advised him to select only the Protestants. Even within a mixed business certain jobs might be reserved for Protestants. I was told the story of a young Catholic, working in a shirt factory, who had taken his own life after being refused a position as a shirt cutter. Afterwards a friend remarked angrily, 'He should have known he wasn't ever going to be permitted to be a shirt cutter! Catholics don't get those jobs!'

So far as many unionists were concerned, the fact that Catholics did not 'get those jobs' was not a matter of discrimination at all. It was simply the way things were. Many of the 'unionist jobs' had been done by the same families for many years and when a position became available a worker would recommend a friend or relative. There was no question of Catholics even applying for these jobs. The Harland and Wolff shipyard, whose huge yellow cranes still dominate the Belfast landscape, is a case in point. In the late nineteenth and early twentieth centuries Catholics were expelled from jobs in the yard during periods of sectarian unrest. Over time they stopped applying for those jobs, and they became the natural preserve of unionists without active bias having to be applied.

Harry Murray started work at Harland and Wolff in 1937. He described conditions in the yard to Bobbie Hanvey: 'People used to earn their pay, or they didn't get it, and if they didn't earn it, they were sacked and that was it. That meant working in all sorts of weather, where it poured all day, you got wet right through to the skin. You sat in the open, taking your tea from an old can, out between boats in the cold and wet. You only got a half an hour break, and there wasn't much to do other than religious services, or playing rubby-dub with dice. If you went out, you had no sickness pay, there was no holiday pay, just the wages you had.'

Murray explains how workers had to keep on the right side of the foremen: 'The foremen were a queer lot. Hard. Some of them really took on the mantle of God. If they took a dislike to you, you were out for life. If they didn't like your face, that was good enough to put you out. They seemed to be picked for their hardness, to be able to kick people up the backside. And there was a lot of things that went on that was very dishonest. One foreman used to get brought in butter, eggs, money, just so people could keep their job. In those days people were more humble than what they should have been because they were driven by management and by foremen. Even with getting the wages out of the shipyard, the wages weren't great and if you were unemployed, it was ten times worse to survive.'

Having experienced such conditions, some Protestants feel frustration at being told that Catholics were discriminated against. They look back on their own lives and wonder how they can be considered fortunate. But, in a place as economically deprived as Northern Ireland, even assured basic housing or the guarantee of a lowly paid job in industry could amount to meagre privilege.

Higher up the ladder, the senior posts in the local authorities were filled almost exclusively by Protestants, as were the upper ranks of the civil service, and nearly all the judgeships. I was told of a Catholic lawyer who was passed over for a position as a judge because the incumbent Prime Minister had already nominated one Catholic judge for a judicial post 'and couldn't bring himself to nominate another'. The National Health Service was similarly blighted. A nurse at the Royal Victoria Hospital, which according to my tour guide had been a model of equality, remembers: 'There was a vacancy for a sister. Someone said to matron that this very good staff nurse would make an excellent sister, and was told, "There can't be two Catholic sisters in one department."' She also recalls a Catholic doctor who emigrated to Australia 'because he wasn't getting any promotion'.

Finding routes barred to them, Catholics often had to use their wits to create work for themselves. According to a retired civil servant, 'The Protestant community relied on the thought that the government was *their thing*, and it would look after them. Employment in the old days was very much on the lines that "Willie" is retiring after many years working in the workshop, and he says he's got a nephew, "Sammy", who's very much the man. But things were different in the Catholic community. For many years Catholics thought we'd better get on and do things for ourselves. And nowadays the Catholic working class is more up and doing than their Protestant equivalent.'

Some attitudes have clearly not changed a great deal over the centuries. In the seventeenth century the expression 'nits make lice' was used to justify the killings of Irish children by settlers. In the 1930s the first Prime Minister of Northern Ireland, Sir James Craig, warned the Australian Prime Minister to watch the Catholics in his country. 'They breed like bloody rabbits,' he said. And in 2009 I was told a story about a recent Protestant wedding in Armagh. Several guests had been sitting in a limousine in formal dress, when a group of Catholics spotted them and started shouting abuse. A girl in the back of the car leant forward and said to the driver, 'You'd better drive into them! They'll just breed!'

These are variations on a theme – and they could be multiplied ad infinitum – but they reflect only one side of a mutual antipathy. Northern Ireland was built on sectarianism, both Orange and Green, with roots hundreds of years old. Sectarianism is the raw essence of today's identities. Years ago it was expressed freely and without apology. Nowadays it is reserved for those who feel the same way, or else it is turned into a joke. Twice I was told the same joke, once by each side:

Q. How do you know ET's a Catholic/Protestant?

A. Because he fucking looks like one.

Probably the most shocking joke I heard in Northern Ireland was repeated to me by a Catholic man who had heard it from one of the Shankill Butchers when they briefly shared a prison wing:

Butcher: What's the difference between a Catholic and an onion?

Man: I don't know.

Butcher: I cry when I slice up an onion.

While I was in Belfast I met a man named Joe Graham. He is a writer, historian, storyteller, and a veteran of the civil rights movement. He is, above all, an old-fashioned republican and political activist. I sat interviewing him, chain-smoking his cigarettes, in his tidy house in Andersonstown filled with Country and Western memorabilia that he picks up on trips to Nashville. The only part of the house that isn't tidy is a cubby-hole beside his study which is crammed with shelves of books, audio tapes, and videos on Irish history, and equipment for the interviews he records himself. Graham is a friendly man in his mid-sixties with wavy grey hair. He has a huge physical presence, and the words 'Belfast' and 'Ireland' tattooed on his hands. While I could not mistake his allegiance, he had a knack for consistently scuppering my preconceptions – by suddenly telling me, for example, that in his younger days he modelled himself on the pop singer Tommy Steele.

Joe Graham is very good company, which was just as well because I arrived thinking that we would chat for an hour and eventually staggered out of his front door ten hours later. He began by sharing his memories of growing up in Ballymurphy, a housing estate in west Belfast, built after the war. Ballymurphy is now an urbanized republican area, but back then it was a mixed area on the edge of open country. Graham remembers: 'We were the last houses before the countryside. The mountains came right down on us. The big mill dam. The water was crystal. Two rounds of bread, a milk bottle of cold tea, and away you went up into the mountains. All the local kids. Ten of you, you didn't know who was who, running about, swimming. There was an old mill, and the part that housed the big wheel was the dungeon. It was a beautiful thing of childhood – but every now and again you'd get a *reminder*, and you were acute enough to take it.'

He describes a reminder: 'One beautiful sunny morning when I was 11 I went up the street. All my mates were Protestant, because all our street was Protestant except us. So I went to wee Billy Smith's house, and Mrs Smith said to me, "He's away out, Joe, son." I said, "Dead on." The same thing happened at the next house. Then, at Jimmy Reilly's house, I knocked on the back door: no answer. His Aunt Tilly was at work, but Jimmy and his wee sister should have been there. Where were they all? So I ran down the dividing fence to the garden next door. Just as I vaulted over the fence into that garden, I saw the curtains flicker in Jimmy's bedroom. So I came back over the fence, climbed on top of the coal shed, leaned over and banged Jimmy's bedroom window. He opened it – and it was all the boys sitting there, red, white, and blue everywhere. "What the fuck's going on?" "Joe! Joe! Get off!" they said to me. So I jumped down and stood in the garden, until Jimmy came down. He said, "We're going to let you in, but for God's sake, don't let my dad know." "Why? What's going on?" "We're making flags!" There was a big football match at Windsor Park, the Six Counties versus England – so they were on a winner either way. I went up into the bedroom and there were thousands of these mini Union Jacks, and the boys were on a couple of pennies each to staple them together. *But that wee Fenian bastard Graham wasn't to be seen about the place.* Hurtful. Because these were my best mates. Hurtful. But I helped them to staple these things. And then, in turn, I said, "Don't tell my mummy and daddy I helped with these …" But it meant fuck all. Even now, it would mean fuck all. A man trying to make a few quid for his family selling Union Jacks? So what? But the sad thing was that in doing so, he hurt a child. He marked a child –

and he did no good to the Protestant kids, because they – in adulthood – must feel guilty.'

For Graham the divide was often emphasized casually but firmly nonetheless. 'I went to St John's School. At the foot of the street there was a huge industrial complex belonging to James Mackie, who employed 99.9 per cent Protestants. You were playing on that street during lunch break and the workers were coming out to go to their dinner, you would get a cold, icy look, as if you weren't there. Yet local people would rub your head fondly. "Hello, wee man. How you doing? Are you being good today?" There was that difference. That coldness from *the other people*. You were aware that this place was totally split.'

Graham, and others like him, could sometimes take advantage of the split. 'We'd get up in the morning to buy pigs' feet. We would hoof them and singe them, we would scrub them and cook them, and me and Paddy would sell them around the bars. But not on the Falls Road! These people had no work and the Catholics didn't eat meat on Friday. So we went down the Shankill, the Old Lodge Road, Sandy Row, where all the Protestants who had shillings lived, and we sold the pigs' feet in the bars down there. That was an education. To get a shilling for pigs' feet, we had to go to these people.'

In 1953, the year of her coronation, the Queen visited Belfast. Graham can remember buses of unionists coming down to the Springfield Road, where a big banner was placed across the road and Union flags flew everywhere. 'It was so British,' says Graham, 'you'd have thought you were in the Midlands.' But for Graham's family 1953 had a different significance: 'It was the anniversary of the 1803 rebellion, and I watched my father going up the stairs with a long pole. He went into the girls' bedroom and set it across the bed, and he opened a wee cubby-hole and he took out the national flag. It was the first time I'd been so close to the national flag, and he set about pinning it onto the pole. Then he got a cable and a lightbulb, and pinned it onto the top of the pole, and put it all out through the bedroom window. I thought it was a carnival thing – but within two hours, the cops were belting up the street in their sedans, demanding that he take it down. My father was a very sedate, serious countryman, and he said that the flag would be flying tonight, and it would be taken down tomorrow morning. By then the Protestants had all gathered, and some were standing in the garden. I'll always remember the cop, a big, ginger-haired bastard, saying, "That's a foreign flag! It'll have to come down!" "Why does it have to come down?" "We've got reports that people are offended." My father asked our neighbour Mrs Rossbottom, "Are you offended?" "Not at all, Jim!" But some of the Protestants started getting angry and shouting at the cop, and my father said, "Why are youse all offended? Have you come all the way from the Springfield Road to be offended?" In the end they left, and the flag flew. That was the first flag that flew in Ballymurphy – and it flew with the grace of the Protestant neighbours. There was no ill intent towards the house.'

Graham speaks of having an acute awareness of inequality as he was growing up: 'We Catholics did get a raw deal by design. They planned it so, but in planning it, they made it "us and them".' It annoys him that today there are those who rewrite history to make out that things were fine before the Troubles started. 'There was nothing bright and beautiful about being a Catholic living in these six counties. There were things that took away your heritage. Things like the Special Powers Act. We weren't allowed to have a rebel song LP. It was confiscated, you were charged. You weren't allowed to read certain newspapers; if you were caught in possession of the *United Irishman* – an eight-page newspaper – you could have got two years in prison. If you had a bit of money found in the house, money to buy a horse and cart to create a livelihood, had the peelers come in at any time and found that, that would have been confiscated. It could have been seen as having a political purpose. You couldn't display the national flag – *yet theirs could be thrust in our faces 24 hours a day.'*

It is interesting to compare Joe Graham's recollections with those of Gusty Spence, a one-time member of the UVF, who served a life sentence for the 1966 killing of Peter Ward, a Catholic barman. Spence subsequently repudiated violence to become a loyalist politician and advocate of the Good Friday Agreement. In an interview he gave to Bobbie Hanvey, he describes his youthful attitude to Catholics: 'Catholics had horns and were in some way inferior to Protestants. We were always led to believe this. At the back of your mind, you knew that it was wrong – but at the same time you lived in that grime and squalor that we lived in, and it was good to feel superior, even at the expense of another human being.'

When he left school Spence started work in a linen mill, where he came into contact with Catholics for the first time. He met a Catholic boy named Jimmy, who talked to him about Irish history. Jimmy told him that the United Irishmen were Protestant. 'I had no knowledge, and of course, I thought he was telling lies.' The two young men used to go swimming together in a Catholic area: 'Jimmy and I had something in common. We both had tattoos. He had a tricolour on his arm, and I had a Union Jack on my arm. Falls Road baths had good facilities for swimming and whenever I went there to swim with Jimmy I had to get a sticking plaster to cover over my Union Jack. So despite what people say about the good old days, about there being no problems, it's a load of nonsense. We lived in an abnormal society. Jimmy had to teach me to say something about a Hail Mary, so as I could bluff my way through, otherwise I would have got a duffing up.' A Protestant from Derry, about the same age as Spence, told me of a duffing-up he had received while dressed in his school uniform: 'I was walking through some playing fields. Two chaps stepped in front of me, who I later found out were Catholic. One of them pointed to the other and said to me, "He wants a fight!" To which I replied, "Then why doesn't he fight you?" To which they both landed punches on me ...'

Spence knew that he would have to start work in the mill once he left school: 'The family needed money desperately so there was no question of where you were going.' He went down to the Labour Exchange with his birth certificate and school-leaving card and received a new set of cards. After presenting them at the mill he began work the next morning. 'Someone referred to them as "dark Satanic mills". I wouldn't disagree with that description. I started work in the spinning room, which was a very, very hot place and a very wet place. You worked in your bare feet in filthy conditions, and there was no recourse to wash-ing, so you returned home from work the same way as you went. The hours were eight o'clock in the morning to six o'clock at night and to twelve-fifteen on a Saturday. All you were supposed to do was keep your head down, keep your mouth closed and earn your sixteen and eight [£0.83] a week.'

However superior Spence might have been taught to feel, his home life hardly felt privileged. 'My ma was a great pawner. All the women of her generation were great pawners because they didn't have the course to anything else.' He describes the Sunday School trip as the only light relief in a grey world. When his mother accompanied the group on one of those trips, she had to borrow a coat to make herself respectable: 'If a woman had a coat, it was a big deal. I'm not overstating the case. Those things hurt. If people would only realize the indignities and the hurt that people felt at having to borrow some other woman's coat.'

Spence regrets the fact that for a Protestant to criticize social conditions would – even today – be regarded as disloyalty. 'You would be called a "closet republican" or a "card-carrying commie". The continuance of the union would be our main philosophy. However, within that, why does one have to be anything *peculiar* to articulate a political philosophy?'

The answer lies in the need to express unity. Unionists were not really a homogenous people. They came from all classes of society and they attended a multitude of different churches, from Presbyterian to High Anglican. They had ranged their wagons in a circle to defend the status quo – and they could not encourage self-examination or internal dissent, for fear of showing weakness to the enemy. Safer to present a united front by placing emphasis on shared values, such as loyalty to the Crown and Protestant supremacy. As Sir Edward Carson, the early twentieth-century unionist leader, had once warned, if divisions within unionism 'became wide and deep, Ulster would fall'.

This united front, and the interests of the Protestant people, have been historically guarded over by the Orange Order. Three hundred years old and named after William of Orange, the Protestant king who defeated the Catholic King James, the Orange Order was formed to unite Protestants against demands for an independent Ireland. Members come from all levels of society and from (currently) eighteen Protestant denominations. When members join, they receive an initiation which spells out the aim of the Order as 'the mutual defence, support and protection of Irish Protestants'. It is also made clear: 'You have promised … never to attend any act or ceremony of popish worship.'

The Order borrows freely from the ritual and terminology of freemasonry; members call one another brethren, they attend lodges, they take oaths, and they can attain the position of grand master. The brethren used to wear orange silk sashes, like the one worn by William III at the Boyne, but more recently they have come to wear orange collarettes and bowler hats. Bowlers are Edwardian symbols of respectability, harking back to the period when the Order began to wield its greatest influence. The early years of the twentieth century were a time when dire labour and housing conditions might have created social disorder, but the Orange Order, and its large numbers of working-class members, were concentrating on other issues: fear of Home

Rule, and the desire to maintain supremacy. Almost every person of influence in Northern Ireland was a member. In 1932 Sir James Craig announced in Parliament that he was 'an Orangeman first, and a politician and a member of this parliament afterwards'.

A very rare unionist politician who was not an Orangeman was Samuel Hall-Thompson, a minister of education responsible for post-war educational reforms. In 1949 a meeting was called by the Sandy Row Grand Orange Lodge to protest against his proposals concerning the payment of Catholic teachers. The Prime Minister attended and, under pressure, promised to revise the plans. He then sacked Hall-Thompson, who became a high-ranking victim of the Orange Order's grass roots. In Britain the working classes came to voice their struggle through the trade unions. In Northern Ireland the trade union movement carried little weight. The unionist working class expressed itself through the Order, and the Order was not overtly class conscious. It is little wonder that in Gusty Spence's experience it was 'peculiar' to articulate a political philosophy. Andy Tyrie, the one-time leader of the UDA, was once asked what he thought was the difference between Catholics and Protestants. The only difference, he replied, was that Protestants couldn't complain.

However firmly unionists stood together, and however robustly the Northern Ireland government asserted its claim to be master of its own house, there was always one party with the capacity to undermine it: the British government. While Britain was allowing the province free rein, little complaint could be heard from Stormont. But in 1940 a proposal from Winston Churchill's wartime government horrified unionists, and threatened to end the life of their young state. As Britain and her colonies stood alone against Hitler, and the people of Britain braced themselves for a German invasion, Churchill's war cabinet offered Eire an undertaking towards a united Ireland, in return for Eire's abandonment of wartime neutrality. The

Northern Ireland cabinet reacted furiously at the perceived treachery. In the event Eire, already keener on reunification in theory than in practice, rejected Churchill's offer. After only twenty years of existence, Northern Ireland had Eire to thank for its survival.

The incident seemed to confirm the unionists' worst fears concerning Britain's attitude to her loyal province. I considered the nature of Britain's attitude as I wandered around the Stormont Parliament buildings. From the ceiling of Stormont's Great Hall hangs a huge gold-plated chandelier, which had been a wedding present from the German Kaiser to his cousin King George V. This chandelier had spent a few years hanging in Windsor Castle until it was taken down at the start of the First World War, when German light fittings fell out of favour. Eighty years later an inventory at Windsor found the chandelier to be missing, but there was no record of where it had gone. Much has been said about Northern Ireland's strategic and economic significance, but its use as Britannia's informal dump has not been so well recorded.

While the British government had the power to destroy Northern Ireland, another organization had the desire to do so. From the time of the creation of the State until the advent of the modern Troubles, the IRA made sporadic attempts to shoot and bomb its way to a united Ireland, but the organization always remained small and received little support from the Catholic community. Joe Cahill joined the IRA in 1938 in west Belfast. He was one of several men convicted of the 1942 killing of a police officer, and was sentenced to death but later reprieved. Just one man, Tom Williams, was hanged for the murder. Cahill described his experiences to Bobbie Hanvey: 'There were actually eight of us arrested on Easter Sunday 1942. Easter Sunday was a period when parades were banned. Our idea was to fire shots over security patrols in three areas, to draw all the security forces into those areas, leaving the other two areas free where parades could be held. So we fired shots over a patrol car. When that was finished, we retreated. There was a bit of a problem then; it just didn't work out as we had planned, and we all finished up in a house. The house was surrounded, there was a bit of shooting, and a policeman was shot dead. We were all arrested and taken to the police headquarters, and brought before the court and charged with murder. We were remanded, and brought before the court on several different occasions right up to the High Court, which lasted three days. Eventually the jury came back in, and six of us were found guilty and sentenced to death.'

For four and a half weeks Cahill shared a condemned cell with Tom Williams. He describes the conditions: 'It's fair to say that the food was much better in the condemned cell. You got two bottles of stout a day, or a half and a whisky. You had hospital beds. And along with the two prisoners, there were three warders there, twenty-four hours a day; even when you were sleeping they were still there.' Cahill already knew Williams; they had gone to dances together, and in prison they became closer still. They passed their days exercising in the yard and had access to chess, draughts, and cards. 'It's fair to say the day was fairly well spent. It normally started off with Mass, then in the evening we had devotions. We had two visits a day, there were so many relatives and people wanting to see us.'

Cahill describes the prospect of death: 'I'm not being boastful about this, but once you made your peace with God, I think death is very easy to face. The only way I can equate it, is often I've heard people saying, "He died a lovely death" because they were prepared to die. Once you're prepared to die, I think death is easy faced. That's where religion plays a big part in my life.'

On a Sunday afternoon, all of the condemned were brought into the solicitor's room. 'The solicitor looked at the six of us. He says, "I have good news for everybody except Tom. The rest of you have been reprieved. Tom," he says, "you'll die." And it was a shock to everybody. At this stage we didn't expect to be reprieved; we thought we were all going to be executed because it was only three days away. There was a tremendous silence and the first one to break the silence was Tom Williams. He says, "This is how I wanted it from the start. Don't grieve for me," he says. "I'm happy to die." And that was the saddest moment in my life. We were taken away from him and we were given a guarantee that we'd see him again before Wednesday. The authorities never kept their promise. We didn't see him again. We were taken to the penal servitude wing. The last memory I have of Tom Williams was on the day of his execution. The chap in the cell above me rapped on the floor and he says, "Joe, jump up to your window." I jumped up to the window and I looked out and I saw his funeral going to the back of the hospital for burial. That's my last memory of Tom Williams.'

One man who volunteered to combat the IRA was Wallace Clark. Clark was a member of the B Specials, the largest of three arms of the Ulster Special Constabulary. He entered the constabulary in 1950, the third generation of his family to join, and became a District Commandant. The B Specials had a sinister reputation; they were greatly feared by Catholics. In an interview with Bobbie Hanvey, Clark challenges the reputation: 'The general view of the Catholics was that the B Specials were heavily biased, tending to brutality, and did a lot of quiet killing – which is all untrue if you look at the statistics. But they were all so frightened of the Bs, which gave us a very strong moral position, in that a B man was very rarely attacked in his house. They were stewing in their own juice, they demonized the Bs so effectively. We did a lot of our work at night dressed in black or very dark green. That's one reason it was so easy to demonize the B Specials. It created the "bogeymen" image.'

Clark explains why he joined: 'I think sort of family pride, like it applied to a lot of men in the B Specials. It was public service, the country was under threat. I felt I could do my little bit in putting down terrorism.' The B Specials were a part-time force. 'They operated around home, they kept their rifles at home, their uniforms at home, and turned out to parade locally. Initially, we drilled a lot in Orange halls but not because of any tremendous connection with the Orange Order. We were sometimes accused of being run by the Orange Order, which was absolute bunkum. The Orange Order hadn't the organization or structure to run a force like the B Specials.'

As a commandant, Clark had eight sub-district commandants under his command, each of whom commanded about thirty men. 'With that organization, and with the rifles at home, we could put down twenty-four roadblocks within ten minutes of getting the alarm. Because the men could turn out quickly. We had these funny old uniforms with a stand-up collar, and you could pull it over your pyjamas, and you could pull on your black trousers. We patrolled the roads, and guarded the checkpoints, or key points at times of high tension. We had two categories – "drill category" when the IRA weren't in the active stage of warfare, and "patrol category", when we were turned out every night, walked along the roads, checked cars, and had a good look at enemy movements. We could switch from drill category to patrol category within twenty-four hours.'

In 1956 the IRA began a border campaign – Operation Harvest – with the intention of forcing British troops out of Ireland. At this time the IRA was only a shadow of what it was to become. Internment was introduced in Northern Ireland and the Irish Republic, and within two years the campaign had ground to a near stop. According to Clark: 'The IRA lost that campaign and they made a formal declaration of defeat in February 1962. They weren't very effective, and they weren't getting popular support. They were limited in the amount of weapons and ammunition they had, and I never like to under-rate my enemies, because there are plenty of clever and brave men in the IRA, but it didn't show in that campaign. They missed lots of opportunities where they could have done a great deal more damage. The funny thing was, you'd mix with IRA men locally. You'd go down to the post office, and see fellows who had been IRA-active, and I would have no objection to having a chat with them.'

The most famous IRA operation of the campaign was the unsuccessful attack on Brookeborough RUC barracks, carried out on New Year's Eve 1956. Two IRA men were killed during the attack, which quickly entered the annals of romantic republicanism; thousands of mourners attended the funerals of the two dead southern volunteers, and Dominic Behan wrote the song 'The Patriot Game' about one of them, Fergal O'Hanlon from Monaghan.

Paddy O'Regan, an IRA volunteer, was wounded in the leg during the attack by two bullets from a Bren gun fired by a police sergeant. He considers that Operation Harvest was 'an honourable campaign in as far as we could make it, and I suppose that was reflected in the fact that there were very few people killed on either side'. The IRA had a policy of non-sectarianism at the time: 'We were instructed not to attack the RUC because they were a police force, but they were given a number of days to stand aside, and when they did not, they became targets. On the other hand, the B Special constables were looked on as a Protestant sectarian force, so we were told that we were *not* to attack them at all.'

The IRA's next campaign would prove to be a much longer and more bitter affair, with far fewer rules of engagement.

4

THE REFORMER

As western democracies underwent a social shift in the Sixties, away from the conservatism of the past, it appeared as though Northern Ireland was being dragged along with them. Terence O'Neill, the fourth Prime Minister of Northern Ireland, took office in 1963 and spoke of introducing 'bold and imaginative measures'. He began visiting Catholic schools, having his photograph taken with nuns, attending civic receptions in Catholic towns, and attempting to introduce what he described as 'long overdue reforms'.

O'Neill's attitudes were not those of a lone man crying in the wilderness. In the early Sixties some young Protestants were even willing to countenance a united Ireland. One man who attended Foyle College, a Protestant school in Derry, remembers: 'Most of my school friends were very pro a united Ireland in those days. We'd have discussions, and we decided that we would still hold onto British culture, but we hoped for a united Ireland where both cultures were valued and accepted. I expect that after the Troubles started, many of these people retrenched back into more black-and-white attitudes.' But even before the Troubles, most people in Northern Ireland were not so liberal in their outlook. O'Neill's attempts to bring the province into the twentieth century were darkly observed by a man whose feet were planted somewhere in the seventeenth: the Reverend Ian Kyle Paisley.

O'Neill and Paisley were very different men. Educated at Eton, a member of the Guards during the Second World War, speaking with an English accent, O'Neill was at the Anglo-Irish end of unionism. To read his autobiography gives a touching sense of the man; his genuine belief in reform shines through, and he writes in an endearingly Pooterish manner: 'For some years we had been in the habit of taking the car to Britain for a holiday in August. Our second stop was with Jean's cousin Jack ...' The overall impression is of a quiet, well-meaning man, who became involved with events and personalities far bigger than himself.

One of those big personalities was Paisley, the son of an itinerant preacher father, and a Scottish Presbyterian mother. Like his father, Paisley became a fundamentalist preacher, and a hugely charismatic one. In this 1969 sermon Paisley – a fine performer in his own right – tells the morality tale of an ungodly actress:

'Some years ago, outside a very famous hotel, in Durban in South Africa, a gospel evangelist was giving out gospel tracts. In that hotel there was staying a very famous actor, and down at the quayside was a great liner called the *Durban Castle*. And that famous actress had booked a passage and had a ticket on that liner, and she came out through the door, to get the cab to take her to board the vessel, and this Christian gentleman stepped up, and he handed her a gospel tract. And when she saw it, she threw it on the pavement and she stamped her heel through it and she said, "Damn your God!" She went aboard the *Durban Castle*. But when it docked at Southampton, she had disappeared. There was an inquiry, a steward was arrested, he was tried and he was found guilty of murder. And he murdered that actress, and it was found that he had pushed her dead body through the port-hole. And she had been buried in the briny deep. Her name was Gay Gibson, a famous actress. "What think ye of Christ?" "Damn your God!" My friends, you don't need to use such a blasphemous expression, but tonight, by turning your back on Christ, you can go to the same hell that that Christ-rejecting actress went to! SHE

DIDN'T KNOW THAT SHE WAS ON HER LAST JOURNEY! And her body perished in the depths of the sea, but her soul baptised in the waves of infinite wrath, for all eternity paid the penalty for her doom and for her Christ-rejection. Friends, how is it with your soul? Men and women, eternity! Eternity! WHERE WILL YOU BE, IN ETERNITY?'

Yet as well as being a hell-fire preacher with the ability to inspire and terrify his congregants, Paisley has also been the most influential Protestant politician of the past fifty years. It has often been difficult to gauge where his politics ends and his religion begins. When he has thundered against Catholicism in sermons – 'Romanism is the enemy of liberty! Romanism is the enemy of this province! Romanism is the enemy of God!' – he has been speaking as both cleric and politician. He has articulated the political fears of his people with an evangelical fury: 'The Protestants of Ulster are not going to be trifled with! We are in no mood to permit anything that is going to hinder our defence and preservation of Ulster as part of the United Kingdom!' The Troubles might not have been religious in nature, but the wily, ambitious Paisley certainly was, and his presence was one of the major reasons why Northern Ireland careered into chaos at the end of a decade that had promised hope.

At the beginning of his tenure, O'Neill made speeches promising that his government would no longer be acting solely in the interests of unionists. His words were received positively by many Catholics, but this only served to make him unpopular with the harder-line unionists. It was a matter of basic mathematics that if he were to bring more jobs, more houses, and more votes to Catholics, that meant fewer of each for Protestants, and this fact was never lost on loyalists.

These were the fears that Paisley was able to articulate, while turning himself, in the eyes of some of his supporters, into a prophet of semi-biblical proportions. In 1964 he threatened to march his supporters to the republican headquarters in west

Belfast to remove a small Irish flag that had been spotted in the window. The police had decided not to intervene, but under pressure from Paisley they smashed the window and removed the flag. Riots ensued and attitudes hardened on all sides. There are many, many incidents which have been said to have led to the Troubles. Of all of those commonly cited, this is probably the earliest.

In 1965 O'Neill invited the Taoiseach (Prime Minister) of the Irish Republic, Sean Lemass, to Stormont. It was an attempt to normalize relations between north and south, and to promote economic cooperation. Previous prime ministers of Northern Ireland had refused to meet leaders of the Irish Republic, on the grounds that the Republic still laid constitutional claim on the north. The visit was controversial and was only publicly announced as Lemass was arriving at Stormont. Even the Northern Ireland cabinet had not been informed until that morning. Grasping for the right words with which to welcome his guest, O'Neill rejected 'Ulster' and 'Northern Ireland' and settled on 'Welcome to the North'.

The visit was considered a success by many unionists, including the Grand Master of the Orange Order. Paisley, however, was furious. He staged a protest, waving a placard saying 'No Mass, no Lemass' in front of television cameras. He made a speech announcing that O'Neill had declared war on loyalists, adding ominously, 'They [the government] may control the police force, they may control the judiciary, they may control the powers that be, but we are determined to remain free. Thy can spill as much printer's ink as they like, but we are prepared, if necessary to spill our blood.' Paisley and his supporters were prepared to sever the Red Hand of Ulster once again in order to secure the province. They believed that normal relations between north and south would be the first step on the blasted road to Irish unity. In fact, by normalizing relations, the south was acknowledging that two states existed. The Republic was effectively accepting partition.

Perhaps Paisley and his friends ought to have been congratulating O'Neill, instead of condemning him.

In 1966 a lengthy investigation appeared in the *Sunday Times* entitled 'John Bull's Political Slum'. Printed to coincide with a visit by the Queen to Northern Ireland, it warned of 'an underlying sickness that will remain to be cured after the loyal cheers die away'. It detailed the gerrymandering and the discrimination in jobs and housing, and it ended by saying: 'Any real liberalization of the Ulster regime will only come after some vigorous prodding from Westminster. O'Neill may put a brake on Paisley's virulence, but the grass-roots strength of Paisleyism has undoubtedly shaken the Northern Ireland government, and what little reforming zeal it ever had is in danger of burning out.' The investigation is notable for its singularity; the British press mirrored its government, in that it had little interest in, or knowledge of, Northern Ireland.

In early 1968, while on a visit to a unionist association in the Shankill, O'Neill was attacked with a hail of missiles by Paisley supporters, who also set fire to a photograph of him visiting a convent. He was fortunate to leave the scene with just a cut under his eye. But it was not just Paisleyites who were causing the Prime Minister concern; the conservatism of his cabinet colleagues was preventing him from introducing genuinely reforming measures. As a result nationalists were questioning whether he was really intent on making changes.

It was within this atmosphere that the civil rights movement came together. A younger generation of Catholics, disillusioned with the Nationalist Party's ineffective style of opposition, was coming to the fore. Nationalists had spent many years dreaming of Irish reunification, but no progress had been made. This new breed, accepting that Irish unity was not an imminent prospect, had decided that equality was a workable alternative, but were adamant that they could not simply rely on favours from unionists to achieve it. They had to take responsibility for bringing

about change through activism and participation. At the fore-
front of this new drive was John Hume, a teacher from Derry,
who would one day play a significant part in bringing the Troubles to an end.

The Northern Ireland Civil Rights Association (NICRA) put
forward a number of demands, including the eradication of the
local electoral voting system, the disbanding of the B Specials,
the repeal of the Special Powers Act, the redrawing of electoral
boundaries, and the fairer distribution of housing. None of these
demands had yet been addressed by O'Neill's government, and
NICRA quickly attracted large numbers of Catholics to its ranks,
as well as a few politically minded Protestants. In an era of civil
rights marches in the United States and street protests in Europe,
Northern Ireland was about to experience much that was unfamiliar.

The first civil rights march came about in response to an incident that highlighted the prevailing inequalities. A house in Cale-
don, East Tyrone, had been allocated by the local council to a
single Protestant secretary, over the claims of two Catholic families. Austin Currie, a Nationalist MP, proceeded to stage a squat in
the house and when he was forcibly removed by police a civil
rights march between Coalisland and Dungannon was organized.
When the march arrived at Dungannon it was met by a crowd of
five hundred Paisley supporters singing 'God Save the Queen'.

The next march, in Derry, attracted huge controversy. As an
RTE cameraman filmed events, the RUC first blocked the
marchers and then began to baton those at the front of the crowd,
before using water cannon. One of those who was cracked over
the head was Gerry Fitt MP, of the Republican Labour Party,
whose bloodied face became a symbol of police brutality and
state oppression. The story of how Fitt came to be attacked has
been told to me by a man who was present. He alleges that Fitt
had been standing in the front line of marchers with his legs
apart. Behind him stood a member of the IRA who wanted to

provoke the police into lashing out. The IRA man kicked through Fitt's legs, making solid contact with a policeman's groin. The policeman reacted by clubbing Fitt across the eye.

This story begs the question of how prominent the (still very small) IRA was in the civil rights movement. The likelihood is that while IRA members took an active part in events, seeing them as an opportunity to cause agitation, it never had any kind of control over the movement. Indeed it would be surprising had members of the IRA not been involved. A civil rights movement dedicated to challenging the established order must have been irresistible to republicans with overlapping, if more radical, intentions. It is also worth bearing in mind that many within the IRA of 1968 were more wedded to political agitation than they were to creating a united Ireland by force – as would be demonstrated by the split of the following year.

As the dramatic events of the Derry march brought the civil rights movement to the world's attention, Joe Graham brought the protest into a unionist citadel. Graham told me, 'The man who allocated houses on behalf of the Belfast Corporation, Mr Lazenblatt, had a big office in Linenhall Street. We decided to get into his office and nail ourselves in, as a protest. I goes in with my six-inch nails and my hammer. Mr Lazenblatt was a wee small man, and I closed the door and put two nails in the door. He never moved. He just sat there. He knew what the agitation was about. I said, "Mr Lazenblatt, we'll be here for a while." "Well," he said, "that's OK. Are you feeling well?" "Yes," I said. "Yourself?" "Yes." So I sat down. I'd phoned all the television and radio studios and the newspapers before I'd done it. I had a loudspeaker, and I opened the window, and I was shouting out the window about civil rights agitators, about getting up off our knees, all good stuff, and the wee man pulled a drawer open, and he said, "Would you like a little sandwich?" And he gave me a cup of tea, and said, "Here you are, Joe. Now what exactly is this about?" I couldn't raise my voice in anger to that poor man, so

I said, "Well, there's no 'One Man, One Vote', Mr Lazenblatt, and you know you're not allocating houses fairly, and thereby, you're discriminating not just in housing but in voting too." "Yes," he said, 'I'm very aware of these allegations, Joe." And when the cops all started coming, I pulled the nails out, and let them in, and they pounced on me and took me down the barracks.'

If Mr Lazenblatt was surprised by this encounter, one can only guess at Eileen Paisley's reaction after her meeting with Joe Graham. Eileen, Paisley's wife, had won a seat on the Belfast Corporation in 1967. Graham remembers the day their paths crossed: 'We went into City Hall when they were creating another Orange Lord Mayor. We decided to protest, so we were up in the public gallery with all the finery below us, the mink, the ermine, the knickerbockers. In the end, we got carried away; we jumped over into the well of the chamber. The Lord Mayor fell on his arse. The gobshite with the mace threw it up in the air. The cops climbed on top of us, hitting each other to get at us. As they were dragging me out – I'm ashamed to say it now – I went past Eileen Paisley, who was a councillor at that time. She was a devil, and I gave her an earful she'll remember for the rest of her life. She was ranting and raving – can you imagine what she thought? A dirty low Fenian shouting at a superior being like herself?'

Confronted by increasing activism and conflict, O'Neill persisted with his attempts to introduce reform, even though he privately felt that his policy of trying to improve community relations now lay in the gutter. He tried to convince his dubious cabinet of the importance of selling concessions to the unionist people, but he received one concession only; he was allowed to call a meeting of local authorities at which he persuaded the Derry Corporation to introduce a system of points allocation for housing, as already existed in Britain.

In the meantime O'Neill was coming under pressure from the British Prime Minister, Harold Wilson, and his Home Secretary,

James Callaghan. He was 'invited' to Downing Street, where he was threatened with the removal of British subsidies to Northern Ireland if he did not accelerate the pace of reform. The British government was finally taking an interest in Northern Ireland. O'Neill himself noted disapprovingly a common Ulster attitude towards Britain, which he described as 'Keep out of our affairs and give us some more money', but he managed to secure cabinet agreement to a package of reform, which he later described as 'small and timid'. It did not include the major reforms demanded by the civil rights movement, yet it was enough to infuriate many unionists, including the Minister for Home Affairs, William Craig, who declared that Northern Ireland should resist British efforts to dictate policy. Now that Britain had roused from her slumber, Craig was effectively leading unionist calls for Northern Ireland's independence.

In desperation, O'Neill made a television broadcast, in which he declared that Ulster stood at a crossroads. He promised that reforms would be implemented, and he attacked those who believed that Northern Ireland could survive without Britain: 'They are not loyalists but disloyalists; disloyal to Britain, disloyal to the Constitution, disloyal to the Crown.' He then sacked Craig, who subsequently complained that the province's problems had started when O'Neill had invited Lemass to Belfast. O'Neill was under pressure from every side – and the pressure was about to intensify.

At the beginning of 1969 a socialist branch of the civil rights movement, the People's Democracy, organized a march from Belfast to Derry. Ian Paisley had mounted vociferous protests to the previous civil rights marches, but on this occasion he allowed his collaborator, Ronald Bunting, to organize the opposition. Perhaps aware that serious violence might ensue, Paisley was standing back from events. Bunting was an odd character. A retired army major, he had once worked for Gerry Fitt and the Republican Labour Party before forming his own political party, which was dedicated to promoting harmony between Catholics and Protestants. He then executed a sharp about-turn to become one of Paisley's most trusted lieutenants. As the civil rights march moved westwards, Bunting organized bands of loyalists to badger it. Then, as the march approached Derry, he arranged for it to be met by an ambush of men – some of them off-duty B Specials – carrying rocks, sticks, and cudgels spiked with nails.

Joe Graham was on the march and remembers the approach to Burntollet Bridge, where the ambushers were waiting: 'Up on the hill, the bastards had big mounds of quarry stones and, as we came round, we spotted what was happening, so the fellas all moved to the front. And then they started throwing their stones. The peelers moved back, exposing us. The peelers wanted to make us disperse, and that would have been it. And we seemed to have dispersed – some people were in the river, some were running away. From the expressions on the cops' faces, I think they thought they had ended the march, but some people came out of the river, others ran back, and we managed to keep the pressure on. There was argy-bargy, allegations being made, and in the end the peelers saw that we weren't going to be dispersed, they saw there could have been loss of life, and they would have been held responsible, so they started pretending to move the bastards off the hill. They disappeared into the trees, and we carried on walking. As we came into Derry itself, we walked past these new council houses, and suddenly it was like the Zulu war. Over the roofs came hundreds of bottles. Then a mob came up towards us – and we thought we were dead ... but they were Catholics from the Bogside who had heard what was happening, and had come to meet us. They lined up either side of us, and we went down the middle. So we went right into Derry, into Guildhall Square. The spirit of 1916 lived on – that was our inspiration. The most beauteous moment of my life.'

Under pressure from almost every direction, facing death threats from loyalists, and calls for his resignation from MPs of his own party, O'Neill looked to the people to reassert his authority; he called a general election. The Ulster Unionist party split into pro-O'Neill and anti-O'Neill candidates, and O'Neill hoped that candidates in favour of reform would inflict heavy defeats on their rearward-looking opponents. In the event they won a majority, but it was not resounding enough to consolidate O'Neill's position. In his own constituency he was challenged by Paisley, whom he only narrowly defeated. Unionism's united front, maintained for almost fifty years, was fracturing. The fault line was the issue of Protestant supremacy. When Paisley stood against O'Neill he described himself as a 'Protestant Unionist'. The 'Big Man' understood his people.

It was in this election that Denys Rowan Hamilton stood as a pro-O'Neill candidate. O'Neill was, says Rowan Hamilton, 'a quiet, responsible man who wanted to sort out the Irish problems – but he was never a serious politician'. Rowan Hamilton was standing in East Down, where his opponent was Brian Faulkner. Faulkner was O'Neill's chief rival within the Unionist Party and had been attempting to bring him down for six years. The count was held at the Old Town Hall in Downpatrick, and Rowan Hamilton received very few votes. 'It was embarrassing for me,' he says. 'After the vote was announced, Dennis Faulkner, Brian's brother, stood up and said that I didn't know what I was doing, standing against Brian Faulkner, and there were cheers from the mob. I turned round to my election agent, a very nice chap, and asked him what I should say in reply. He told me to say nothing. There was nothing much *to* say.'

There was not much left for O'Neill to say either. After the election his colleagues pressed him to remain in office, but in his view 'the game was up'. Before he resigned he managed to squeeze 'One Man, One Vote' through Parliament. At around the same time a series of explosions devastated electricity and water instillations around the province. These explosions were assumed to have been caused by the IRA, and when O'Neill suggested to a senior police officer that they might have been the work of loyalists, the policeman replied that loyalists would never destroy their own country. Several months later it was discovered that the bombs *had* been planted by the loyalist UVF with the intention of destabilizing O'Neill. The Red Hand was being severed once more. One of the men responsible for the explosions was Thomas McDowell, a member of Ian Paisley's church; McDowell was burnt alive while attempting to blow up a hydroelectric power station across the border in the Republic. Paisley has always denied having had any knowledge of who was responsible for the explosions.

As he left office O'Neill made a televised speech in which he praised the clergy of Derry for a recent display of ecumenism. 'This simple act of Christian friendship,' he said, 'was a shining example of what would have been possible, but for the machinations of wicked men who have preached and practised hatred in the name of God.' It was quite clear to whom O'Neill was referring. In his autobiography he only ever refers to his nemesis as 'Paisley', the only individual not to be granted a Christian name.

O'Neill left behind him a province of empowered nationalism, furious unionism, and feelings of fear on both sides. He had been brave enough to attempt reforms, but not strong enough to achieve them. He could not convince loyalists – or even many more moderate unionists – of the need to make concessions. Many years later, however, hard-line loyalist politicians would cooperate with nationalists and republicans in the interests of peace – and they would be led by Ian Kyle Paisley. O'Neill's tormentor would one day sit as the First Minister of Northern Ireland, with an ex-IRA member as his deputy, both men presiding over a democratic assembly. O'Neill would never have believed that such a thing was possible. In April 1969, as he resigned, tensions in Northern Ireland were high. Before long they would erupt into terrible violence – and become the Troubles which have defined the north of Ireland ever since.

5

THE TROUBLES

Ian Paisley and Gerry Fitt appeared together on Terry Wogan's BBC television chat show in the Eighties. On screen they played their parts, Orange and Green, but away from the cameras, in the Green Room, they smiled, they laughed, and they asked about one another's children. The man with the cracked head, and the man who supported the men who cracked his head, were quite friendly really. This should probably not come as a surprise. For one thing Fitt and Paisley must have encountered each other countless times over the years and would have developed some sort of relationship independent of politics. And the fact is that Ian Paisley is extremely charming in person.

I met Paisley in 2009, when I was invited to attend his annual St Patrick's Day Breakfast. Held at the La Mon Hotel, and attended by a broad range of public figures, Paisley made a speech about the relevance of St Patrick to *all* Christians, after which a nun named Sister Briege stood up and spoke on a similar theme. The preacher and the sister then ate their breakfasts side by side. This shiny, new, ecumenical Paisley is quite unrecognizable from the man who once rounded on O'Neill for shaking hands with the likes of Sister Briege. After a demonstration of Irish dancing, which Paisley seemed to enjoy, I was introduced to him. I asked him what he had thought of his breakfast, although in truth I was wondering what he and his breakfast companion thought of each other. He gripped me by the hand, stared into my eyes, and said, in the world's most unmistakable voice, 'I had the porridge. But they wouldn't give me any c-rr-aaa-yyy-mm!' He started to laugh his infectious laugh, and I started laughing too. Next year, we agreed, he would have his cream.

As I spoke to more and more people in Northern Ireland, something began to stand out; not many are boring. As somebody who has spent years standing in silence on the London Underground, I was suddenly finding it difficult to buy a bus ticket without a conversation ensuing. The fabled Irish charm is real enough – but it has a corollary; however inflexible the individual, no matter how many terrible things they had said or done, there was a good chance that I would end up enjoying their company. Some were as hard as granite, and could have snapped me in two with a glance. A few had tempers that were visible just below the surface. There were one or two I could picture pulling a gun on me in other circumstances. But we met in 2009 in front rooms and cafés, pubs and social clubs, and charm is charm, wherever it's found – even if its purpose is to show the charmer in a good light in a soon-to-be-published book. And if Ian Paisley and Gerry Fitt – or more recently Ian Paisley and Martin McGuinness – can chuckle together, then perhaps everybody here can, some day, laugh with everybody else.

Just as I liked people I didn't expect to like, so I enjoyed places I didn't expect to enjoy. Derry is the best example. Or should I say Londonderry? Or L'Derry. Or the Walled City. Or the Maiden City. Or Stroke City. If Northern Ireland is a place of contradictions, then Derry is its capital; residents cannot agree on a name. It is known as *Derry* to nationalists, as *Londonderry* to unionists. Those other names are awkward compromises. Translink, Northern Ireland's public transport company, is alive to the problem; if you plan a journey on its website and type in the name 'Derry', your itinerary will thereafter refer to 'Derry'. It remembers. But if you call the place 'Londonderry', so will the journey planner. If you want the site to crash, tell it you're travelling between the two. In this book I have referred to Derry; it is shorter, it is an older name, and it is the form used in the titles of both the 1689 Siege of Derry and the Apprentice Boys of Derry. There is no bias intended. I would like to think that nobody will be offended by my decision, but that's just what I would like to think.

My preconceptions of the city, whatever it is called, were of a sullen, grey, bomb-shattered purgatory. But I found something very different. It is beautiful. The centre is contained entirely within seventeenth-century walls, and the bombs have failed to dislodge its fine Anglican cathedral and its rows of lovely Georgian houses. It is steep and hilly, set on the curve of the River Foyle, in the shadow of the Inishowen mountains. It is small enough that you continually encounter the same people. I bumped into John Hume three times in one week. And it is friendly. Pass somebody in the evening on Shipquay Street and they will say hello. Even I was doing it after a while.

In the middle of my journey I spent a few days in Ardara, a town across the border in Donegal. To get there I drove from Belfast, and the contrast was striking. Belfast is a hard city of stone and traffic; it feels British. Ardara is a sleepy town of music, tweed, and random conversations; it feels Irish. Derry, geographically, in size, and in personality, is somewhere in between. In demographics too; despite the historical importance of the city to Protestants, the most recent census records that 77 per cent of those in the Derry urban area are Catholic.

The first three people I noticed on my arrival in Derry could not have had less in common. I had taken the bus from Belfast, and I wandered into the imposing Guildhall Square, just outside the walls. As I stood taking in the atmosphere, looking like the tourist I was, I was approached by a little old man who started chatting before showing me a succession of sleight-of-hand coin tricks. After he had wandered away my attention was gripped by an obese man wearing a T-shirt the size of a barrage balloon which read: 'I beat Anorexia.' I've never been a fan of comedy T-shirts, but as they go, this was a good one. As I walked past him towards Waterloo Place, I became aware that somebody had started walking alongside me, inches away. I quickened my pace and so did my shadow. I was holding a book with a large sticker saying 'London Library' on the cover, and I turned my head a fraction, to see that the shadow, a man in his twenties, was staring down at the book. Suddenly he jumped in front of me and spat 'Fucking Limey!' in my face, before running off. I think that's what he spat, but I was putting so much effort into not looking alarmed, that I might have misheard his last word. But there was no missing his point; I was a Londoner in a city where, for many people, the role of the English in their recent (and not-so-recent) past has not been forgotten.

I felt homesick for a couple of hours after this little chain of events, but over the course of many stays in Derry, I would encounter nothing but warmth and hospitality. The sleight-of-hand man proved to be typical, not the furious spitting man. Even on my frequent trips into the Bogside, the resolutely republican area beneath the city walls, I was made to feel welcome.

While in Derry I stayed with Peter and Joan Pyne, who own a number of bed-and-breakfasts in the centre of town. At the end of each day I would relate to them my tiny adventures, and I began to feel very much at home. Peter gave me a sense of what it was like to live in Derry at the height of the Troubles. One of the couple's properties, a Georgian house in Great James Street, had witnessed more than your average B&B. On one occasion a bomb planted nearby blew a soldier through the front door and onto the stairs, where he sat for several minutes, dazed. Another time the bakery opposite was blown up after men entered the shop and told the staff to tell police that they were being robbed. When the police arrived a bomb hidden in the doorway was detonated. In yet another incident an explosion blew a piece of shrapnel into the wall above the sitting room door. Peter Pyne had wanted to keep it there, as a memento for his guests, but, to his disappointment, the builders removed it.

These were not unusual experiences for people trying to make a living in Derry. Another man I met, a shopkeeper, had twice been visited by people intent on destruction. The first time, three men in Mickey Mouse and Donald Duck masks walked into his shop and started tossing petrol around. They ordered everyone out, before lighting a match and dropping it. Another time two men carried a bomb down into the basement, 'with the result that my shop ended up in the street'. On both occasions the shopkeeper had to clean up as best he could and continue trading. He would only receive compensation once he had opened up again – which meant that he could not afford simply to give up and move on. None of these attacks was specifically targeted at individuals. The IRA's intention had been to reduce the city to a state of unworkable chaos, and the men and women who ran the businesses had to take their chances.

Another shopkeeper explained how a large number of businesses in the north would pay sums of money to organizations on either side, to protect themselves from attack. In their accounts, these businesses would describe the payments as 'security costs', for which they did not have to show any paperwork. They could then set these payments against tax. I wonder how many taxpayers were aware of the extent of their contributions to the IRA and UVF.

It is very difficult, walking around Derry today, with its shopping malls, its restaurants, its wonderful Tower Museum, its Millennium Forum theatre, and its sushi bar – opened by an optimistic Swedish woman married to a Derryman – to imagine the city in the grip of the Troubles. The relief at Derry's rebirth is profound for almost everybody – except for those who cavil at the peace process. But one local businessman struck a discordant note. During the Troubles, he told me, the hooliganistic acts were directed at the police and the army; they were not directed 'anti-socially'. These days, he said, he will no longer walk around the city centre at night, for fear of attack. He spoke of the past almost with nostalgia, of the days when the communities used to clamp down on thieves and muggers. For many years Northern Ireland was deprived of 'ordinary' crime.

Back in the old days of community justice, I would not have risked walking into the Bogside. Even a few years ago I might have ended up in a small room being closely questioned as to my intentions. A couple of Bogside residents said they could tell I wasn't 'Irish' as soon as they saw me, even though I was dressed – or I thought I was – like everybody else. Jeans are jeans, aren't they? The American journalist Elizabeth Shannon once described the Bogside as 'so tribal, so incestuous about its relationships, that even a stranger feels in some way "at home" there'. I think I understand what she meant. I was already used to feeling like an outsider in Northern Ireland. But now I was in a place that itself feels like an outsider. It is a dangerous bond. I can't remember a place where I felt so comfortable but had to watch my words so carefully.

Part of the Bogside's intensity comes from its location, lying directly beneath the city walls, at the feet of its one-time masters. The Apprentice Boys' Memorial Hall, an emblem of Protestant supremacy, sits above it. The Apprentice Boys are a similar fraternal order to the Orange Order, founded in 1814, to commemorate the lifting of the siege of Derry. Outside their hall the Apprentice Boys fire a symbolic cannon – over the Bogside – every December. The Bogside is built, as its name suggests, on wet, marshy ground. It grew up as waves of Catholics started arriving in the late eighteenth century from surrounding rural areas. Its modern notoriety derives from the fact that it was the spot where thirteen unarmed men, taking part in a banned civil rights march, were killed on 30 January 1972 – Bloody Sunday

– by members of 1st Battalion, Parachute Regiment. A four-teenth victim died as a result of his wounds months later. Bloody Sunday, the civil rights movement, and Derry's recent national-ist history are recorded in the heart of the Bogside, in the Museum of Free Derry. It is a stark and emotional museum, filled with personal relics and with the actual sounds of Bloody Sunday; a recorded soundtrack of the day plays on loop. In a back office, away from the soundtrack, I met 60-year-old John Kelly, whose life was changed on Bloody Sunday. His brother, Michael, was one of those shot dead.

John Kelly is a quiet, dignified man, with the sense of humour apparently obligatory in Northern Ireland. He told me that he had been born in a house just outside the Derry walls, before his parents moved to Creggan, a large post-war estate built for Catholics within the gerrymandered South ward. 'We had a very basic upbringing,' he remembers. 'My father, like all men at the time, found great difficulty finding employment, and I was one of thirteen children.' His house had three bedrooms, a living room, a kitchen, and a bathroom. There was lino on the floor. 'It was like thousands of other houses around this place. There were us boys in one room – we were lucky. Me and Michael would be lying side by side, and I can remember waking up with a warm back. The nine girls were in another room. It had a couple of big beds, and all the girls were squeezed into them. My mother and father had the third room. It was a happy family. My mother and father hadn't got very much, but they clothed us and fed us, and looked after us very, very well.'

The Kelly family lived a basic life: 'I remember hardship. But at Christmas time I remember my father creeping in and putting something into a stocking at the end of the bed, an apple or an orange. And there was always a toy.' Kelly attended the Christian Brothers' School in the Bogside. He would walk to school in the morning, walk back home for lunch, and return in the after-noon. 'My mother would say, "What are you going to have for your lunch, son?", and I would say, "Ma, give us a couple of sandwiches, a bit of ham." I would have that continuously, until I had to turn round to say, "Ma, you couldn't give us something else?"

When he was eight or nine his mother brought home a television on hire purchase: 'We were the first in the street to have one, and all the other children were looking into the window at it. It was fascinating – *Billy Bunter*, *The Cisco Kid*. They were happy times. We hadn't the money to go away, but every day in the summer we would go out into the countryside and play among the fields and the wee streams, playing in trees, picking up tadpoles. It was a healthy way of living. I went out the door and my Ma wouldn't see me until six, when I came back for my dinner.'

As a youngster Kelly had no involvement with politics: 'We were brought up in our little haven of a nice wee house in the Creggan, and my Ma and my Da looking after us, happily playing on the street. When I was 15, I left the Christian Brothers and I went to work in a local factory called the BSR, where I was trained as a toolmaker. And that was my life, you know, no involvement in foul play, no discussion about politics within the house.' One day Kelly became aware of a neighbour, a boy with whom he had grown up, walking down the street in a uniform. The boy was a Protestant, who had joined the B Specials. 'I played with him on a daily basis, as equals, without ever arguing about religion. When I saw him in his uniform, I found it fairly strange to be truthful.' His parents would take him into town on the anniversary of the Battle of the Boyne to watch the Orange parade. 'It was just the situation of Ma and Da with their family watching the bands. It wasn't a situation where they'd turn round and say, "They're all Prods!" I didn't even know what an Orangeman was until I was 16.'

When he started work in the factory Kelly came into contact with more Protestants. 'But even then there were no arguments about politics. You just knew that one was a Prod and one was a

Catholic. It was the way it was. The only thing I remember was a Protestant telling a joke about Our Lady, and that annoyed me. But then it calmed down, it was OK, and we became friends. At work we'd laugh and we'd joke with each other, but we never mingled afterwards. It was never, "I'll see you for a game of snooker" or "I'll see you at the dance." But that was because of where you lived. If I'd lived in the Waterside, I'd probably have hung around with these guys, but because I lived in the Creggan, it was a different game. OK, there were certain areas you didn't go to, there were certain dance halls you didn't go into. You were just careful where you travelled. But, for me, it was no big deal. You accepted who people were.' Kelly wishes that there could have been more integration throughout society: 'Had it been a normal society, the children should have been educated together. Catholic or Protestant – it shouldn't have mattered.'

As he grew older he began to become aware of the political situation. 'You were living in your own wee world – and then you were educated. Because you didn't realize these things were actually happening around you. I remember going up to the town, walking down the High Street, and seeing people trying to evict other people from a house. And a group came in, supporting the people who lived in the house. And then you started asking questions about what the hell was going on here.'

Kelly's real awakening occurred as he was having his hair cut by the local barber – who was the father of 1970 Eurovision winner Dana. It comes as something of a shock to find that Dana – who sang the lovely 'All Kinds of Everything' – grew up not in an unearthly glade scattered with fairies, but on the Creggan Estate. It was while in the barber's shop that John Kelly heard that a civil rights march had been attacked on the Waterside. 'After that I started paying attention, and it created in my mind an annoyance, and an anger. That's how it was for me, and for thousands of other people. I'd only just reached the age for voting, and I was awakened to the fact that I was denied the vote.

I had a job – I was lucky, but I started to become aware of the discrimination. Something within me was lit, and I started joining the civil rights marches along with the other people.'

In January 1969 the words 'You are now entering Free Derry' appeared on the gable end of a house in the Bogside. They were coined by the socialist activist Eamonn McCann, who explained: 'Free, in the first instance, had meant freedom from the RUC and the oppressive state whose authority it enforced.' Before the civil rights marches, the RUC had been generally accepted by Catholic communities, but that tolerance soon melted away. Roads leading into the main Catholic areas of Derry were barricaded, and an autonomous 'Free Derry' was declared, closed to the RUC and regulated by its own vigilante patrols. The barricades came down after the intervention of the Derry Citizens' Action Committee, under the leadership of John Hume.

The situation quickly deteriorated. In April 1969 Samuel Devenny, a quiet, 42-year-old undertaker and hearse driver, was attacked by RUC officers in his home. Kelly recalls the events: 'Some of these young guys were rioting against the police, and the policemen went after a few of them up William Street. Sammy Devenny's family lived in William Street, and the door was open, and some of them ran through it. The police came in and went after them in the house, and in the process they beat up Sammy Devenny and his family.' Devenny died from a heart attack brought on by his injuries three months later. 'That was horrible,' Kelly recalls. 'You hardened to what was happening around you. Some people would say that Sammy was the first casualty of the Troubles.' In the aftermath of the attack, the police withdrew from the Bogside, but they resumed carrying out patrols. In the summer, as the community's fears heightened, the barricades were built up once again.

On 12 August the Apprentice Boys prepared to march through Derry to mark their annual celebration of the lifting of the siege. On the eve of the march Patrick Macrory, who would one day write an excellent account of the siege, asked an Orangeman whom he considered kind and decent, why it was necessary to mount such an obviously provocative celebration. 'He looked at me in mild surprise and then said grimly: "We have to show them who's master, that's why."'

The parades of the Orange Order and the Apprentice Boys had been fraught affairs on many previous occasions, but rarely as fraught as they were in 1969. Catholics barricaded roads in the Bogside and armed themselves with petrol bombs, stones, and nails. Protestants looked down and felt under siege once more; Catholics looked up in anticipation of an invasion by police, loyalists, and B Specials. The march began peacefully – but problems started when marchers, coming along the walls, tossed coins down into the Bogside. Catholics began throwing stones up at the Apprentice Boys and police. In an instant a violent confrontation was under way. The police tried to dismantle one of the barricades, and it seemed to Catholics as though an invasion had begun. John Hume wandered around the city, pleading with rioters to disperse, as buildings were set ablaze by petrol bombs, and police fired CS gas for the first time in the United Kingdom.

In the midst of the chaos the Irish Taoiseach made a radio broadcast announcing that: 'The Irish government can no longer stand by and see innocent people injured and perhaps worse.' In the Bogside – and in Protestant areas – this was understood as a declaration that the Republic's army was coming to liberate Derry – and there were those in the Irish cabinet who argued that Derry *should* be taken by Irish troops. Indeed declassified documents reveal that an Irish government plan was drawn up, first to mount guerrilla attacks on targets in Belfast (including the docks, the airport, and the BBC studios) which would draw security forces away from the border, and then to launch an infantry assault on Derry and Newry. The plan was never carried out; it was ultimately considered 'militarily unsound'.

Sam Malcolmson was a policeman from a rural area, who had been drafted into the Bogside on that day. He told Bobbie Hanvey: 'We went in, we were beaten out, we went back in, we were beaten out. Looking across the barricades, it did astonish me – the hatred on the faces of people. A guy standing in front of me had a petrol bomb, and I was wearing my visor so as to get a better look at him. I lifted the visor, and that was all I could remember until I was being dragged off, and thrown in the back of a Land Rover, and taken to Altnagelvin Hospital.'

John Kelly, who had got married a week before, had helped to build the barricades: 'You helped – like thousands of other people who lived in Derry at the time.' He remembers the fighting: 'I was living in a flat up in the Marlborough area, and I looked down and saw the place on fire. Because we were just married I was being careful not to get involved, but I came down to see what was going on. I was choked on the CS gas, and I can remember the noise, and being really pleased with the comradeship of the people. People were moving as one, and going with the flow to protect themselves from invasion by the RUC and loyalists groups. A shout went out that St Eugene's Cathedral was being attacked by loyalists, so everybody, including myself, went down to help protect the place. I was standing at the top of Great James Street, and there were loyalists and police at the bottom, when shots rang out and a guy I knew was hit in the leg by a bullet. And after that the British army was brought in.'

Once British troops moved in, the trouble was quelled, but only after the people of the Bogside had prevented the police and the B Specials from entering the area. The 'Battle of the Bogside', as it became known, was seen – by both sides – as a victory for the Catholics, in the city which had denied them entry in 1689. In the midst of the fight civil rights activists appealed for demonstrations to take place elsewhere to 'take the heat off Derry'. Their call was heeded in west Belfast, with horrible consequences. Mobs of Catholics gathered on the Falls Road while mobs of Protestants gathered on the Shankill Road. Both sides were motivated by the fact that the Bogsiders had resisted the authorities.

The Shankill Road and the Falls Road run parallel to each other, but in 1969 there was no 'peace wall' between them. The riots began in west Belfast – as they had in Derry – with Catholics clashing with police. They spread along the divide. At some point loyalists followed police down the streets connecting the Shankill and the Falls, throwing petrol bombs into Catholic houses as they went. Shots were fired from Catholic areas, and the police deployed armoured cars, which opened fire more or less indiscriminately. Their bullets killed a 9-year-old Catholic boy who was lying in bed in his family's flat in Divis Tower, a block at the bottom of the Falls. People from both sides were killed. Houses in Catholic streets, or in the Catholic ends of Protestant streets, were burned to the ground. Catholic families in predominantly Protestant streets, and Protestant families in predominantly Catholic streets, left their houses never to return. Refugees took shelter with relatives or in church halls. Belfast became a war zone. One man recalls the aftermath: 'The only way to describe it is that it was just like the photographs of Dresden in the Second World War. There were just skeletons of houses and factories, the whole lot had been burned out.'

It is important to understand the significance of fear in the events of August 1969. Catholics feared that their communities would be wiped out. Protestants feared losing the upper hand – which, in reality, also amounted to fear that their communities would be wiped out. People are driven by fear, and fear is the parent of cruelty and hatred. Yet Joe Graham remembers a brief moment of unity in the midst of the hell: 'While this town was burning to the ground, I had to visit a Protestant man called Davy Murray, a trade unionist, an old socialist who ran a wee print shop and a sweetie shop. I went the back-ways to get into the Shankill. Nobody in their right sense would have done it, and when I got there the sweetie shop was open. I walked on in, and Davy and his wife were sitting drunk. I didn't know them to be drinkers, and Davy said, "Ah, Joe, what's it like on the Falls? Is the Falls burning?" I said, "Aye, Davy," and he started crying, "Our poor people, Joe, they'll never get back together."' Unable to control the situation, the Northern Ireland government, now led by James Chichester Clark, asked James Callaghan to send British troops onto the streets of Northern Ireland to relieve the police. Callaghan did so, but, as he presciently told Gerry Fitt, it was very easy to put the troops in but it would be a devil of a job to get them out again.

Gregory Campbell is today a DUP member of Parliament, but in 1969 he was a 16-year-old shop assistant in Derry, marching in his first Apprentice Boys parade. In a 2009 speech he recalled watching Catholic rioters who 'seemed intent on creating mayhem and insurrection'. The Battle of the Bogside was not, in his view, a case of disadvantaged people confronting the state as a last resort; it was, rather, the start of 'an open-ended rebellion against the rule of law' which strangled any prospect of a shared community with a brighter future.

For Brendan Hughes, a 20-year-old Catholic from west Belfast who was to become a leading member of the Provisional IRA, August 1969 had a different impact: 'There wasn't any political thought in my head at all at that period. But I felt for the people who were being bombed out ... Here it was, the B Specials on the streets, the RUC on the streets, and on the Falls Road, the RUC actually opening up with machine guns, and the next morning the casualty list, the burnt-out houses and so forth. I toured the areas helping people out with the furniture they had left, into the safer areas of west Belfast. I felt anger, bitterness. I can articulate it now, I didn't then.' Hughes and Campbell, two men who could never hope to agree on an interpretation of events, seem to tally on one detail. In Hughes's words, 'That whole period of '69 brought about the conflict.'

Catholic communities tended to look on the IRA as an ally in difficult times. When times were not desperate, for example during Operation Harvest, the IRA received little support. But when the communities felt under threat, as in August 1969, they expected it to be there to defend them. On this occasion, however, they were disappointed. The IRA stayed very quiet. 'IRA – I Ran Away' appeared chalked on Belfast walls. The reason for the near silence was that the IRA had moved in a Marxist direction away from its roots, as its leader at the time, Cathal Goulding, explained to Bobbie Hanvey: 'We wanted to move away from violence, to shift the emphasis back on the civil rights movement. We felt that was the only way we were going to make any progress. If we could break down that attitude of bigotry and hatred that existed between Irish Protestants and Irish Catholics, particularly in the six counties, then we wouldn't have to bother about talking about the unity of the six, and the twenty-six counties. It would come as a matter of fact.'

Nevertheless, many within the republican movement – including Joe Cahill and the young Gerry Adams – disagreed with Goulding's outlook. They wanted to return to the physical-force republicanism of the earlier IRA. At the end of 1969 the IRA split into two distinct organizations: the Official IRA, which followed Goulding's Marxist line, and the Provisional IRA, which adhered to old-style republicanism. The Provisionals vowed to defend the Catholic communities and, although the Officials remained in existence, it was the Provisionals who would become the principal enemy of the British army over the next thirty years of conflict. It is poignant that today words similar to Goulding's are uttered by one-time Provisionals now that they have, in turn, moved away from violence.

As the IRA built up its strength the British government kept up the pressure on the Northern Ireland government to introduce reforms. As a result the B Specials were abolished, to be replaced the following year by the newly formed Ulster Defence

Regiment (UDR), which, depending on one's point of view, was the B Specials by another name, a pale shadow of the B Specials, or a responsible, non-sectarian, part-time security force. One British officer, who arrived in Northern Ireland in 1969, describes why he believes the B Specials were disbanded: 'It was because they were incompetent, and because they inflamed the nationalist minority, who saw them as being a Protestant militia, *which is what they were*. When you see so-called policemen throwing stones back at rioters and calling them "Fucking Fenians" – I saw this happening – the British quite rightly decided they wouldn't use them.' The same officer describes the logistical difficulty in disbanding the force: 'The great thing was to get all of the B Specials on parade at the same time throughout the province, with their weapons, and then to disarm them. People thought this could be dodgy, and I'm not sure they ever got *all* the weapons, but basically they got most of them.'

With a rejuvenated IRA, with loyalist groups poised to respond in kind, and with the British army on the streets, the scene was set for the thirty-year cycle of violence. When British soldiers first arrived, however, they were seen as saviours by the Catholic population. According to Joe Graham: 'It's true that the Brits were welcomed by the vast majority. On the night they arrived I was on the Falls and they came in and they were welcomed overwhelmingly – but I didn't like it. There's a traffic light on the corner of Springfield Road, and the Brits put barbed wire across the Falls Road – so I climbed up and stuck a tricolour there. And people were shouting, "What are you putting that up for? The soldiers are here for us! Go fuck yourself!" People definitely believed they were here for them. The soldiers probably thought they were here for them.'

In Derry, John Kelly remembers most Catholics welcoming the army, while a few warned that they were invaders. 'But it was a relief, you know, because people were tired. For a couple of days and nights during the battle, they had been fighting with the RUC and loyalists. People were getting hurt, gassed, ending up in hospital. So it was a relief when the army came in and created a cordon. But it was a surreal situation, and something that I didn't fully understand, to be truthful.' Carol Lynn Toland was a young girl in Derry when the troops arrived. 'The excitement was great. My mother was bringing them out tea and sandwiches. The Saracens [six-wheeled armoured vehicles] were outside our front door – and the soldiers were very nice to us. We had our pictures taken with them. They told us stories and let us try on their helmets.'

Over time the 'honeymoon' period of good relations came to an end. In Belfast events on the Falls Road in July 1970 hastened the separation. The army entered the Lower Falls to search for IRA weapons. As a crowd gathered, soldiers reversed a Saracen, crushing a local man to death. A riot developed and the army fired CS gas, which drifted into houses in the narrow streets. Both the Official IRA and the Provisional IRA opened fire and the army responded, killing four unarmed civilians, one of them a press photographer. The British commander then deployed a tactic that had been used successfully in colonial conflicts – the curfew. In many previous conflicts, however, the army had not been attempting to win 'hearts and minds', nor had it been exposed to media scrutiny. For a day and a half residents were kept off the streets, while troops dismantled houses in search of guns. The consequent bad feeling led a *Sunday Times* Insight team to record that the affair turned 'what was perhaps only an increasingly sullen Catholic acceptance of the army into outright communal hostility'.

According to a sergeant in the Royal Green Jackets, attitudes were also changing within the British army: 'A lot of us had a lot of sympathy with the Catholics. But it's always the same when someone starts shooting at you; you're tired and you're bitter. Everyone's got their own tribe, their own group identity, and that's the strongest thing we all cling to at times of stress.' An army officer who arrived in Belfast just after the curfew, told me of trying to separate the two sides during a confrontation at the edge of Ballymurphy: 'Huge crowds were gathering on both sides, hurling stones and abuse.' At one point hundreds of loyalists began waving union flags 'as a means of provocation. I was trying to stop them. And then Ian Paisley arrived. I said to Paisley, "Thank God you've arrived. Can you please stop your people doing this bloody flag-waving? It's a red rag to a bull!" And Paisley said, "That's an absurd request! That's most offensive behaviour! You are denying my people the right to wave the flag of our Queen and country!"'

Reflecting on the period, the same officer told me with sadness in his voice, 'The viciousness with which they [the Catholics] attacked us! *And we were trying to defend them!* We were seen as specifically defending the Protestants, but we were trying to keep the sides apart! It's so pathetic, when you're trying to help and nobody wants to be helped!' Yet Joe Cahill, the survivor of a British condemned cell in 1940 and, thirty years later, a senior member of the Provisional IRA, says, 'People soon realized that they [the British army] weren't in there for the defence of the people, they were there to bolster up the Stormont government, there to bolster up the RUC, and people soon realized that it was still the same enemy.' While the role of the British troops *was* to keep the sides apart, in doing so they were, in effect, bolstering up the Stormont government, which had lost control of its province. This was why, no matter how well or badly the army behaved, it was probably always destined to fall out with the Catholic population. In 1970 the Provisional IRA was preparing to resurrect the struggle for reunification, but it had not yet got the weapons, or sufficient support from the Catholic community, to begin the job in earnest. It was keen, in the meantime, to be seen as the true defender of the Catholic people, and to deepen the rift between the army and the Catholic communities. Events such as the curfew, when the army behaved with little sensitivity, made its job easier.

The IRA was also keen to warn Catholics against 'fraternizing' with the enemy. John Kelly recalls: 'Girls used to go to army dances over at the Ebrington barracks. They became known as "army dolls". At the beginning it was fine, but when things started to change, it pretty well became a mortal sin. There were even girls from republican families that ended up going with soldiers, and that was really frowned upon.' Some girls who fraternized had their heads shaved before being tarred and feathered. A nurse at the Royal Victoria Hospital remembers: 'The tar was a thick diesel oil, and we used to use Swarfega to get it off. The hospital's pharmacist became annoyed that we were using more Swarfega than any other department in the United Kingdom – but no other department was dealing with tarring and feathering …' For all that, Kelly tells me that there are ex-British soldiers married to Derry women, who live in the Creggan today. 'They were accepted after a while – but it was really traitorous.'

For Kelly in Derry, the souring of relations between Brits and Catholics was a 'steady progression'. At first he wondered, 'Why turn on the Brits when they were seen as the saviours?' but, after a while, 'They started battling with the young guys, and they started killing people like young Cusack and Beattie.'

Seamus Cusack and Desmond Beattie, two young Catholics from Derry, were shot by the army on the same day in July 1971. An unofficial inquiry, chaired by Lord Gifford QC, found that both men had been unarmed when shot. Carol Lynn Toland remembers: 'The "honeymoon" didn't last a terribly long time. It soon became clear that the army was just as oppressive as the police. So the young fellas started this rioting – throwing stones. Des Beattie was rioting in the Bogside when he was shot. He was going steady with my cousin, he was her first love, he lived around the corner, and he used to babysit me. In July '71 I was 9 years old, and while I was lying in bed I heard the adults crying and I knew there must be something wrong. That set the tone for the rest of my life – because I used to be afraid when I heard this crying. It happened a few times. I asked Mammy what was wrong and she said, "Go back to bed!" and I said, "You'd better tell me what's wrong!" and she said, "Des Beattie was shot."'

By the time Beattie was shot, a combination of republican provocation, lack of army restraint, and sheer inevitability had produced the situation experienced by one British soldier on patrol in Ballymurphy: 'Everyone didn't like you. Old grannies in the street would spit at you, and young children would spit at you. The environment, the atmosphere, was more frightening than the gunmen.' This, in turn, meant that individual soldiers' attitudes, and consequently their actions, hardened. According to an army captain, 'It became hard to justify to the soldiers – no, justify would be the wrong word – to produce the right context whereby the boys would realize … that it was not a battle in the conventional sense of the word, and that restraint was always necessary.'

As 1971 wore on, the regular riots began to be supplemented by much deadlier encounters. The first IRA man to be shot dead by the army, 21-year-old James Saunders, and the first soldier to be shot dead by the IRA, 20-year-old Robert Curtis, were both killed on the same day in February. In March three off-duty soldiers were killed in an attack, chilling in its cynicism. The soldiers, two of them brothers aged 17 and 18, were lured out of a Belfast bar by female IRA volunteers. The women invited the soldiers to a party and telephoned some male friends to drive them there. The entire group drove out of Belfast, and while the soldiers were relieving themselves by the side of the road, they were shot in the head by the 'friends'. One of the dead soldiers was allegedly found propped up by the road with his beer glass placed in his hand. Although these killings may have been carried out without the authority of the Provisional leadership, it was quite plain that the modern Troubles were going to bear little resemblance to the IRA's Harvest Campaign of a decade earlier. In 1971 alone, 180 people were killed in the province;

107 by republicans, 45 by the army, 22 by loyalists, and one by the police.

For John Kelly, and for many people who considered themselves nationalists, the introduction of internment in August 1971 was the point at which the British army truly became the enemy. Brian Faulkner – Terence O'Neill's nemesis and Denys Rowan Hamilton's election opponent – had become Prime Minister in March. He was aware that the British government, dismayed by the chaos erupting in Northern Ireland, stood poised to impose direct rule. He moved to appease the British by offering cabinet posts to liberal unionists, as well as a single post to a member of the Northern Ireland Labour Party – the first non-unionist ever to hold a cabinet position. He also offered the chairmanships of two new policy and legislative committees to nationalists. These political concessions were a sop to Catholics; Faulkner also intended to introduce stern security measures in the belief that he could bring order to the province. Foremost among these measures was internment – the rounding up and indefinite detention of suspects without trial.

As Northern Ireland's Minister of Home Affairs, Faulkner had introduced internment during the Harvest Campaign. It had helped to neutralize the IRA on that occasion, but those had been very different times. For one thing, the Irish Republic had simultaneously introduced internment; it had no intention of doing so this time around. For another thing, the Catholic communities in the north were readier to identify with the IRA than they had been for fifty years.

Early on the morning of Monday, 9 August soldiers accompanied by members of the RUC Special Branch, descended on the homes of IRA suspects. Three hundred and forty-two arrests were made. One of those arrested was Paddy Joe McLean, who told Bobbie Hanvey: 'My mother-in-law was on her death bed in hospital in Omagh, and on Sunday night I sat with her, and I came home about four o'clock on Monday morning. I don't think my eyes closed before the noise came at the door, and I went down, and it was the army and the police. I got time to put my clothes on, and I didn't get handled roughly. I was just told, "You're coming with us."'

In the days that followed, Faulkner justified internment on the basis that Northern Ireland was 'quite simply at war with the terrorist and in a state of war many sacrifices have to be made'. There are several problems with this statement. First, these sacrifices were to be felt only by Catholics. Only two Protestants were arrested, and they were both civil rights activists. No loyalists would be arrested for a year. Catholics had long complained that they were victimized. Now internment appeared to highlight their grievance. Second, the chief sacrifice to which Faulkner was referring was the move beyond the rule of law, a legal state of affairs with no place in a supposed liberal democracy. What had been acceptable in 1956 was no longer acceptable in a society familiar with the concept of human rights. Third, Faulkner's reference to a 'war' had the effect of offering weight to the IRA's claim that it was engaged in a legitimate struggle; this, presumably, was not the impression that he was intending to give.

Quite apart from all this, internment was to fail in its express purpose. The leading members of the Provisional IRA remained at liberty. The intelligence relied upon by the RUC Special Branch was hopelessly inaccurate, with the result that the innocent, the old, and the irrelevant were arrested. In some cases soldiers were sent to the wrong address, where they ended up arresting a father or a cousin of an IRA man. Of the 342 people detained, over a hundred were released within two days. Over the following six months over 2,000 more people would be arrested, most of whom would also be quickly released.

Of those detained twelve were selected for interrogation techniques that would subsequently be judged 'inhuman and degrading' by the European Court of Human Rights. One of the men chosen was Paddy Joe McClean: 'It lasted for roughly five days.

There was about twenty-four different forms used. No food, no sleep, light all the time, unbearable noise, sounds of riots, sounds of gunfire. I resolved not to cooperate. I no more spoke, sat, walked, or did anything. Any time I had to be moved, I had to be lifted. I was medically examined there, and the doctor who examined me, said, "If I'm needed to dispatch him, you'll find me at the country club." I never forgot those words. In my mind, there's only one meaning for "If I'm needed to dispatch him".

Across the province, Catholic fury grew. Violence erupted in Belfast on the Monday morning. Gun battles raged between the army and the IRA, buses were hijacked, barricades were built, and plumes of smoke rose over Belfast. On the Tuesday eleven people were killed in the city. As the violence spread, so did fear, the underlying currency of the Troubles. During August up to 2,500 families moved home into 'friendlier' areas and Northern Ireland became more divided than it had ever been. Many mixed areas simply ceased to exist. Ironically, given the purpose of internment, young men began to join the IRA in greater numbers. Republicanism came to fill a vacuum which the Social Democratic and Labour Party (SDLP), the successor to the Nationalist Party, could not. Even though far more of Northern Ireland's Catholics would vote for John Hume, Gerry Fitt, and their SDLP colleagues than would ever admit to supporting the IRA, the course of the next thirty years would be more tellingly defined by those at the extremes than by those in the peaceful centre. The eventual rise of Sinn Féin to power – and the level of trust that would one day be placed in the more extreme politicians – is testament to this.

One senior British army officer to whom I spoke admitted: 'Internment was a disaster. The intelligence was insufficient to justify the numbers that were taken. It just helped the republican cause enormously, because it didn't stop anything, and it was hugely offensive to the Catholic population.' Another British officer described one obvious change: 'Prior to internment, we could meet known terrorists on the streets, and talk to them daily, without any powers of detention or arrest. But the moment that internment was introduced, all the known terrorists disappeared from the scene. The pattern of life became for them to be living undercover, mounting operations as and when they planned them.'

Once internment had been introduced, John Kelly, a man who had once been confused by the situation, became much clearer in his thinking: 'Internment was a massive turning point for me. That's when I saw what the Brits were doing. I realized it wasn't right. So I was one of the guys out on the street in the Creggan, battling with them, throwing stones, building barricades, defending your area, and keeping them out. It was a movement against the British army, against the unionists, and against the British government for what they were allowing to happen here.'

Kelly witnessed the growth of the IRA: 'There had been very few guys I knew as being IRA. But then, with internment – that's when things started. The British army were seen as being enemies to everyone. And the republicans saw that as an opportunity.' Kelly came to view the IRA as defenders of his community: 'I seen these guys, they were patrolling the area, they were seen with their weapons on a daily basis, and they were actually protecting the people.' He was surprised by the identity of some of these people: 'These were guys you knew – but you didn't know. Do you understand what I mean? They wore their masks, and I was shocked when I found out who some of them really were. I couldn't believe it. These were civil beings. If it wasn't for this situation, these guys would *never ever* have joined a paramilitary organization like the IRA.' The atmosphere in Derry, once a peaceful city, was now different: 'It was always very, very tense. You were going to work, and you didn't know if you'd be coming back again. You'd get caught up in gun battles on a daily basis. You had to dive for cover. You seen buildings going up in the air. It wasn't normal.'

After internment the Free Derry barricades were built up, stronger than ever. Free Derry came to encompass the whole of the Bogside, the Creggan, and Brandywell. Kelly remembers it fondly: 'The people who organized Free Derry were ordinary human beings, ordinary people with jobs, who saw it as the right thing to do, to keep the Brits out, keep the RUC out, and protect their own area. Everybody joined in that. But you travelled in and out of Free Derry all the time. You had to go to work. You had to feed your family. Women had to go and buy the food. You weren't stuck inside Free Derry.'

According to Kelly, Free Derry was not an excuse for anarchy: 'It was well organized, and well controlled. There were guys – I'm not talking about members of the IRA – policing their own area. There was very little crime, because of the people. If there were break-ins, the people dealt with it. You had your courts, and it was the people in the area who actually sat in these courts, and chastised the people to ensure that they didn't do it again. Some people left the area because of some of the things they did, and they knew what was going to happen to them if the right people got them. But it wasn't a case of guys running around with guns and shooting people willy-nilly.'

For Kelly, and for other residents of the Bogside and the Creggan, Free Derry represented freedom within the unionist state, their own tiny republic. It is little wonder that the Bogside still feels like a place apart, and that Elizabeth Shannon remarks on a place that is 'incestuous about its relationships'. Within Free Derry Kelly felt 'totally safe, but when the Brits moved in and broke down the barricades I felt open to fear. The greatest fears were the British army and the RUC. They could come and go as they pleased, whereas before, there was protection out there.'

For many Derry Protestants, living across the river from the walled city in the Waterside district, or in the Fountain Estate – a small enclave beside the Bogside – the early days of the Troubles, and more specifically the actions of the Catholics, brought alarm. Billy Moore, a senior Apprentice Boy who was a young Waterside resident in 1969, told me, 'There was great fear and concern throughout the Protestant community in Londonderry. There was rioting, burning of shops, businesses, and as Protestants we thought this was an attempt by Irish nationalism and Irish Catholics to destabilize and destroy the state of Northern Ireland, which we believed was our country. In my community – I was only 17 – I looked to people who were senior, and they were fearful that this was the beginning of all-out civil war. The small Protestant communities felt that it was only a matter of time before they would be attacked and forced out of their homes. So people were out trying to create vigilante groups. Volunteers were required to patrol the street at night time, and everyone was put on a rota and did their turn. We did what everyone believed at that time was necessary to defend our community; we were being betrayed by the British government that we had always supported, and by many of our politicians who didn't appear to show much concern for working-class Protestants. We felt stranded with no support from anywhere. We, in the Protestant community in Londonderry, were close to the border, and we feared that the Irish army was about to come across the border and attack us.' As it turns out, such fears were not fantastic, and not far from being realized.

Loyalists throughout Northern Ireland were fearful and uncertain. The resurgent IRA was feared, unionist politicians were resented for pursuing British policies, the Orange Order was considered toothless, the B Specials had been disbanded, and the British army was thought to be standing by as republicans attacked loyalist communities. In Belfast, in September 1971, over 3,000 people showed up at a meeting intended to coordinate the small working-class Protestant vigilante groups that had sprung up. Most people could not gain entry, but out of the meeting was born the Ulster Defence Association, an organization created to defend its communities, and which came to mirror the IRA in that it contained a spine of hard-liners who would take the fight to the enemy. The UDA was organized into a British army-type structure of battalions and companies, as was the Ulster Volunteer Force – an organization that had been re-formed several years earlier on the fiftieth anniversary of the Battle of the Somme.

Unionists and loyalists had been heartened by the introduction of internment, but in fact Catholic support for the IRA had increased, and so had IRA activity. The army very quickly became aware that its greatest weapon against the IRA would be intelligence. The conflict would be very difficult to win militarily, and containment would be best achieved by detailed knowledge of the enemy's intentions and personnel. Even in the earliest days of the troops' presence, when Anglo-nationalist relations were still reasonable, the British were attempting to infiltrate the various levels of republicanism. Gordon Corrigan had arrived in Derry in September 1969, an officer with the Gloucestershire Regiment. His company was billeted in a ship on the River Foyle. Another company was billeted in a public toilet in the centre of town: 'It was wasn't a particularly pleasant place. But being soldiers, they got it cleaned up very well … and there was no shortage of crappers …'

Corrigan became the intelligence officer with battalion headquarters. He could pass as a local man: 'They bought me civilian clothes in local shops, and I did some agent running. At that time the IRA was beginning to stick its head up, but its security was appalling. So I could get away with doing things then that you could certainly not get away with doing two years later. Robert Nairac was doing pretty much what I was doing – but he got caught.'

Corrigan lived in a boarded-up sweet shop that had been derelict for some time. It had a single room and a telephone. His job was to work closely with RUC Special Branch, keeping tabs on what was happening in Derry. He would draw up an assessment and feed it to the military. His cover story was that he was a horse buyer: 'That seemed to work reasonably well. You talked to people, and kept your ears open. The great thing about the Irish is that they love drink and they love intrigue. Irish informers generally don't do it for the money – although some did it for the money – they did it because they loved conspiracies. I took on a couple of sources and I found a couple of my own, but you find them by sitting in pubs. As more and more drink was consumed, if somebody let something slip, then you might get something on them and apply a little bit of pressure.'

Once Corrigan had an informant, he had to be careful: 'There was a telephone number that my wretched sources could get me on, and we'd fix a meet. I knew the rules. I wasn't going to have a meet somewhere that I could be jumped. And I never paid for specific information. If you paid for specific information, they would tell you anything to get money. When they were short of money, they would give you something which might be total crap. So, every so often, you gave them a wad of cash.'

A lot of Corrigan's work involved going to republican meetings: 'I was a member of three republican clubs. Semi-social but political organizations. They were technically open meetings, but they would frisk you at the door, and look at you. If somebody turned up who was clearly a Brit, they wouldn't let them in, but I got in all right. You would hear very inflammatory stuff, but sometimes something that would lead to something. "We're having a demonstration. If anybody wants to help, please stay behind after the meeting." Well, of course, I stayed behind. That gave you good intelligence on general intentions. But the real nasties you got from sources that you were either paying or sometimes blackmailing. It might be that he was shagging somebody's wife. Or it might be that he was in financial trouble. Once you had bank account numbers, then you were away, because Special Branch had their way of checking bank accounts and running them back.'

In these early days Corrigan found the IRA reasonably easy to infiltrate: 'It was all fairly small stuff compared with what happened later. The IRA got much more difficult to infiltrate. Riots were most days. But shootings were still a rarity.' On one occasion Corrigan discovered information about the smuggling in of weapons from the United States: 'There was an American base near Londonderry, and there were weapons being smuggled in for the IRA by American military personnel. I actually got hold of this. I went to the hand-over. I hid in a bush and watched it. But I thought, this is big! This is not something I can deal with, so I pushed it up to MI5. I was told, "Right! Back off! You don't know anything about this. MI5 will deal with this."'

While walking around the city Corrigan frequently chose not to carry his pistol: 'If they twigged who I was, I thought they might just beat me up if I didn't have my pistol. They might not top me. The police told me always to take my pistol, but I didn't think they were right. It might have been a misappreciation, because Nairac *did* get topped.'

Corrigan was forced to leave Northern Ireland very suddenly in 1970: 'I was sitting in a pub in the Bogside, quaffing a pint of Guinness. I don't like Guinness, but you have to drink it because that's what they drink. A chap came in who had been at prep school with me. He was the local undertaker, so he could move either side of the sectarian boundaries. He said, "Gordon Corrigan! Didn't you join the army?" He didn't mean to make things difficult for me, but a couple of chaps in the corner put their pints down, and started reaching down … so I legged it very quickly. I had a little police radio, and I sent the code word, and they came and got me out. I was blown. They told me that I had to go back to Britain. I couldn't just go back to the unit. They would have gone for me because they had thought I was one of theirs. And that was that.'

In the wake of internment, and the failure of Special Branch intelligence, the army realized that it needed far more accurate and comprehensive information. One army officer described how he 'turned' a minor IRA figure who had been arrested while joyriding in a car that had been stolen for IRA purposes. The man was offered two options: he could be handed over to the police and brought to trial, or he could be turned loose and dealt with by an uncompromising local IRA commander. 'I suggested that it would be a kneecapping, or perhaps even a headjob in his case.' As a third option, the British officer suggested that the IRA figure could work for the British army. The man chose this.

The man was moved to an army barracks, where he identified IRA suspects from behind a screen: 'He gave me the lowdown on most of the IRA leaders, and this helped with the immediate arrest of the unpleasant commander.' The man was also taken out on patrol in the back of an armoured vehicle, from which he would point out IRA men on the streets. For six weeks this arrangement continued, while a cover story was created for the man's absence.

Seven weeks after the imposition of internment, a bomb was planted and detonated in the crowded Four Step Inn on the Shankill Road. Twenty-seven Protestants were injured and two were killed. Neither of the dead men had any connection with the security forces or the paramilitaries. The Northern Ireland Civil Rights Association and John Hume were quick to condemn the attack as an attempt to stir up sectarian hatred. The IRA never claimed responsibility but the blame could hardly be thought to lie elsewhere. On the day after the attack Ian Paisley addressed a crowd beside the ruins of the bar and announced the formation of his new political party, the Democratic Unionist Party. The loyalist mood was one of fury and disbelief. The funerals of the two men attracted an estimated crowd of 50,000; the coffins' procession was accompanied by members of the Orange Order.

Just over a month later revenge was taken. Fifteen people were killed when the UVF exploded a bomb in McGurk's Bar in the centre of Belfast. None of the dead had any connection with the IRA; McGurk's was a quiet bar, with no republican links. A nurse who arrived on the scene can remember people digging with their bare hands trying to pull survivors out of the wreckage. Back at the hospital, she was caring for three men who had lost their wives in the attack: 'We had a wee man who was out with his wife for a drink, and when the explosion happened he felt his wife's hand and he knew he'd lost her. We had Mr McGurk; his wife had been upstairs and he didn't know she was dead. Wee Mr Irvine was there as well; he'd lost his wife. Three widowers in one ward. It was very difficult to cope.'

Attacks such as these, committed first by one side, then by the other, in ceaseless reply, would become the pattern for the next thirty years. This was the fuel that spurred the Troubles on, the bloody manifestation of 'whataboutery'. And these two particular attacks – on ordinary drinkers in ordinary bars – were nakedly sectarian. They could in no way be described as attacks on paramilitaries or agents of the state. The antagonism being felt in Northern Ireland was becoming more intense as 1972 drew near.

One British officer, responsible for his men during the frequent riots that were taking place at this time, decided that he would have to act firmly to take control of his area. He felt that he had been handling the situation inadequately, being too defensive in his patrols. The rules for opening fire, as he understood them from the Yellow Card, the army's official rules of engagement, were that a soldier could shoot when he could identify a target, and when that target was in the act of threatening, or had just threatened, life. This officer decided to 'vary' policy in one way. He told his men that when they could identify the direction of the fire but could not pick out an exact target, one soldier should fire two rounds into a high wall, in the area where the shooting came from. He describes this as a 'quite unofficial rule', outside the rules laid out in the Yellow Card. He felt that this action would have several benefits. First, he wanted local people to know that his men were professional, and would return fire; second, it might make the enemy 'a little jittery on the trigger'; third, it would buy his men more time to react, as local children would be pulled off the streets in advance of an incident, if his company had a reputation for returning fire; and fourth, it gave his men the sense that they were doing something, and were not perpetually on the receiving end. The officer was aware that a 'showdown' was coming: 'In fact, we were shot at on seven occasions that evening. We returned fire on every occasion we were engaged. I like to think that we asserted a grip on that area, that we were never to relax on the remainder of our tour.'

As security became tougher and attitudes continued to harden, an event was about to occur which would irrevocably destroy the relationship between the British government and the nationalist people of Northern Ireland. Bloody Sunday might have been only one terrible event among many over many years of the Troubles. It did not cause the highest death toll of any incident; the Omagh bomb in August 1998 was responsible for twenty-nine deaths. It cannot be said to stand out for the grief and misery it caused; thousands of deaths, many of them all but forgotten, were to change the lives of countless people. But Bloody Sunday marks a moment beyond which rapprochement seemed impossible. It gave rise to a terrible increase in violence; 1972 would see the deaths of almost three times as many people as the previous year. It would see a sudden growth in, and support for, the IRA. It would see the British embassy in Dublin burnt to the ground to the cheers of a mob. Just as the outrage caused by the Omagh bomb would one day help to bring the Troubles to an end, the horror and fury brought about by Bloody Sunday would grant them a long and bitter momentum.

6

THE MARCH

Wandering around Derry today, you can still walk down the streets whose names became famous in the weeks after Sunday, 30 January 1972: William Street, Rossville Street, Chamberlain Street, Little James Street. Many of the original Bogside buildings are no longer there, although the 'You are now entering Free Derry' gable end still stands. You can have your photo taken beside it, or buy its image on a key ring or a tea towel. The barriers through which the paratroopers stormed have long gone, and 'Aggro Corner' is nowadays nondescript. But it does not take much imagination, as you stroll around with your bag of souvenirs, to imagine the events of that day.

The atmosphere in Derry had been tense in the build-up to Sunday. A week earlier 3,000 people had taken part in a civil rights march to Magilligan internment camp near Lough Foyle, where they were met by soldiers of 1st Battalion, Parachute Regiment, who had been brought in from Belfast. The marchers had refused to follow the route designated for them and, when they tried to make their way down the beach towards the camp, they were confronted by paratroopers wielding batons and firing rubber bullets. Such a reaction was reminiscent of the old days of the B Specials. It signified a new and tougher approach from the British military authorities.

One of the reasons for the tough approach was that civil rights marches were now illegal. So, in fact, were *all* marches in Northern Ireland, including Orange parades. But NICRA remained defiant. It arranged another anti-internment march for the following Saturday, along a route from the Creggan down into Guildhall Square in the centre of town. Three days before the march was due to take place two policemen were shot dead by the IRA. On the same day the decision was taken to bring the Paras into Derry to deal with the riots which would undoubtedly accompany the march. The army's plan was to reroute the march down Rossville Street to an ultimate gathering point at Free Derry Corner. The rioters, it was safely assumed, would break away from the march as it turned down Rossville Street, attracted by the barriers manned by soldiers. As the rioters threw their stones they would be 'scooped up' by paratroopers who would break suddenly through the barricades.

The Parachute Regiment is not made up of average soldiers. One ex-paratrooper describes them as 'the Rottweilers of the army', as 'shock troops' who have 'built up a reputation for asserting themselves'. I asked one officer, who was serving in Northern Ireland in 1972, whether the Paras' actions on Bloody Sunday had surprised him. 'Not really,' he answered, 'because I just knew that was the way they did their business. They have an ethos of thuggery. They were simply not suited for that form of operation. They were much better suited to war; but this wasn't war.' The same officer had witnessed the Parachute Regiment's method of house searching, which was quite different from that of his own regiment: 'Kicking down the door, kicking the dog, waking the children. Bang, crash, wallop!'

The Catholic chief of police in Derry, Frank Lagan, was desperate to ensure that the march would not be marred by trouble from either the Provisional IRA or the Official IRA. He approached local businessman Brendan Duddy who, in turn, approached both wings of the IRA with a request that their guns be taken out of the Bogside. He then waited for a reply. According to Duddy: 'They have this wonderful way, the IRA, of saying, "I have a message for you." It would be so cryptic and nearly always a stranger. And he says, "Those guns have been removed."' Duddy was able to go back to Lagan with the message that there would be 'no guns whatsoever in the Bogside on that march' – although the Official IRA did, in fact, retain a number of guns in the area. But none of this was known to the men of the Parachute Regiment. One paratrooper recalls: 'To us what was important was that it was an illegal march. As squaddies, our perception was that probably all the people in republican areas were IRA supporters.' The paratroopers were briefed that they would be entering a 'no-go' area which the IRA would defend with aggression. They were warned to expect sniper fire, petrol bombs, and nails bombs. With their 'bang, crash, wallop' style of soldiering, a peaceful operation was unlikely to ensue.

John Kelly was marching on that day. So was his 17-year-old brother Michael, who was training to be a sewing-machine mechanic. Michael had never been on a march before, and at first his mother refused to let him go. Kelly explains the family background: 'When Michael was a 3-year-old boy he contracted a virus and he was in a coma for three weeks. It was a situation of 50/50 whether he was going to live or die, and at one time he was so seriously ill that the priest asked my mother to give him up to God – and she refused to do so. She wouldn't give him up to God. But he survived and my mother was more protective of him than of maybe the rest of us. So she says, "No! He's not going on the march!", but by pure persuasion from his friends, me, and a couple of my brothers-in-law, eventually she gave in. I remember talking to him, and saying, "Look, if anything happens, get off site!" because he was never experienced with riot situations. So I remember saying cheerio to him, but be careful. This was up at the Creggan Chapel, where the march gathered, and he walked away with his friends.'

John Kelly remembers walking past St Eugene's Cathedral, where he saw the bishop, Bishop Farran, standing at the window blessing the marchers. As he walked down William Street, he had his first sighting of the Parachute Regiment: 'They were installed on the flat roof of the GPO behind the Cathedral. I remember seeing their red berets.' There were also paratroopers on top of a wall at the back of a Presbyterian church which overlooked William Street, and others inside a burnt-out factory next door. Kelly walked along William Street, past the Paras: 'We got down to the bottom, to the entrance to Rossville Street. I remember standing at Chamberlain Street, where the riot was happening.'

As predicted, people had broken away from the march to start throwing stones at soldiers of the Royal Green Jackets who were manning barricade 14, which blocked the path to Guildhall Square. Kelly remembers: 'I stood for a while watching what was going on, but it was an everyday affair, and I decided to walk into the Bogside and go and listen to the speeches at Free Derry Corner.' At some point after Kelly and the rest of the crowd had entered the Bogside, the first shots of the day were fired on William Street. One round was fired by the IRA, hitting nobody. Five rounds were fired by the Paras from the area of the Presbyterian church, hitting two people walking across waste ground. It is a disputed issue as to who fired the first shot; members of the *Sunday Times* Insight team who investigated the events have suggested that the first shots were fired by the Paras. Their investigation suggests that on hearing of the shootings, an Official IRA man grabbed a rifle in fury and climbed to a vantage point overlooking William Street, from where he fired a single shot at the paratroopers on the roof of the GPO. The Official was then tackled by angry Provisionals who accused him of disobeying orders and placing marchers in danger. The Paras, on the other hand, claim that the Official opened fire before they did. But whoever fired first, two facts now seem clear. First, that neither of the people shot by the Paras was armed; one was a 15-year-old boy bending over to pick up a rubber bullet, the other was a 59-year-old man on his way to visit an elderly friend. And second, that at least some of the Paras concluded that the IRA was likely to resist their entry into the Bogside.

At 4.07 p.m. the men of 'C' Company were ordered to advance through Barrier 14. Three minutes later Support Company was ordered through Barrier 12 on Little James Street, to the north of William Street. As this was happening, John Kelly was moving slowly towards Free Derry Corner. He had not been aware of the shooting on William Street. 'As I walked over Chamberlain Street, I met Barney McGuigan. He used to give me a lift to work in the morning. We stood and talked for a couple of minutes, and we walked into the car park of Rossville Flats, towards where the speeches were going to happen. Then the shout went up that the army had moved in. Normally, in those days, the army didn't come into the Bogside. They stopped at the edge of the Bogside, at "Aggro Corner", where riots happened on a daily basis. When the shout went up, I ran. Everybody ran. Because you didn't have to be part of a riot; you would be arrested even if you were on the periphery of a riot, and given an automatic sentence of six months in jail. So everybody ran. I looked to the right, and it was jam-packed with people trying to get through, so I went the other way. And as I ran through the alleyway, the shooting began.'

The army's plan was to send 'C' Company down Chamberlain Street by foot, while Support Company advanced down Rossville Street in Saracen armoured cars. The two companies would then encircle the rioters in the car park of Rossville Flats, which stood in the middle. Members of Support Company claim that once they had jumped out of their Saracens, they came under heavy gunfire and attack from nail and petrol bombs. This is denied by civilian witnesses. Several civilians record seeing a man, *several minutes later,* firing two or three pistol shots from beside a wall in Rossville Flats car park. The existence of this gunman is corroborated by the Paras' own radio log. But neither the radio log nor any civilian witness record the gunfire reported by the Paras, or bombs of any kind. Over the next ten minutes members of 1st Battalion, Parachute Regiment, fired over a hundred rounds of rifle fire into the Bogside.

Kelly says, 'I could hear the shots starting and I ran to where the monument now stands. I lay behind an artificial structure in the shape of an old threepenny bit as the shooting went on. I could hear the "crack, crack, crack, crack". I was keeping my head down. After a while there was a lull in the shooting, and I got up and tried to get out of the area. I ran across Rossville Street, but as I did I felt two bullets whizzing past my head. I didn't feel fear, or anything, I just kept running across and I dived in behind one of the houses. When I got there, a brother-in-law of mine, George Cooley, was standing there. We stood there for a while. We didn't know that anybody had been shot dead; we didn't see any bodies. After another lull we saw a circle of people, and we decided to go back in to see what was going on. As we stepped out, two bullets bounced in front of us. I heard the whacks and I saw the dirt bouncing. They must have been fired from the Derry walls – they couldn't have come from anywhere else. So we jumped back into cover again, and we waited another minute or two.'

The first bullets fired at Kelly had probably come from the Paras of Support Company, who had opened fire on people running away from them along Rossville Street. One of those people was Father Edward Daly, who would one day become the Bishop of Derry. He was charging along Rossville Street, when he saw a young boy alongside him, who was laughing at the sight of a priest running. The boy suddenly 'gasped and threw his hands up in the air and fell on his face'. The boy was 17-year-old Jackie Duddy. Father Daly, realizing that Duddy had been struck by a live bullet, took a white handkerchief out of his pocket and waved it as he edged towards him. The firing continued as Father

Daly administered the last rites to the dying boy. It was at this point that the IRA man with the pistol started shooting from the car park wall; Father Daly and others screamed at him to go away. Father Daly is certain that this man only started shooting *after* the paratroopers had opened fire. A group of men then lifted Duddy and carried him to Waterloo Street, while Father Daly walked in front, waving his now bloody handkerchief. The photograph of this scene, with a helmeted soldier silhouetted in the foreground, and a BBC cameraman filming the scene in the background, has become one of the iconic images of Bloody Sunday.

In the meantime a number of Paras had gathered behind a wall at Kells Walk at the edge of Rossville Street. They were facing a small rubble barricade, seventy yards further down Rossville Street. At this barricade were a number of people, one of whom was John Kelly's brother, Michael. At one point Michael seems to have leant forward. As he did so, he was shot in the stomach by one of the paratroopers by the wall. Others behind the barricade ran off in panic, and came under fire. Several men rushed to Michael's aid; they too were fired upon. Five more people were shot dead at the barricade. Willie Nash was running away as he was hit; John Young was shot in the head while crawling on his hands and knees; Michael McDaid was struck through the cheek; Kevin McElhinney was shot in the buttock as he stumbled away; Hugh Gilmore, shot through the stomach, ran on until he collapsed.

The soldiers who had fired these bullets would give evidence to the Widgery Tribunal – the first judicial inquiry into Bloody Sunday – that those behind the barricade had been carrying rifles and nail bombs. But many years later one of the paratroopers at the wall broke ranks, and offered a quite different account. His controversial evidence was given at a second judicial inquiry, established by Prime Minister Tony Blair in 1998, in response to concerns regarding the original inquiry. The second tribunal, chaired by Lord Saville of Newdigate, began hearing evidence in 2000 in the Derry Guildhall.

The Para who broke ranks, a radio operator with the Anti-Tank Platoon of Support Company, known only as Soldier 027, gave evidence to the inquiry that a soldier had run to the wall, knelt down, and commenced firing without pause or hesitation, towards the centre of the crowd at the barricade. According to 027's statement: 'I stood at the wall and put my rifle to my shoulder. I looked through my sights, scanning across the crowd. I was as keen to find a target as anyone, but I could not identify a target that appeared to justify engaging. I did not see anyone with a weapon or see or hear an explosive device. I lowered my weapon and looked at the guys firing and tried to locate what they were firing at. I still failed to see what I could identify as a target and it caused me some confusion. I have a clear memory of thinking, "What are they firing at?"'

027 feels that two of the soldiers 'had a preconceived idea of what they were going to do that day, and set about doing it as a pair of oppos'. While giving live evidence to the inquiry, he stressed that he saw no weapons or bombs at the barricade. He recalls that once the firing had started at the wall, a corporal ran up beside him and pushed himself between two other soldiers. The corporal 'indicated to me that he thought what was happening was great. He was exuberant.' The soldiers who arrived at the back and joined in the shooting were, in 027's opinion, not able to assess the situation. According to his statement: 'I had the distinct impression that this was a case of some soldiers realizing this was an opportunity to fire their weapon, and they did not want to miss the chance.'

John Kelly was unaware of his brother's plight as he stood with George Cooley on the west side of Rossville Street: 'We ran over to the circle of people we had seen, and we seen a body lying on the ground. It was Gerry McKinney. They thought he'd taken a heart attack, because they didn't see his injuries. They were giving him mouth-to-mouth resuscitation. All of a sudden I heard, "John! John!" It was another brother-in-law of mine, George Downey. What had happened was this: my brother Michael had been shot at the barricade, thirty yards from where I had been lying. I might have seen him if I hadn't been keeping my head down. George Downey had gone to Michael's aid, and helped to carry him from the barricade into a house. As they were bringing him out of the house into an ambulance, he saw me. So, myself and George Cooley ran to where they were bringing Michael out, and we helped to put him in the ambulance.'

Kelly helped to carry two other men – William McKinney and Joe Mahon – into the ambulance: 'I was sitting in the front of the ambulance as it drove out of Glenfada Park and went up Rossville Street. We were actually stopped by the Paras, and I remember putting down the window and telling them to fuck off. I says, "Leave us alone! We're going to the hospital!" I had a feeling that Michael was dead before we got to the hospital. Lying in the ambulance, he was a sort of grey-green colour. There was no response from him whatsoever. Eventually we got there, and we brought Michael and the others in. A doctor checked Michael – I was at the side – and the doctor said, "Sorry. He's dead." I says, "Are you sure? Check him again!" He checked him again, and he said, "He's dead."

Other boys and men continued to die in other parts of the Bogside. Barney McGuigan, the man with whom John Kelly had been chatting as they walked down Chamberlain Street, was killed beneath Rossville Flats while crawling to aid Pat Doherty, who also shot dead. James Wray, Gerald Donaghy, Gerald McKinney (whom John Kelly had seen on the ground), and William McKinney (whom he had helped into the ambulance) were all shot in Glenfada Park.

By the end of the day thirteen people had been killed and another eighteen had been injured by gunfire. John Johnston, one of the men shot on William Street, survived the day, but died months later from his wounds. 027 recalled sitting in the Saracen at the end of the day, where 'there was already a recognition that there was a problem that had to be explained away … The topic of conversation was who had fired what, what number of rounds fired we thought would be acceptable and justifiable, and how to account for the rounds that were fired.'

John Kelly watched the injured arriving at Altnagelvin Hospital. He also remembers paratroopers walking around: 'They were laughing and joking, not giving a damn about what they did. One of them went into the toilet, and we were talking about going in after him, and one of my brothers-in-law held me back. Thank God he did hold me back.' Kelly's father eventually arrived at the hospital, and John told him that Michael had died: 'I remember him sliding down the wall in the corridor. We had to go to the mortuary to identify Michael's body, and what we seen was horrific. There were nine or ten bodies in there. Some were lying on these low trolleys, some were on the higher trolleys. There was blood everywhere. We had to go round each individually, and eventually we found Michael. Then as I was leaving the mortuary, the cops stopped me. They says, "I want to ask you some questions." I told him to leave me alone: "I want to go home with my family." My father was still inside. He must have been saying prayers. And we were sitting there, me and the guy who owned the car, and all of a sudden this army personnel carrier backed up to where we were sitting, and the back doors flung open and they dragged three bodies out by the feet and hands and took them into Casualty. They got them pronounced dead and then they brought them out again, threw them back in the Saracen, and took them over to the mortuary. This was at six o'clock. They had those bodies for an hour and a half. I don't know what they had been doing with them.'

It is possible that part of the answer lies in an account given to the Saville Inquiry by a paramedic. The bodies of three men, McDaid, Young, and Nash, had been picked up from the barricade by paratroopers and tossed into a Saracen, observed by a number of witnesses. According to the paramedic, when she heard moans coming from inside the Saracen, she pulled the door open, but a soldier slammed it shut. She gave evidence that she opened the door again and noticed the foot of one of the supposedly dead men twitch. She claimed that the soldier then pointed his rifle through a flap in the side of the Saracen and fired three shots.

The original inquiry into the events of Bloody Sunday – the Widgery Inquiry – concluded that paratroopers who had identified armed gunmen fired on them in accordance with the rules of the Yellow Card. It concluded that shots had been fired at the soldiers before they began the firing that led to the casualties. It found that while there was no proof that any of those killed had been shot at while handling a firearm or a bomb, there was a strong suspicion that some had been firing weapons or holding bombs. And it found that some soldiers had demonstrated a high degree of responsibility, while the actions of others 'bordered on the reckless'.

According to a local lawyer, Widgery had approached the hearings with the prejudice of an ex-Guardsman, who could not believe that British troops would open fire on unarmed civilians. By describing conduct that 'bordered on the reckless', Widgery's tribunal ensured that the paratroopers would not be prosecuted: in order to convict an individual of manslaughter, an element of recklessness would have to be demonstrated. Soldier 027 alleges that when he came to make to a statement to the Widgery Tribunal, he gave an account of the shooting towards the barricade, but that the lawyer taking the statement said something to the effect of: 'We cannot have that, can we, Private? That makes it sound as if shots were being fired into the crowd.' The lawyer, claims 027, then left the room, before returning with a different statement for him to sign. He was not subsequently called to give live evidence at the inquiry.

On the day that he announced the Saville Inquiry, Tony Blair confirmed to the House of Commons that 'those shot should be regarded as innocent of any allegation that they were shot while handling firearms or explosives'. As I write, eleven years after Blair's comments, the Saville Inquiry's findings are expected shortly. The tribunal retired in late 2004, having listened to the evidence of 921 live witnesses and heard the written statements of 1,555 others. Witnesses did not merely offer their evidence unchallenged; many were extensively cross-examined in an effort to establish the truth. One of those was Soldier 027. It was put to him by the counsel for other soldiers that he was a 'fantasy merchant'. He was questioned closely about his motives for giving evidence in the present inquiry; he denied that his primary motivation was financial, but he acknowledged that he had received an advance payment from a publisher for a book based on his experiences. In addition he accepted that he had received a financial package from the Northern Ireland Office with regard to the present inquiry, but he denied demanding money in return for his testimony. The financial package, he claims, was designed to guarantee the safety of his family.

One witness who was cross-examined at even greater length was the commander of Land Forces Northern Ireland, General Sir Robert Ford, who was responsible for the conduct of army operations. General Ford was questioned about two memos that he had written in 1972. In the first memo, to the General Officer Commanding, Harry Tuzo, written shortly before Bloody Sunday, he had written: 'I am coming to the conclusion that the minimum force necessary to achieve a restoration of law and order [in Derry] is to shoot selected ringleaders among the DYH [Derry Young Hooligans], after clear warnings have been issued.' In the second memo, written in the week after Bloody Sunday, he wrote: 'I believe that we would have had the greatest of difficulty in containing the situation without shooting the crowd.' While these memos do not demonstrate that the events of

Bloody Sunday were premeditated by those in command, they lend support to the suggestion that a tough approach was intended. In his evidence, however, General Ford flatly denied that his intention in using the Paras had been to take a tougher stance. They had been ordered in, he claimed, because they were experienced at carrying out quick 'in and out' operations. Tapes were played to the inquiry of radio conversations between army personnel on Bloody Sunday. These tapes, recorded by Jimmy Porter, a local amateur radio enthusiast, contain the following words spoken by a soldier: 'He [Ford] thought it was the best thing he'd seen for a long time … "Well done, 1st Para," he said, "look at them, twenty-four of them wheeled off …" And he said, "You know, this is what should happen."' In relation to these recordings, General Ford told the inquiry, 'Well, quite honestly, there is no truth in what they said at all. It is highly emotional and inaccurate.'

The Saville Inquiry will return findings on, among other things, the intended role of the soldiers on the day, and whether their use was sanctioned by the British government. Yet whatever their intended role, the fact is that 'the Rottweilers of the army' were sent into what they perceived as enemy territory, in the midst of a march that they knew to be illegal, to 'scoop up' rioters whom they considered supporters (if not members) of the IRA, while anticipating that violence would be used against them. Whether or not their own violence was foreseen by the men who deployed them, it was surely foreseeable.

Another man who gave evidence to the Saville Inquiry was Martin McGuinness, the IRA's second in command in Derry at the time of Bloody Sunday. He gave evidence that, once the British army had shot civil rights marchers, a small number of IRA members, including himself and the commanding officer, sent a message that there should be no immediate retaliation against the British army; the world should be allowed to see what had happened. Liam Clarke, the *Sunday Times* journalist, has alleged that Martin McGuinness had a more active role on the day; that he had provided a number of marchers with nail bombs to attack the Guildhall and nearby shops, but that the nail bombs were recalled when the route of the march was altered; and that he had intended to plant a bomb in a book-maker's shop on Chamberlain Street but had not had sufficient time to plant it when he received the message that the soldiers were coming. McGuinness, for his part, has dismissed Clarke's allegations as fantasy.

In the days that followed Bloody Sunday, the IRA expanded quickly in Derry. According to one local man: 'The IRA in Derry, prior to Bloody Sunday, would have had less than fifty volunteers. In the aftermath of Bloody Sunday people like myself flocked to the IRA; the IRA had to stop recruiting after three weeks. They said, "No, we have too many members. We can't deal with them." I asked this man about his own experience. He told me, 'I had been involved. When my father arrived home [from Altnagelvin Hospital, where he had identified a relative's body], I said to him, "Daddy, tell me why …" and my father said, "I can't tell you why. I don't know." It was the first time I realized that my father didn't have all the answers. I said, "Well, see, if you can't explain to me why they did that, I'm telling you now, I'm join-ing the army!" And my father said, "No! Calm down! Think about this! These things can happen!" I said, "What do you mean these things can happen? Why march in a demonstration when they have weapons and I don't?" And I joined the republican struggle, and I've been involved in the republican struggle ever since.'

As the IRA grew, so did violent attacks. An Official IRA bomb planted at a Parachute Regiment barracks in Aldershot killed five women. A Provisional IRA bomb killed two people and injured 130 in a restaurant in Belfast. As Northern Ireland became ever more lawless, the British Prime Minister pulled the rug from under Brian Faulkner's feet and announced

Direct Rule from London. Home Rule was over and the Ulster Unionist Party's long spell of control came to an end. The power that unionists had worked so hard to exert over their province seemed to be ebbing away. While Direct Rule appeared to be a victory for republicans, in practice it simply meant the IRA could channel its odium directly at the British government.

For John Kelly, the first job after identifying his brother was to tell his mother that her son had died. With her concern for Michael, his mother had actually followed him down to the march, but she had lost sight of him and gone instead into her daughter's flat in Kells Walk. Kelly recalls: 'She stood at the window looking for Michael, and then she saw the paratroopers moving in. According to her, she saw Michael, and she shouted to him, but Michael didn't hear her, and he ran on towards the barricade. Now the point is, where she stood looking out of that window, the paratrooper who fired the fatal shot must have fired it from below her feet. But after a while she went home, and someone told her that Michael had been shot, but only shot in the ankle and he was OK. When we arrived home and told her that Michael was dead, it was total bedlam in the house. And she didn't remember anything for five years afterwards.'

At first the family had to wait for Michael's body to be brought home from the hospital. 'My mother was sedated, and she should have slept for a week with the amount of medication they gave her. She was only a wee woman, less than five foot. Michael's body was brought home that Monday, and he lay out in his coffin, in his bedroom, and that night myself and the brothers-in-law were sitting in the bedroom at about three or four o'clock in the morning, when all of a sudden she came running through the door of the bedroom, and lifted Michael bodily out of the coffin, crying, "Michael, son! Michael, son!" We had to restrain her, and put him back into the coffin again. She didn't remember doing these things.'

Kelly cannot remember the day of his brother's funeral. He vaguely remembers shaking hands with hundreds of people. 'But then we had problems with my mother. She used to go missing, and we would have found her up in the cemetery, sitting with Jim Wray's mother, chatting about their sons. There were times that she would have went down to the police barracks and started arguing with Superintendent Lagan. It came to a point that Superintendent Lagan used to just allow her to come up and rave. She used to go down to the army and roar on to them about killing her son. They got to know her as well. But there was one time especially that really sticks out – she was found walking towards the cemetery with a blanket under her arm. There was snow on the ground and people were asking where she was going with the blanket, and she replied, "I'm taking it up to Michael's grave to put round him to keep him warm."'

John Kelly believed that his mother was going to be another casualty: 'I thought we were going to lose her to a broken heart, and I was the fall guy. I was the guy that had to go up and argue and fight with her to bring her in, because whenever she went off, I'd get the call: "John, come up, Ma's at it again." But eventually she came out of it. And she lived up until four years ago. She died about three months before the Saville Inquiry physically ended, but she was seriously ill for about a year and a half before that. I used to give her an update as to what was happening with the inquiry, and when she was really, really bad, I turned round and I said, "Look, Ma. We won the case! Michael was declared innocent!" She says, "That's grand, son." And she went to her death thinking that Michael's name had been cleared. I had to do that, you know? After Michael was shot, she kept everything belonging to him. She kept his clothes, all his wee bits and pieces, all his textbooks, even a half-eaten chocolate bar. And she made me promise that when she died everything would go with her. So on the day that she was getting buried I placed everything in the coffin. It all went with her to the grave. She went away happy, if you want to call it that.'

Even though other young men reached for the gun in the wake of Bloody Sunday, John Kelly did not join the IRA. 'It never, ever crossed my mind to join the IRA. I'm not a violent person. I was trying to bring my mother along, you know, and I was a young married man with a child and another on the way. I was the breadwinner, so I had to work it all out in my own mind.'

So far as the IRA was concerned, it took inadvertent revenge on the Parachute Regiment seven years after Bloody Sunday. On 27 August 1979 two bombs planted by the side of a road in Warrenpoint, County Down, killed sixteen members of the Parachute Regiment and two of the Queen's Own Highlanders. The revenge was inadvertent in that those who planted the bombs cannot have known that the Paras would drive into them, but not since the Battle of Arnhem in 1944 had more members of the regiment been killed on a single day. The first bomb, hidden in a straw-filled trailer, was detonated by remote control from the far side of the River Newry, as a convoy passed by. The second bomb, which was even bigger than the first, was detonated twenty minutes later, and hidden in the gate lodge of Narrow Water Castle, which the IRA had correctly guessed would become the army's Incident Control Point. The carnage was terrible. According to one soldier who arrived at the scene of the second blast, the human debris amounted to unidentifiable lumps of raw red flesh, interspersed with legs, arms, ears, hands, and heads.

John Kelly's search for justice would continue for many years after Bloody Sunday: 'I always thought in my head that some day things would work out. That we could rectify the Bloody Sunday issue. For the first twenty years people accepted the official story, which we knew was totally wrong. The families would have met up once a year, and we were told that once Widgery was set up, that was it. Couldn't do nothing more about it. Done, dusted, bang. But on the twentieth anniversary people decided to try and do something about it.'

The families spent years gathering support, until Tony Blair agreed to launch the new inquiry. Kelly says that all the families gathered that night 'but there was no great sense of celebration. It was just a relief that Tony Blair had realized that there was something wrong about Bloody Sunday.' Kelly has been a family liaison worker with the Bloody Sunday Trust throughout the life of the inquiry. In 2003 he went to London to hear the evidence of Soldier F, the paratrooper who killed his brother and three others. The bullet that killed Michael had been traced to his rifle. Kelly remembers: 'You had four different families, plus other families, who travelled to London. Me and Michael McKinney were dealing with the families, ensuring they were OK, dealing with the media and so on. I'm not a religious man, but on the morning that Soldier F was due to appear I went down on my knees and asked God to give me strength to get through the next few days. In the morning, because of my job, I was asked to sort out problems, but then I sat down waiting for Soldier F, to see him for the first time, nervous, very tense, and someone comes to me and says, "John, I have a problem." So I had to get up and go outside, but then Gerry Duddy came to me, and said, "John, go back in there, this is your day. I'll look after it for you." So I went back in, and I listened to Soldier F, listening to his evidence, listening to his lies. He doesn't remember. In all cases he doesn't remember. Now, he killed four people that day. My view is, if you were driving along and you killed a dog, you'd remember that for the rest of your life. This guy took four human lives, and he doesn't remember anything about it.'

Kelly believes that when Lord Saville delivers his report, the families will receive a full declaration of innocence. 'I do honestly believe that. Because of the evidence for a start. But also because counsel for the British army, Edwin Glasgow, stood up in his opening submission and said that he would not contest the innocence of the people unless other evidence surfaced during the inquiry.'

He also wants to see Soldier F face criminal prosecution. 'My family wants it. A lot of other families want it, but not all families think the same way. Some families just wanted their day in court. People say to me, "It was thirty-seven years ago. Move on with your life. Forget about it." But my younger brother had his life taken away from him by a soldier. I believe that my family is entitled to it. I think there is a great possibility that I'll see Soldier F again, and I look forward to it. In saying that, whether it happens or not is another thing.'

I asked John Kelly how he would feel if Soldier F is not prosecuted. 'I would be devastated, you know,' he says. As I left him I walked out into the street at the spot where the barricade once stood at which his brother had been killed. I walked up Rossville Street, past Aggro Corner, through Barrier 12, and turned left onto Great James Street, where I was staying.

Derry has changed. You can now buy sushi a four-minute stroll from the spot where paratroopers opened fire. But Bloody Sunday is still alive for many people. It is still alive for John Kelly, and as I walked out of the Bogside it was alive for me. The spirit and quiet dignity of the man had transformed it from a piece of history into a flesh-covered tragedy. I had been planning to go to the cinema that evening, but no screenwriter's words would have had much impact on me. I stayed where I was. Days later, back in England, I decided to go and meet another victim of the Troubles, a woman whose father was killed by the Provisional IRA, the shadowy beneficiary of the Bogside slaughter. She tells her story in her own words. There is little that I can add.

7

THE BOMB

In September 1984 a member of the Provisional IRA planted a twenty pound bomb behind a bath panel in Room 629 of the Grand Hotel, Brighton. The bomb was fitted with an electronic timing device, which triggered an explosion at 2.45 a.m. on 16 October, when many senior members of the British government were staying at the hotel, during the annual Conservative Party conference. The middle section of the hotel collapsed, killing four people. Thirty-one others were taken to hospital, one of whom died a month later. Margaret Thatcher, the British Prime Minister, had been working on her conference speech in the hotel when the bomb exploded, damaging her bathroom but leaving her bedroom and sitting room unscathed. One of the injured was Norman Tebbit, the Industry Secretary, who was dug out of the rubble after a four-hour rescue operation. His wife, Margaret, was left permanently disabled by the blast. In the aftermath of the bomb the IRA issued a statement which ended: 'Today we were unlucky, but remember we only have to be lucky once. You will have to be lucky always. Give Ireland peace and there will be no more war.'

On 11 June 1986, after an intensive police investigation, Patrick Magee was sentenced at the Old Bailey to eight life sentences for his part in the bombing, with a recommendation that he serve at least thirty-five years. He was released in 1999 in the aftermath of the Good Friday Agreement. One of those he killed was Sir Anthony Berry, the Treasurer to the Royal Household and former assistant editor of the *Sunday Times*. I met his daughter Jo in a hotel near to where she lives. This is what she told me:

'I think I was probably slightly difficult when I was young. I went to boarding school, and was very, very unhappy there. I wasn't particularly homesick, but I was very good at getting into trouble for things I just thought were kind of fine. I remember trying to be good and failing dismally, and then getting upset because I didn't really want to be in trouble. My dad wasn't disappointed. I don't think he really thought very much of school anyway. But mum hadn't been reading my letters, which were saying, "I'm so unhappy, please take me away from this place." She was too busy having love affairs and getting into trouble in her own life.

'I used to feel really guilty living in a nice house. There were the poor people down the road, who got all of our Easter eggs, and it was always made me sad. I remember my dad had this Bentley, and once we drove past some gypsies with a pony and little cart, a whole family of them. I must have been about 7, thinking, they look amazing, and I waved to them as we went by. I remember the woman's face, full of anger at me, and realized it was because she saw me for what I represented. It filled me with guilt and shame – but Dad was a great one for accepting people's beliefs. He had loads of friends who were Labour. He was a very accepting kind of person. I remember just before he died, my sister became a very angry feminist, and she used to argue with anyone, but I was never like that. And nor was Dad, so we would talk about things and it was fine.

'I went through quite a lot when I was young. I had really low self-esteem. I once got a razorblade out and I really messed my wrists up, and Mum asked, "What happened?" and I said, "I fell into a gorse bush." She said, "Oh, OK." But at the same time, I was meeting my dad's friends. Michael Heseltine was a close friend, and Peter Walker, and I met Maggie Thatcher. When I went to Buckingham Palace I had to find the right clothes and I had to put a safety pin in my shoes. I don't think I was really ever *that* type of person. I was more Labour. I remember, when I was quite young, asking everybody who came to my dad's house how they voted, and I couldn't understand why everyone voted Conservative, that really confused me.

'I had a connection with my father, especially in the last year of his life. He was a great one for convention – you know, "We're doing this because that's how it's done" – but, still, I found that he really accepted me. He was quite unusual and very important. I was about to go off to Africa, at the time of the bombing, and he said he was worried that I wasn't looking after myself. But then he said, "I understand why you're going," and I said, "Oh, why?" and told me that he'd been to Burundi as part of a government thing, and he stayed with some missionaries who lived miles away from electricity, and they were there without a fridge, so he couldn't have his gin and tonic. For the first time ever! He said that his first thought had been, my God, how can people do this? but when he left he thought, OK, these people are doing it for a reason stronger than the need for a gin and tonic. It's something much bigger than them. And he said, "It's the same with you. There's something bigger going on in your life, and I can respect that."

'At the time of the bombing I was staying with my sister in Notting Hill Gate. She was going off to teach, and she woke me up because she'd heard it on the news. Dad should have been at the Metropolitan Hotel next door, but at the last minute a room was made available in the Grand, so he switched. He shouldn't have been there, really. But we didn't know that. We didn't which hotel he was in.

'So we rang up my brother, Edward, and he was asleep. It was very early, half past six in the morning. He woke up, and he said he had been to Dad and Sarah's [Sir Anthony Berry's second wife] room the night before, and they were in the Grand, so he'd go up to the hotel and have a look. He went up there and he went as close to the grounds as he could but, of course, he could see quite clearly that their room wasn't there any more – a hole was there. Then he saw some MPs he recognized standing outside. It was chaos, you can imagine, and he tried to find out if anyone knew anything. This was before mobile phones, so he would come back to his flat to ring us and say what he had found, and then he'd go off again. And then he rang up from the hospital to say that he'd found Sarah. She was OK, but there was no sign of my father.

'It was a long wait. My sister and I were watching the telly to see if we could see my dad. It was mad really. If Sarah was injured, he should be with her. At one point we saw their dogs on the telly. Someone had found their dogs, and we told Edward. But it was just waiting and waiting. Then, at about two or three in the afternoon, he rang to say that they had found a body with a signet ring on it. Edward had the same signet ring as the one that Dad wore. Dad had given it to him. He didn't want to identify it himself so he gave them his ring and they came back and said, yes, it was the same ring.

'As soon as we found out, I wanted to get out of the flat. I didn't want to be with anybody. I started walking down the streets of Notting Hill Gate, down to Portobello. I was walking and just saying over and over to myself, "Dad's dead." Some builders saw me, and said, "It can't be that bad! Give us a smile!" and I said, "It's worse. My Dad's been blown up.' I stopped at a phonebox and rang some very good friends of mine. I needed to tell somebody. Then I went back to the flat.

'There were loads of problems about who was going to come to the funeral, and who wasn't – Maggie Thatcher and all of them, so there was loads to organize. My brother had to take charge of all of that. I remember a guy coming to ask us about coffins. I was in total shock, because you kind of just don't believe it. You keep on remembering it, and I couldn't sleep and I couldn't eat, and I just felt I wasn't on the same planet as everyone else. I remember getting in my car and howling. The pain was too much. I wasn't used to feeling that much, and I just didn't know what to do with it. I couldn't be this free spirit believing in love any more – this was the real world.

'I always loved being with children, so I rang up Great Ormond Street Hospital, and asked them if I could volunteer to sit with children who were waiting for operations. I thought that would be nice to do. So I ended up spending two days a week with children who were dying; four weeks after my own dad was blown up, they put me with kids with cancer. After about six weeks a child died that I had got close to. And I just walked out of the hospital, and I didn't know what to do. I completely lost it. There was nobody I could talk to, and I was thinking, I'm not normal any more.

'One night, a couple of months after the bomb, I was on the tube and I got off for no reason. I just had a very strong impulse to get out, and I ended up sharing a taxi with a young man from west Belfast. I told him about my Dad, and he told me that his brother had been in the IRA, and been killed by the British army. We found out very quickly that we had this connection. And we talked about our dream for a world where people didn't get killed – or have to kill. As I left the taxi, words came to me, "I can build a bridge!" It was the one way I could help. That feeling gave me a lot of strength, and it gave me the idea to go to Northern Ireland. So I went over to Belfast, and I can remember landing at the airport, and seeing the soldiers and the tanks. It was just another world.

'I went down to the Bessbrook Monastery in South Armagh, to do a workshop with Elisabeth Kübler-Ross, a survivor of the Nazi concentration camps and a brilliant woman. It was a workshop to help people to deal with unfinished business. When it came to my turn, I started off by saying that my father was blown up by the IRA eight months ago. And there was silence. What I didn't know was that I had absolutely terrified everyone there – because nobody mentioned the war. Nobody mentioned it. A few people said they were there because they were abused as children, or they were bullied at school, the same sort of things you would hear in England. But nobody said they were there because of the conflict. There were people there from both sides, but back in 1985 they couldn't talk about it. It was extraordinary.

'Elisabeth Kübler-Ross really wanted people to get into their feelings, not to speak from their heads, so I said, "I'm really going to have to say what's going on with me. I'm feeling really peaceful, this is a lovely place to be," and then I talked about the guy I had met in the taxi. After that, someone said, "Would you like to stay on? I'd like to introduce you to some people in Belfast. It would be really wonderful if you could talk to a group of people I know." So I was taken to a safe house in north Belfast, and then to meet a reconciliation group in Rostrevor.

'After that I met somebody from Sinn Féin. All the time I was talking to him, he was giving this close attention to his special-needs son. And that was almost more important than his words because I could see what an amazing, loving, and devoted father he was. And then somebody who had been at the meeting wrote down what I had said, photocopied it, and sent it around Northern Ireland. An INLA man in Long Kesh prison got hold of it, and he started writing letters to me, saying, "It's not that I'm a really bad person, I never wanted to hurt anyone. I just couldn't see any other way. If you know another way, then let me know." He told me what he'd experienced and why he did it, and he said, "I wish we didn't have to hurt each other." His letters were a great way for me to start "humanizing the other". Both he and the Sinn Féin man said they were really sorry about my dad. But at this time I wasn't telling anybody at home that I was doing this, going to these places. I didn't want to see the looks of disappointment from them that I knew I would get.

'Back then I was asked, "Could you ever imagine meeting the man responsible?" and my answer was something like, "Yes. If it feels right, maybe someday." So the thought was already there. But then I was asked to speak to a group of youth leaders, who said, "No, we don't want to meet her." They thought I was too much the enemy, and they were too angry. That was awful. I realized I was way out of my league. It was the wrong time. Who was I to think about building bridges when people were still so angry? So I stopped going to Ireland. I went to live in North Wales, and I had three children. I wasn't connected to Northern Ireland, except the radio that I could listen to in Wales. But I couldn't get out there.

'For many years I never talked about my Dad. Not to my family or anyone. I never told my children what had happened. I locked it all into a box. And then, one day in 1999, the box opened. Pat Magee had just been released, that may have triggered it, but it all came back to me. And once it started, it wouldn't stop. It was very scary, and I crashed the car the next day. I couldn't sleep, and I was in pieces again. There was rage – "How can somebody think that what they have to say is so important that they can kill my father? How can someone play God?"

'I knew I needed to do something. I met someone from the Glencree community. He had this piece of paper that said, "We're looking for people affected by the Troubles, who come from England, Scotland, and Wales, to come to Glencree in Ireland, and we're going to pay for all your travel and expenses. Do you want to come? This is purely to get support for what you have been through." My partner at the time was telling me that I shouldn't do it – but in February 2000 I went. There were people there who knew what I was feeling. I felt safe and we got very close. It was like opening up more of the box and letting it out. There was a lot of laughter as well as tears and rage, and the more I went back, the stronger I felt.

'I spent a weekend with four blanket protesters and two hunger strikers, which was really interesting. I got as close to them as I could. I didn't want to argue politics, I just wanted to experience them as people. Maybe they thought I was a bit odd! I actually went through masses of betrayal after that weekend. I went through hell. I had this horrible feeling that I had betrayed my father by meeting these people because they could have killed him; they were active IRA men. But what I discovered was that when you go around the other side, these people could be my friends. They were like me. We all could be each other and we betray that when we live in this "us and them" reality. The sense of betrayal is a conditional response to stop me, and once I realize that, it just goes away.

'Northern Ireland is a very small world, and people were saying that they could arrange a meeting with Patrick Magee. I said, "OK," but at first I was told that he didn't want to meet me. But then, after a peace conference in Dun Laoghaire, my friend Anne – the sister of the INLA man who wrote to me from Long Kesh – said that she could arrange it. One day she phoned and said, "He's going to be at my house tonight at seven. Will you be there?" I said, "Yes," and put down the phone. I started thinking, shit! It's the wrong day! I'm not in the mood! But how could it be the wrong day? I'd waited so long for this. So I went off and got the ferry to Dublin, feeling completely scared, wondering if it was the right thing to do. I sat on the ferry, playing cards with two businessmen, who beat me at rummy for an hour, thinking, maybe he'll be more scared than me ...

'I got to Anne's house, which was full of activity, with people coming and going, the phone ringing, her trying to cook, and suddenly she said, "I've got to go. Carry on cooking." When she came back, we sat down to eat, and then there was a knock on the door. There hadn't been any time to prepare. We hadn't even mentioned him.

'Pat came into the room on his own. His friend was parking the car. I got up and shook his hand, and said, "Thank you for coming." He said, "Oh no. I wanted to thank you. Thanks for inviting me." We started off by being very polite. Anne left us to it, and we were together for three hours in this room. Sitting in two chairs, looking at each other. For the first hour he was doing his good strategy bit, the political blah-blah, giving me the Sinn Féin perspective. I was already very familiar with that. I was expecting it. Then I told him a bit about my father, and what I had been doing, and why I had been in Ireland.

'After a while he looked at me and took off his glasses, and he said, "I don't know who I am any more. I don't know what to say. I've never met anyone like you with so much dignity. I just don't know … how can I help? I want to hear your anger and your pain. I want to hear it."

'At that point part of me thought, I want to run away. This is really scary stuff now. I want to go. But another part of me thought, this is what I want! Now it can begin! We can really meet because he has opened himself up! I actually said to him, "We've got something now. This is just the beginning of a long, long journey. I don't know where it's going to take us …"

'I had expected that he would just sit there and defend it all. I'd met plenty of people who were like that, and if he had been like that, we would have shaken hands at the end, and I would never have seen him again. But I had seen him as a human being, not as the "Brighton bomber". I welcomed it and was scared at the same time. I had voices in me going, "What the hell are you doing talking to the man that killed your father?" but also, "It's OK, this will be good for me, this is what I need." On many levels it was extraordinary. The last words I said to him on our first meeting were, "I'm glad it's you …"'

8

THE BOMBER

Having met Jo Berry, I wanted to meet Patrick Magee, the man responsible for changing her life. I had his mobile phone number, which turned out to be very similar to my mother's – but nobody's perfect. Aware that he was in London, I phoned him and asked him to meet me at my flat while I was on a trip home. On the morning of his visit, as I dithered in Tesco's, unable to decide which biscuits would be best for *someone like him*, I received a text message that read, 'Sorry. Can't make it. When you're next over?' I was frustrated – partly by the offhand message, and partly because I wasn't sure that this interview would ever take place. Magee must, I thought, have spent much of his life shunning routine and evading commitments in order to keep himself safe. He would think nothing of dodging a persistent and annoying stranger. On the plus side, friends came over in the afternoon for tea and seemed to enjoy the biscuits.

Magee subsequently agreed to meet me at the Europa Hotel in the centre of Belfast. I arrived at the hotel hoping that he would too. I had come straight from London, and I paid for a room on the eighth floor with a view over the railway lines and the hills. I settled down at a little table by the bed and ran through questions relating to his early life, his IRA activities and his attitude to his past. As I did so, I was interrupted by a text message. It was Magee telling me that he was around the corner and would be in the lobby in two minutes. The Europa, notorious as Europe's most bombed hotel, was about to play host to Europe's most notorious hotel bomber.

The judge at Patrick Magee's Old Bailey trial described him as 'a man of exceptional cruelty and inhumanity'. Sean O'Callaghan, a one-time active IRA man and police informer, called him 'highly intelligent and cool, but a strange, moody individual'. Magee is well known in England, but not by his given name. Like the Yorkshire Ripper, the Stockwell Strangler and the Moors Murderers, his deeds have denied his humanity. He is the Brighton Bomber.

Magee's attack on the city's Grand Hotel in 1984 brought the Troubles to a new level. It was not an attack on a 'soft' police or army target, nor was it one of the tit-for-tat killings that characterized the conflict. The chronology of *Lost Lives*, the scrupulously researched encyclopaedia of Troubles-related deaths, is illuminating. It betrays a dismal predictability. Open it at a random page and read of the death of a Protestant, followed by the death of a Catholic, followed by the death of a soldier, followed by a lull, which is broken by the death of another Protestant. On it goes. Such predictability has led to a perception of the Troubles as a game with its own rules, its own momentum, and its own internal resistance to resolution. Certainly, shifts in strategy were limited on all sides, with the result that the British army came to view the conflict as a valuable training ground for its soldiers. The prospect of decisive victory for either side usually seemed as distant as the prospect of a negotiated peace. The Brighton bomb, however, halted the game – if only temporarily. It was a thing apart. It shattered complacency by striking at the heart of the British establishment. Had it succeeded in killing Margaret Thatcher and members of her cabinet, as it so nearly did, the repercussions can only be imagined. As it was, it represented a very real blow struck by the IRA against the British government, rather than against its foot soldiers. Alan Clark, a member of that government, wrote admiringly in his diary: 'What a coup for the Paddys. The whole thing has the smell of the Tet Offensive.'

While the actions of one man in a hotel bathroom can hardly stand comparison with the sudden advance of 100,000 Vietcong, the real impact of the Tet Offensive was not military – it was a failure in that respect – but in its political and psychological effect on the people of the United States. Similarly, the Brighton bomb reinforced the belief among politicians and ordinary people that Irish republicanism was capable of a great deal more than 'routine' localized killings. In fact the IRA never again attempted to kill Margaret Thatcher – but its point had been made.

For all of its strategic significance, and despite the republicans' insistence that it was an act of war, it is difficult to understand the explosion in the Grand Hotel as a military operation. Carried out by a man in civilian clothes who planted the device a month before its timed detonation, it took the lives of noncombatants who had no discernible connection to Northern Ireland, and no responsibility for Ulster policy. I wanted to speak to the man responsible, to discover his attitude to having claimed the lives of such peripheral figures.

Two minutes after receiving the text message, I took the lift down to the lobby to meet Patrick Magee, a short man who walked with the aid of a stick. He had a distinctive bearded and spectacled face, and I watched for the reactions of those around us as I accompanied him back to the lift. The sight of Magee, I thought, might merit a reaction from the staff of a hotel bombed thirty-three times over twenty-two years – but nobody seemed to pay us much attention. When I later asked him whether he had ever bombed the Europa, he declined to answer – but perhaps he should. The hotel's own literature bears such proud witness to its bomb-ravaged past that, were he to claim responsibility, he might end up with a carvery named after him.

Up in my room we sat at a table beside the bed and began to talk. I realized that anything Magee said would come filtered through his reputation. Many other republicans and loyalists are able to discuss their pasts, aware that the darker incidents are known only to themselves and comrades. Magee is different. Whatever he chooses to do with his life, wherever he goes, he is the man who bombed the Grand Hotel. I wanted to view him as I found him, to avoid the worst effects of the diabolical – or for that matter romantic – prism. So, while Sean O'Callaghan, himself a controversial figure, might have considered Magee a 'strange, moody individual', to me he came across as a quiet, polite, and intense man. One of the first things he did was to remark on my computer screensaver, an assortment of photographs of nineteenth- and twentieth-century paintings that I had taken in various galleries. He would like to take similar pictures, he said, but he was wary of using a flash in museums. Irony out of the way, the conversation settled down along pleasant lines, and I naively began to wonder whether he was behaving self-consciously 'normally' for my benefit and that of anybody who reads this book. But why would this be true? Should it come as a surprise that Patrick Magee is capable of feelings as mundane, sensitive, and downright ordinary as yours or mine?

More surprising is the discovery that he grew up in England. His family moved there from Belfast when he was four, so that his father could find work. 'My Da was at the end of his apprenticeship [in the shipyard] and he always maintained that he couldn't get a job because he was a Catholic.' The family ended up in Norwich, and Magee remained in England until he was 19. 'I was never happy in England. I was always resistant to it. I was 6 or 7 before I twigged that we weren't going back to Belfast. I can remember my mother trying to discourage me from saying "Mammy", which is a very Belfast expression.' As a child he was known as 'Paddy' to other children, but he developed an English accent – which he worked hard to rediscover years later, when engaged on his 'mainland' campaign.

Magee returned to Belfast in 1971. 'I honestly did not return here to get involved in the violence. I just wanted to see what was happening.' What he saw alarmed him. 'I saw very poor people in very poor districts totally ignored by the state. In fact the state was at war with them. There was no work for Catholics, except in the most lowly paid jobs.' He went on a few training schemes and was struck by the arrogance of the Protestants he met there. 'The first thing, they're straight in your face asking where you're from. They knew. They could nearly smell what you were. But I wasn't going to back down. I told them I was living in Unity Walk, and then they smiled *that* smile, and I knew something was going to happen.' It didn't happen to Magee, it happened to another Catholic man. 'We were doing a welding course, and they had fiddled with one of the machines, and they nearly electrocuted this guy. He was cursing and all these men were laughing.'

By the time Magee returned to Belfast, the Troubles had been raging for some time. 'The crying need,' says Magee, 'was for defence. The people were just being left to themselves. The Provisionals were people from the poorest working-class ghetto areas – the front line – where they were needed. There was this idea that the IRA was parachuted in from across the border, that they weren't part of the community. That was just propaganda.'

Unity Flats, where Magee was living, was a small Catholic enclave at the bottom of the loyalist Shankill Road. It is one of those 'flashpoint' or 'interface' areas which saw so much trouble over the years. On 12 July 1969, the anniversary of the Battle of the Boyne, Orange marchers from the Shankill halted in front of the flats and began taunting the residents, who responded by pelting the marchers with missiles. A group of loyalists then tried to force their way into the flats, but were held back by police. The violence continued into the night, as the police struggled to contain the situation. Three years later, Magee recalls loyalists marching past the flats. 'That was a frightening experience. Thousands of them marching in ranks with their accompanying bands. And what was the state's response? To hoard us in. Big hoardings all round us. We weren't allowed to leave our district. That was the contempt the state had for us.' Magee has no doubt why British troops were sent into Northern Ireland: 'Britain sent troops in, ostensibly, to separate the two sides – but really to prop up the state. And they turned their attention on us – so we were at war with them.'

'People were shot, murdered, and their bodies dumped all around us to scare us,' says Magee, remembering a friend whose body was left in a car at the back of Unity Flats. One event which affected him deeply was the killing of Louis Scullion, a local IRA man, who was shot dead by the Royal Marines. 'He was coming out of a club at one in the morning, dandering across the road, and they shot him dead. I heard the shooting, but I didn't bat an eyelid, you heard it all the time. But then somebody came to the door and told me he was dead.' The next morning Magee went down to the spot and dug one of the bullets out of the wall. 'Louis was accused of opening fire on them – but that wasn't true!' Magee is adamant on the point: 'It didn't happen!' Shortly afterwards he watched a patrol of Marines walking through the New Lodge Road, spitting on the ground. 'I remember the anger it generated in me – and I felt powerless to do anything.'

Magee had decided exactly how he was going to empower himself, when he was arrested and taken to an interrogation centre. 'It was very common, it was called "going for your tea". The army would continually round up people in the district, trying to gather information, trying to get an overall picture.' He was thrown into the back of a jeep and stamped on by the arresting soldiers, and then handed on to the police at the interrogation centre. 'The Special Branch knew that I wasn't connected. But I was treated with utmost contempt the whole time, like a sub-human, like I was second-class.' The experience shook him up, particularly as he was thinking in terms of a new life. 'I was so glad that I didn't know anything. I said to myself, "What if I had been arrested and knew things? Could I have put up with this?"' After his release he spent a couple of weeks sifting through his doubts and fears. He questioned himself: 'Could I kill somebody? Could I withstand torture? All of those questions. You have to know your own mind.' Settled on his answers, he joined the Provisional IRA.

As I listened to Magee I believed that he was talking sincerely, that his experiences of Belfast in the early Seventies, and his reactions to them, were truly remembered. But while it is true that the Provisional IRA saw itself as the defender of the Catholic people, and that Catholic communities in Belfast and Derry regarded it as such, the defence of its people was not the IRA's long-term objective. Its primary aim was the removal of the British from 'the six counties' and the reunification of Ireland. At the time Magee was joining its ranks, the Provisional IRA had become involved in a bombing and shooting campaign to get the Brits out, and the more provocative the IRA became, the more ordinary Catholics were at risk from violent reprisals from loyalists or the security forces. Far fewer Catholics were killed during IRA ceasefires than at other periods of the Troubles. These facts do not necessarily contradict the IRA's claim to be the defender of the Catholic people; the republican struggle was intended to bring about a secure state for Catholics, meaning that a short-term increase in suffering could be considered a price worth paying on the road to genuine security.

There is a darker possibility to consider, though. Might the IRA have been deliberately provoking attacks on Catholic people in order to justify its own existence? Did it pursue a strategy of attracting support by placing its own people in danger? According to one ex-IRA volunteer: 'If we provoked them [the security forces] enough, if we attacked them enough, at some point it wasn't just us they were going to be shooting at, it was the people … And we agitated and agitated until we got to that situation.' Once again the image comes to mind of people cutting off their hands in order to claim Ulster.

Patrick Magee, however, saw himself as a witness to what was happening on the ground, and he wanted to become part of the resistance, and a force for change. 'I wasn't in it because I was Irish, or because I was anti-British. I was in it because there was this great disparity in power. A lot of people saw the enemy as the loyalists more than the British – but I would ask, "Why is this happening? Who has the power interest here?" and it was the British state. They had long-fingered the whole situation for decades by handing it over to the unionists. The British didn't want to deal with it.'

His fight for a united Ireland was, Magee says, a political struggle for the extension of democracy. For nationalists, content to work within the given political framework, an end to partition would have been enough in itself, whereas for Magee it would only be the starting point towards a more accountable society. 'By the very nature of the six-county state, democracy was impossible. The whole state was a gerrymander. It was set up with an inbuilt majority and the unionists were not going to let it go. You could not work within the state to change it.' For this reason, and because Britain was determined to 'use the stick' to maintain unionist supremacy, Magee felt that 'militant republicanism had to take the lead in the matter'.

As I listened I wondered whether subsequent insight had crept into his recollection. I asked him whether he had been motivated by something more visceral than a sense of politics. 'A lot of the early motivation would have been absolute anger and hatred for things you'd witnessed. When you had to grit your teeth and say, you know, "You'll get your chance later." And there's been times when all I had to sustain me was hatred – but it's never enough. We were chipping away at a very powerful enemy, so there had to be deeper analysis and deeper motivation. But one of the rings *was* hatred.' He remembers being troubled when a prominent IRA member told him that feelings of hatred kept him going. 'But I don't believe for one second that hatred controlled this man's whole career in the movement.'

He is clear about the sort of people who joined the Provisional IRA: 'I don't want to glamorize it, but the best people in the district were in the republican movement. Decent people, with high morals and values, who cared about their community. Very few of them would have drifted into any sort of criminal life. I've only known a few psychopaths, people who were dodgy.'

Magee had already spent time on the fringes of the movement before joining, watching riots unfold and absorbing all that he could, while demonstrating that he could be trusted. 'You didn't become trusted by asking a lot of questions or wearing your beliefs on your lapel.' And so, when the time was right, he decided who to contact and said he was interested in joining. He was told that if he joined, it would go one of two ways. He would either end up in jail or dead. 'They will always try to dissuade you. They don't want to be burdened by somebody who is going to behave as some sort of tourist. They were very cagey because of infiltration. And it took a lot of resources to train somebody.' A man who had spent much of his early life resisting English influence must have seemed a fitting volunteer for an organization dedicated to doing much the same.

The first training Magee received was in a house with other new members. They entered one by one and sat around a room as weapons were brought in and somebody sat on a bed and demonstrated them. They then took turns to strip a weapon before filing out again in single file. For three or four days a week he received arms and explosives training. He sometimes went to a spot in the country where he was picked up and taken to a training camp.

Since Magee is known for one particular action, I asked him whether he had been chosen specifically to work with explosives.

'Many volunteers were really terrified of *the gear*,' he told me. 'In 1972 we lost more people than in any other year, and many of them were because of premature explosions. Three or four people sitting huddled around a bomb that went off. Nobody else wanted to do it – so I did it.' Magee considers himself to have been competent: 'There wasn't that much to know. Just basic circuitry. But it's all about a certain calmness and focus – and I had that.' As we sit chatting it is certainly hard to imagine him flustered. He stresses that there was an element of self-preservation to explosives work. The alternative was to give the job to someone who might have got him killed. 'But this idea that I was the only one capable of doing what I went on to do is ridiculous. There were others who could have done it. I just happened to be the guy who was active in England.'

In 1973 Magee was interned in Long Kesh prison camp. He was 23 years old. Internment, as we have seen, had been introduced two years previously in order to allow suspected terrorists to be detained indefinitely without trial. Brian Faulkner had declared that Northern Ireland was 'quite simply at war with the terrorist', and over the next few years Long Kesh, with its internees housed in rows of former RAF huts, became a de facto prisoner-of-war camp. At the time of his arrest Magee had been on the run in Belfast. 'There was a period of six weeks where every single day I had to bail over a back wall or something to get away from the Brits. That's what it was like. It was so intense.' One day, as he was crossing the New Lodge Road, making his way to a safe house, army jeeps pulled up and soldiers raced towards him. He was frogmarched into a Protestant area, where a large crowd of loyalists cheered as he was taken away.

Internment remained in force until December 1975 – and while it kept some known republicans from the struggle, it did not bring the IRA to its knees. In reality it boosted the IRA in the Irish Republic, in the United States, in Northern Ireland, and in Long Kesh. In the Republic, IRA men on the run were able to move about freely, in the United States the flow of money and weapons to the IRA increased, in Northern Ireland new recruits were attracted to the movement, and in Long Kesh a university of military and political thought was created.

Magee says that his real political education came inside Long Kesh. The camp was divided into 'cages' (compounds) made up of four huts, each cage run by the prisoners and holding over a hundred men. Magee spent time in a cage with Gerry Adams, who was brought to Long Kesh in July 1973. His first impression of Adams was of a hippy. 'I mean this was the leader, and this guy had long, straggly hair, a beard, a colourful T-shirt and bell bottoms. It just didn't fit.' Whether the image fitted the position or not, Adams had authority in Long Kesh. Magee remembers fifty or sixty men sitting around while Adams was speaking: 'Very relaxed, Adams says, "Does anybody in the room think that this war will be over in two years' time?" Nobody said anything. And he says, "Well, OK, does anybody here think that it's going to be over in ten years' time? Twenty years' time? No takers?" Well, everybody was a bit concerned because you had already got the message. Long haul. He knew that it was going to take years. He was already planning his political agenda. That was the thinking – and all the changes that occurred within the movement. The British weren't predicting it.'

Magee was witnessing the birth of a new republican strategy that was to define the future course of the Troubles, and it was quite different from the strategy being pursued at the time by leaders on the outside. In February 1975 those outside were embarking on an eleven-month ceasefire. In the build-up to the ceasefire, the British government, frustrated and short of ideas after the failure of a political settlement known as the Sunningdale Agreement, had sent out feelers to the Provisional leadership, who agreed to discuss terms, believing that the British would now be willing to contemplate a withdrawal from the province. As a result the ceasefire was imposed. Surprising words came from the British negotiators, including a statement that 'the tendency is towards eventual British disengagement'. Billy McKee, a member of the Provisional Army Council at the time, believes that the British were serious in their intentions, although Brendan Duddy, the man who had acted as a secret middleman between the authorities and the IRA on Bloody Sunday and was doing the same on this occasion, believes that 'the British weren't ready for it' because loyalists would have caused more problems for the British in the event of a British withdrawal than the republicans had ever caused them. In the event, even without any agreement, loyalists embarked on a sectarian campaign against the Catholic community, and the talks and the ceasefire fell apart.

Many republicans outside of the Army Council believed that the ceasefire and the negotiations had merely been an attempt by the British government to run down the IRA's fighting strength while buying time to gather intelligence. And in Long Kesh, as Patrick Magee witnessed, Gerry Adams was laying down an alternative strategy – the 'long war' doctrine. This involved a realistic assessment that the British were not going to be quickly defeated, and a counsel to republicans to settle down for a long and bitter guerrilla struggle that would wear the British down. But this strategy was not simply an extension of the deadline for British withdrawal. The Provisional IRA was to be reorganized. The old detachments, the large-scale battalions and companies, would be phased out and replaced by Active Service Units (ASUs) made up of a handful of volunteers. These smaller units would possess only limited knowledge of overall strategy and would prove much more difficult – in theory – for the British to infiltrate. Another branch of the new approach was to develop Sinn Féin, the IRA's political organization. Within a few years the increased emphasis on politics would evolve into a joint military and political strategy, which was plainly articulated in 1981 when Danny Morrison asked delegates at Sinn Féin's Ard Fheis (conference): 'Who here really believes we can win the war through the ballot box? But will anyone here object if, with a ballot paper in one hand and the Armalite in the other, we take power in Ireland?'

In reality the republican struggle had already been one of 'armed politics' for some time. In the early days of the Troubles the IRA's intention might have been to defeat the British militarily, but it was soon realized that such a result was impossible given the relative sizes and infrastructures of the IRA and the British army. A more realistic ambition was to cause the British so much difficulty and suffering that a favourable political settlement must follow. 'The whole struggle,' as Magee stresses, 'was about maximizing our political side.' But it was only at the time of the second hunger strike and Morrison's Ard Fheis speech that 'maximizing the political side' came to mean the fighting of elections. Before 1981 Gerry Adams opposed Sinn Féin's participation in electoral politics. After it, he encouraged electoralism to the point where eventually it came to smother the armed struggle. When Sinn Féin did well in elections, republicanism was boosted and the IRA came under pressure not to jeopardize the gains. When Sinn Féin did badly in elections, this was often deemed to be the result of public distaste for IRA operations – and this too had the effect of reining in the IRA. The legacy of the 'long war' strategy would be to make the Provisional IRA unsustainable and the Good Friday Agreement possible.

But initially the 'long war' doctrine had a pragmatic as well as a strategic basis, and this involved a concern relating to the IRA's own people. At the time when Magee became involved in the movement there had been hundreds of young men queuing to join the IRA. For many it had been a teenage hobby, a passionate hobby, but a hobby all the same. As the decade wore on, as these young men grew older, they found jobs and settled down with families, and they began pulling out. The IRA found itself haemorrhaging members, and the 'long war' strategy represented an effort to create a more professional IRA, made up of disciplined and committed volunteers.

Magee recalls his time in Long Kesh as spent 'fuming and thinking and reading'. He did not have many visitors. 'I was a bit isolated simply because my people were in England. I mean you're in a hut full of guys from Derry and Belfast, all of whom had known each other throughout their childhood, played games together, dated women together. They all had a shared background – and I was this guy from England.' He suspects he was mistrusted. 'People would have been watching you. There was this kind of paranoia all the time. I remember a guy saying to me, "Only trust someone you've known all your life." I was aware of the difference, certainly.'

When he was released he travelled the few miles back to Belfast, had a cup of tea, and reported straight back to the Provisional IRA. 'I had become deeply politicized. All I wanted was to get back and get involved.' The ceasefire was coming to an end, and within twenty-four hours he was sitting in a room with a gun in his hand. 'There was such a well of motivation built up, it just carried me through. It was a very intense period for me. It was like a form of madness, actually, because I had no fear. All I had was contempt for the British and the state. They couldn't have scared me, you know? The Brits were just watching you and recording it all. I was being arrested on a monthly basis. And not even so much to interrogate or to get information, but more to disrupt. But eventually that wears you down.'

Magee and others like him came to be worn down by the British government's hardening attitude; it was not only the Provisional IRA that was altering its approach. The British accepted that they could not defeat the enemy by direct confrontation, as had been attempted in various colonial outposts; to do so would cause suffering to the wider nationalist community, and provoke condemnation across the world. Instead it introduced a policy variously described as 'normalization', 'criminalization' and 'Ulsterization'. Since British troops had arrived in Northern Ireland in 1969, the army had been carrying out a large amount of the security work. From now on much of this work would be transferred to the police force and the locally recruited Ulster Defence Regiment. Terrorist suspects would be arrested, robustly questioned by detectives at interrogation centres before trial, and on conviction imprisoned in the new Maze Prison near Lisburn, with its H-shaped blocks, the rebuilt version of the old Long Kesh camp. In the Maze they would be treated as ordinary criminals and no longer as special category prisoners. De facto prisoner-of-war status was coming to an end.

These measures were intended to contradict the IRA's portrayal of itself as a liberation army engaged in a colonial war, and to turn the perception of political struggle into one of criminal activity. The IRA could, in this way, be marginalized, and the Troubles relegated to a little local annoyance. In April 1976 Roy Mason, the 'Barnsley Brawler', was appointed Secretary of State for Northern Ireland, with the belief that he could crush the IRA. Allegations began to proliferate that the security forces were acting increasingly outside of the law, and that the RUC were extracting confessions from terror suspects under torture. Magee speaks of being taken to Castlereagh Holding Centre, where he was 'treated like a piece of dirt'. One republican, interrogated at Castlereagh in 1976, recalls: 'I had a form of torture that was brutal and it was a relief when I was finally taken to prison, to remand.' Magee remembers being impressed by the fact that his Castlereagh doctor faithfully recorded every mark on his body, including a bruise on his back from a baton blow which affected him for years afterwards. 'And I know one guy – he's dead now, actually – who received electric-shock treatment.' But the fact is that the IRA did not take prisoners. When a British soldier was captured, he was interrogated and shot. What right did the IRA have to complain when the British state did not behave in an exemplary fashion? 'It's because the British had sovereign power and they abused that power,' says Magee. 'They had options. We didn't have options. One isn't a mirror image of the other.' A young British officer who served in Northern Ireland in the Nineties sees the matter differently: 'It did used to stick with me that we would spend all this time making sure that we upheld the provisions of the law, and they [the IRA] would do the most vicious and disgusting things – but then would immediately expect the full protection of the law as soon as they decided it suited them.'

The direct measures introduced by the British (as well as other factors such as improved intelligence) had a profound and immediate effect on the level of violence. One hundred and thirteen people were killed as a result of the Troubles in 1977, compared with 307 the year before. An ex-IRA man from Derry told me, 'At the time it seemed that the RUC and the British army were raiding everywhere, rounding up as many men as possible and capturing weapons. By the end of 1977 we were almost beat. They had nearly crushed the IRA. But the creation of the small cell units made a change. How the hell the IRA ever got back and turned it around from then onwards was unbelievable – because the army at that time was so close to defeating it.'

A British army captain, serving in 1977 as an intelligence officer in Derry with a staff of eighty, recalls that his section was having a great deal of success. He remembers his response to a spate of shootings in the city. By plotting the instances he was able to work out that most of the shootings were taking place within three hundred metres of St Eugene's Cathedral, and he decided that there must be a cache of weapons nearby. His men had already searched the area well – except for the cathedral complex itself, which was out of bounds. He then looked at the dates of the shootings and spotted a pattern – so he could predict that on one of two weekends, between ten at night and one in the morning, there would be an attack around the cathedral. He withdrew his soldiers from the area, except for small covert patrols that circled the three-hundred-metre area. On the second night a car drew up and went into the Cathedral School, where its occupants pulled up a manhole cover and retrieved four Armalites and four M16s. 'We got them. I was very proud of that,' says the major.

Patrick Magee, in the meantime, had met his first wife within a few days of his release from internment. They were married eighteen months later. She was 'an active republican' when they met, but 'she gave that up when she met me. It was tough. I mean, you couldn't maintain a normal relationship.' At this time Magee was on the run, and the uncertain life started to wear him down. 'By 1980 I was absolutely burnt out. I had been on the run for three years. There was no certainty in anything, and your options are totally limited. For a period of a year in the north, I was in a different house every night.' A very small number of people would have known where he was at any one time: 'The person whose house I was staying in, the person who brought me to it, and somebody else might have had to know. But you can only sustain that for a certain period, and after so many blows, you just say, "I can't do this any more." I had reached that point in 1980, and I decided to forge a life for myself. I didn't think I could contribute any more – in fact I felt that I was a danger to people around me. And one of the myths around the IRA is once in, always in.'

There are parallels that can be drawn between the bleakness of Magee's life on the run and the dehumanized state experienced by British soldiers on their tours of duty. One army officer told me, 'I was always in uniform. Every time I went out, I'd get a helmet on and a weapon and a flak jacket and all the rest of it, and people would look at me – but they wouldn't see *me*. They would see another soldier, and it was a freaky psychological experience. You were a figure of hate for some people, a figure of support for others, but you were never an individual. We had a moustache-growing competition – and I won it, but it actually made me feel even less like myself than I had done. I lost my libido, and didn't feel like a man. I became a kind of robot. I think we all felt lost and isolated.' When he was first sent to Northern Ireland this officer had been in a relationship which promptly ended when his girlfriend phoned him to ask what the time difference was, and whether he'd taken enough traveller's cheques with him …

While on the run, Magee wanted to go to live in the United States. 'I actually applied for the visa, and – somehow – I got it, but in the end I didn't have the money to go to the States, and I ended up in the Netherlands. I've read that I was supposed to be setting up cells over there, but that wasn't the case. I was over there trying to build a new life for myself, my wife, and my son.'

Magee was arrested in the Netherlands and a warrant was issued for his extradition. He was held for four months, during which time committees were formed to campaign for his release. The extradition attempt failed, but fearing 're-arrest or worse', Magee was smuggled out of the country, through France, and into the Irish Republic. Once there, he was immediately targeted by the Irish police. 'They knocked on the door one day and introduced themselves. There would always be one guy shouting at you and you'd be shouting back at him, and the other guy would be standing back, weighing you up. They'd got their different agendas, the British and the Irish, but there was lots of collaboration. Of course there was.' One consequence of Magee's extradition battle was that he returned to the struggle reinvigorated. 'After beating that and returning to Ireland – and getting out during the hunger-strike period – I suddenly got my motivation back. It was the hunger strikes, and the things that were happening on the ground, it was terrible times. Children being killed with plastic bullets. All of that.'

At this point I raised the subject of Magee's military activities within the Provisional IRA, but I was politely kept at bay: 'I wouldn't talk about the operation at the Grand or indeed any operation.' He says that at the time of the explosion in the Grand Hotel, he was in Ireland: 'My reaction was relief. Just sheer relief. The responsibility I had for this operation – a massive operation – and if it had failed I would never have been trusted again. I would have had to go and live on an island somewhere, Skelligs Rocks or somewhere like that.' He explains the republican thinking of the late Seventies and early Eighties that led to the operation: 'Quite clearly the British strategy was containment. They wanted to contain the war to pocket the six counties, dampen it down, get it off the front pages. But if you were able to bring the war *to them*, you could stir it up. And if you were to demonstrate to them that you were going to keep on coming back, that you could sustain it, then they would have to deal with you at some point.' The reference to bringing the war 'to them' alludes to the fact that the British were more likely to pay attention to attacks mounted on targets in England than to an endless cycle of tit-for-tat killings in Northern Ireland.

Viewed as a single incident, the Brighton bomb did nothing to end the Troubles. It was never going to force Margaret Thatcher to the negotiating table. But, according to Magee, it was not anticipated that it would: 'There was no one operation, even an operation that went for the jugular, that was going to achieve your ends. You had to sustain it. It was all about negotiating from strength.' So while the bomb was an upping of the military ante, it was intended to further underline that the IRA could not be defeated, and Alan Clark's diary entry suggests that, in the eyes of some, it had the desired effect. Certainly, the eventual peace process was made possible by a British acceptance that the Provisional IRA was not going to be beaten, and the IRA's ability to carry out operations on the scale of the Brighton bomb was a factor in that acceptance. But equally the process resulted from eventual republican recognition that the British state was not going to abandon its unionist subjects and walk out of

Northern Ireland – out of respect for the rights of the majority, and out of fear of civil war. That such a fear was realistic is clear from the existence of a 1994 document drafted by the UDA – the 'Doomsday scenario' – which declared that in the event of a British withdrawal from Northern Ireland the organization's aim would be to 'establish an ethnic Protestant homeland' within which the stranded Catholic population would be 'expelled, nullified or interned'. Over the years it became clear to republican leaders that no amount of ferocious attacks would simply conjure a united Ireland into being. Peace was born out of stalemate, purchased at the cost of lives, some of which were taken by Patrick Magee.

Yet while Magee has been at pains to stress that the struggle was intended to 'maximize our political side', it is probable that had he killed Margaret Thatcher and her cabinet, political negotiations would have been impossible for many years to come. The British government could not have contemplated speaking to Sinn Féin – in which case the peace process could not have happened. In these circumstances the Brighton bomb would have nullified the 'long war' strategy of which it was an integral part. Such are the contradictions inherent in the strategies of the Troubles.

Magee was arrested in Glasgow eight months after the bombing. 'I was preparing for the next job. I was on active service when I was caught. Somebody was followed across from Ireland, met me in England, and they followed us back to the others.' Magee was traced to the bombing by a palm print left on a Grand Hotel registration card bearing the name 'Roy Walsh', under which he had booked into the hotel. He was eventually released from prison in 1999, in the wake of the Good Friday Agreement.

In Magee's eyes, the war had, by then, been won. 'The British were always ahead of us in terms of resources at their disposal. But a few hundred people were able to take on this very powerful enemy and – I think – to beat it. To draw a comparison, if you're in a bar and you see a fight, and there's some wee guy who's fighting some hulk, and they end up getting separated, you look at their two faces, and this wee guy is still standing, and the other guy looks a bit marked. Who won that fight? Would you be in any doubt who won that fight?'

One republican who might be in some doubt is Anthony McIntyre, a writer and commentator, who spent many years in Long Kesh, having been convicted of a 1976 murder. McIntyre has written: 'The political objective of the Provisional IRA was to secure a British declaration of intention to withdraw. It failed. The objective of the British state was to force the Provisional IRA to accept … that it would not leave Ireland until a majority in the north consented to such a move. It succeeded.' To call on Magee's allegory, the little guy had failed to kick the hulk out of the bar.

But just as arguments have raged about who 'won' the conflict, so there are men and women of every shade of green and orange who will tell you that their side is 'winning' the peace, and there are others who will tell you the opposite. Magee chooses his words carefully in his analysis of the peace process: 'I think the Good Friday Agreement goes a long way. It gives a vision of what is possible.' And what is possible? 'Well, there was this idea that the movement could deliver on its own – and we couldn't. We could only do it through combining with other interested groups: the rest of nationalist Ireland, and the "Irish diaspora". That's what the peace process was about: broadening the base. That's what the Hume-Adams talks were about – except they should be called "Adams-Hume" in my opinion.' If the very deepest roots of the peace process – from a republican point of view – reach down into the cages of Long Kesh, then its shoots can be observed in talks that took place over a number of years between Gerry Adams and John Hume, the civil rights activist who became leader of the nationalist SDLP in 1979. The talks began in January 1988, brokered by Father Alec Reid, a priest at

John Beresford-Ash, a wonderfully old-fashioned character, impeccably mannered, entertaining and honest. He died in April 2010 as a result of a fall in the grounds of his beloved home, Ashbrook.

Top Killyleagh Castle, a fairy-tale fortress of towers and dogtooth walls in County Down.
Bottom left Denys Rowan Hamilton, the former master of Killyleagh Castle; a reluctant but principled politician.
Bottom right Archibald Hamilton Rowan, an earlier master of Killyleagh Castle; a Protestant and fervent republican whose heroic destiny failed to materialise.

Joe Graham, republican, historian, civil rights veteran, and storyteller.

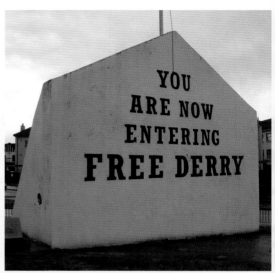

Top left John Kelly, a gentle and dignified Creggan resident whose life was changed on 30 January 1972 – Bloody Sunday.
Top right Words which appeared on the gable end of a terrace in the Bogside in January 1969. When the barricades were in place, the Queen's writ did not run in this part of Derry.
Bottom The view from on top. The Bogside and the Creggan (including St Eugene's Cathedral) photographed from the Derry city walls.

Joe Cahill. Reprieved from a death sentence in 1940, Cahill became a leading Provisional IRA figure three decades later. He is photographed outside Sinn Fein headquarters in Dublin.
© Bobbie Hanvey

Top A Shankill mural depicts the story of the Red Hand of Ulster; it is the tale of a man who wants Ulster so badly that he is willing to cripple himself in order to lay his claim.

Middle left A mural on the Shankill estate commemorates the life of Stephen 'Top Gun' McKeag.

Middle right A stretch of 'peace wall' in Belfast decorated with the lyrics of an old Belfast song sung by Van Morrison, and with the scrawled names of numerous visitors.

Bottom left A mural in the Ardoyne representing the 1916 Easter Rising; Harold Nicolson once wrote, 'The Irish have no sense of the past … For them, history is always contemporaneous and current events are always history.'

Top The mural of Bobby Sands on the corner of Falls Road and Sevastapol Street in Belfast. The author asked a local man about the graffiti on the mural. 'Don't worry,' he was told. 'Whoever did that'll be dealt with.'

Bottom left Adrian Callan, ex-Provisional IRA volunteer, prisoner, and a man of warmth and intelligence. He told the author of arriving home from prison, and experiencing a weird sensation as he approached his house: he had not walked on a slope for more than a decade.

Bottom right A 'Catholic back garden' in Ardoyne backing onto the peace wall. On the other side of the wall lies a similar garden in a different world.

Alternative Altars. **Top** Presbyterian. Martyrs' Memorial Free Presbyterian Church on Ravenhill Road in Belfast. Built in 1969, this church was founded by Ian Paisley. **Bottom left** Catholic. St Columba's Church, Long Tower, Derry. Overlooking the Bogside, a church has existed on this site since 1786. The present building dates to 1907. **Bottom right** Church of Ireland. St Columb's Cathedral, Derry. Built in 1633, the Cathedral served as a rallying point for besieged citizens during the 1689 Siege of Derry, and today houses many artifacts from the time of the siege.

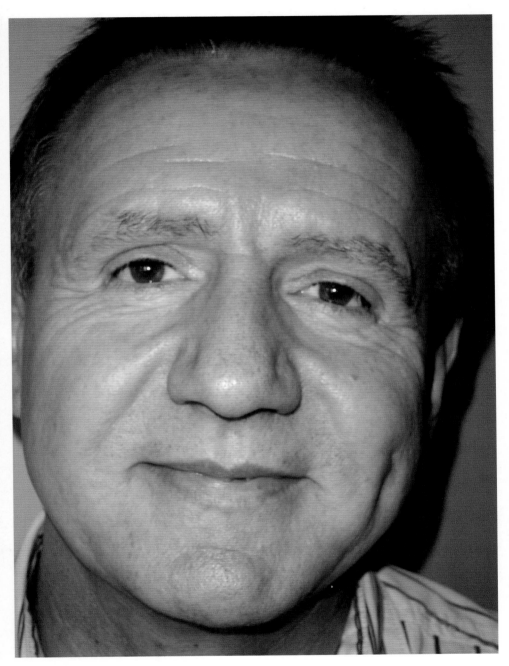

William McKee, a former governor of the Maze Prison. He is a touchingly sensitive man, a long way from the stereotype of a prison officer.

Top and middle right The scene as the Royal Irish Regiment marches through Belfast on its return from Afghanistan.
Middle left and bottom The annual burning of an effigy of Robert Lundy in Derry. Lundy, the Governor of Derry, deserted the garrison during the 1689 siege, and to this day a traitor to the Protestant cause is known as a 'Lundy'. © Claire Price

Gerry Foster, an ex-member of the Irish National Liberation Army. He is a man with strong views on the current levels of hypocrisy and denial relating to the past.

Ken Bloomfield, ex-head of the Northern Ireland Civil Service, and the subject of a 1988 IRA assassination attempt. He is a thoughtful man, willing – unlike most other interviewees – to accept that he has, on occasion, made mistakes.

Top left The shiny, new, ecumenical
Ian Paisley, photographed at a St
Patrick's Day breakfast in 2009 at
the La Mon Hotel near Belfast.
© Bobbie Hanvey
Top right A statue outside Belfast
City Hall reflecting the city's
shipbuilding heritage.
Middle The Stormont Parliament
Buildings, built in impressive
classical style, and opened
in 1932.
Bottom The huge, gold-plated
central chandelier in Stormont's
Great Hall which was once
discarded by Windsor Castle.

Anna Lo, a Member of the Northern Ireland Legislative Assembly. A liberal, a woman, Chinese, and Daoist by birth, she is an unusual MLA in socially and religiously conservative Northern Ireland, but she says, 'I am seen as someone without an axe to grind.'

David Johnston. Raised in loyalist east Belfast, he may have distanced himself from traditional beliefs but he has always been a passionate observer of his home city.

Top The author stands at the 'Top of the Hill' in Derry. From this spot, it is hard to reconcile the city's beauty with the rage and hatred that has coloured it.

Middle left A pillar in the Bogside daubed with graffiti in support of the Real IRA. A peace mural sits in the background.

Middle right A view into the Bogside – a place 'so tribal, so incestuous about its relationships, that even a stranger feels in some way "at home" there'.

Bottom The rebuilt bandstand in Regents Park, London. The original was blown up by the Provisional IRA on 20 July 1982. Seven bandsmen of the Royal Green Jackets were killed.

© Lionel Levine

Clonard monastery in the heart of republican west Belfast, and they showed that at least one senior republican genuinely wished to begin a process of negotiation.

When the talks started there was a vast gulf between the republican approach of Adams and the nationalist approach of Hume. Hume and the nationalists believed that Britain had no selfish interest in remaining in Northern Ireland. It was the unionists, they argued, who insisted on retaining British sovereignty. As a result it was pointless attempting to bomb Britain into withdrawing; a united Ireland would have to come about through agreement and cooperation between Catholics and Protestants. This was a difficult concept for republicans, long accustomed to believing that British occupation of the six counties was rooted in self-interest, and that only an armed struggle would loosen the colonial grip. In a 1992 BBC Radio Ulster interview, in which Adams and Hume shared a studio, the fundamental disagreement was clear for all to hear. As Adams hammered home his belief that the Brits were the problem, Hume simply repeated: 'But we are a deeply divided people ...'

Yet it is conceivable that by the time of this radio interview Adams had already come to accept Hume's position. According to author and journalist Ed Moloney, Father Reid had arranged for brief but meaningful contact to be made between Adams and the British government several years earlier. Moloney claims that a representative of the British government sent Adams a document stating that the government had no 'political, military, strategic, or economic interest in staying in Ireland' and that it would be prepared to withdraw from the 'central forum of political debate' so that the parties to the conflict – nationalists and unionists – could engage in their own agreement-making. In other words, British withdrawal from Ireland could, in the first instance at least, be political rather than physical. This concept runs counter to the traditional republican insistence that a British withdrawal would have to be physical, swift, and total, and it may have offered Adams a pragmatic vision of a future peace process that could be sold to republicans. It certainly describes the actual path that the peace process has taken – and continues to take.

Brendan Duddy, who for so many years was the secret link between the British government and the Provisional IRA, told me that during the Eighties and early Nineties he repeatedly told militant republicans that unionists felt like 'disinherited sons' and that the task of republicans was 'to remain in a passive peaceful situation until people begin to relate to each other', which, he stressed, is just what is happening at the moment. But whatever the influences on Adams might have been, he was clearly serious about working with Hume, and they began to issue a series of joint public statements. In April 1993 they set out their basis for a future agreement involving all parties. They underlined the right of the Irish people to 'national self-determination', but stressed that the exercise of that right was a matter for agreement between the people of Ireland, and that such an agreement was only achievable if it could 'earn and enjoy the allegiance of the different traditions on the island of Ireland'. These words confirm that Adams had started to acknowledge political realities: no longer were unionists being dismissed as simply the dupes of the British. While the statement fell short of stating that unionists must be able to give their consent to any agreement, it laid the foundations for the republican acceptance of such a principle, which would eventually come to underpin the Good Friday Agreement.

I asked Magee whether the ultimate achievement of the Hume-Adams talks was that they led republicans to recognize the rights of unionists. 'There was another very important side to those talks,' he says, 'and it's a side that is completely overlooked. The British strategy for decades was to undermine and marginalize the republican movement. The SDLP was part and parcel of that undermining of Sinn Féin, and the SDLP would have been happy with some sort of compromise that changed nothing, just paying lip service to ending partition. So the big battle that we had was to win the argument within nationalism for inclusion. Only when that was tackled and won, was progress possible. Sinn Féin was at the helm of the struggle to gain a broad front strategy. Adams and Sinn Féin led the peace process.'

Yet Sinn Féin could not have led a 'broad front strategy', let alone a peace process, had it not understood the strength and sincerity of unionist belief. It had certainly not always done so. In fact, as late as 1990, one senior republican remarked: 'The British government has one simple role: to convince the Irish people who at present subscribe to some hazy idea of British-ness that the British connection is going, and they have to come to some sort of accommodation with the other people with whom they share this island.' Such a view did not reflect reality. Unionists considered themselves British whatever anyone else thought, they had lived in Ulster for four hundred years, and they constituted a majority of the people of Northern Ireland, and they weren't going anywhere. How could these points simply be ignored? The answer lies in the fact that republicans did not think in terms of – or even recognize the existence of – North-ern Ireland, but chose instead to think in terms of the entire island of Ireland, on which unionists were a minority with no right to dictate terms. This might explain Sinn Féin's patroniz-ing proposal, made in a 1987 policy document, for the intro-duction of 're-settlement grants' to allow unionists 'to move to Britain'.

I asked Magee about the changing republican attitude to unionists. 'Well, it was important to take on board the fact of these one million or 900,000 Protestants. I've no difficulty in accepting that republicans had unrealistic views about how they could negotiate with unionism. But there's no perfect war. There's no perfect strategy – because the other side have their agendas too.'

Does Magee think that unionists will ever agree to a united Ireland? 'The big, big reason why there will be a united Ireland is because you cannot extend democracy in any meaningful sense in this part of the world unless you get rid of partition. Partition stymies true radical politics – so I think it will happen. Do I think that's the end of the matter? Of course it's not. It's just the beginning. And I don't think it matters when it happens.' This reasserts Magee's belief that there *should be* a united Ireland; it does not explain why unionists will ever agree with him. I pressed him again and he said, 'A united Ireland can only happen when fewer people from the unionist background are fearful of it as an outcome. You need them. Why would you want to do it without them?' This is an odd question from a man who spent much of his life trying 'to do it without them'.

So *how will* unionists be persuaded into a united Ireland? 'You've got to make the idea attractive to them, and obviously that's going to be a long-term effort. I think the economic argument is strong. I think all sorts of ties with Britain are important too. The Good Friday Agreement recognizes the north–south dimension and the east–west dimension. Any long-term solution has to take on board all of those dimensions.'

It must be difficult for many republicans to reconcile the current political situation with what went before. For all of Magee's emphasis that the 'long war' consciously prepared the ground for political negotiation, the Provisional IRA never deviated from its position that the armed struggle would continue until British control of the six counties was at an end, prior to reunification. Yet the British are still in control of the six counties, and the Provisionals' armed struggle is over. Some republicans are still hopeful of imminent reunification: one Derry republican told me that his target date is 2016, the hundredth anniversary of the Easter Rising. 'Everything is possible,' he said, 'and I'm one of these people who is very positive. Never say never.'

All the same, compromises have had to be made, and they run deeper than a premature end to conflict and an extended deadline for a united Ireland. Magee has said that 'the real strategists within the movement were radicals and socialists'. He was never a nationalist, he says, because nationalists were content to work within the 'given political framework'. He was not content to do so. Yet now he is offering support to a republican leadership which is doing precisely that. The movement has come a long way since the days when it believed that a reunited Ireland would serve as a barrier against capitalism. As well as being radicals and socialists, the strategists have proved to be pragmatists and politicians.

It is significant that neither Magee nor the leadership is prepared to be – or perhaps even capable of being – explicit on the strategy or the timescale for reunification. Anthony McIntyre believes that no strategy exists and that 'the activities [Sinn Féin] is now involved in are designed to gain a better deal for Northern Irish Catholics under British rule.' But perhaps a strategy *does* exist, predicated upon – just as Magee has said – making Irish unity attractive to unionists. Doing so might involve a gradual fusion of northern and southern institutions, taking place so naturally and mutually beneficially, that the unionist majority consents as the border withers away.

There are, of course, republicans who feel betrayed by a peace without British withdrawal, and by the sight of former comrades working within the political system. At a gathering in April 2009 in Derry a Real IRA volunteer wearing a black balaclava read the following to a small crowd: 'Let us remind our former comrade [Martin McGuinness] of the nature and actions of a traitor. Treachery is collaborating with the enemy, treachery is betraying our country … No traitor will escape justice regardless of time, rank or past actions.' Patrick Magee seems to have little sympathy with such dissident sentiment. 'Of course there are people who are not happy with what's going on – except that none of them seem to be concerned about building politically.

Somebody will sidle up to you in a bar and will want to engage you in politics, and you'd say, "Ach, Jesus, here we go again." But you try to be as open and honest as possible. I would try to engage with them, and just point out that I support what is happening, I believe that it is the only course, and I would throw it back on them: "What's the alternative?" None of them has been able to come up with anything viable as an alternative.'

A reply (of sorts) to Magee's question has come from Marian Price. Price, an ex-IRA volunteer who was jailed for her part in the 1973 London bombing campaign, is an outspoken critic of the peace process. She is a leading member of the 32 County Sovereignty Movement, an organization that is believed to serve as the political wing of the Real IRA, much as Sinn Féin once served as the political wing of the Provisional IRA. In a speech in April 2009 she said, 'We are constantly asked – what is your alternative? The answer depends on who is asking the question. To those who call us traitors we say: "Any alternative but yours." To those who call us anti-democratic we say: "Let us negotiate without pre-conditions." To those republicans who genuinely seek an alternative, we say: "Let us construct one together." This final remark seems to confirm that the dissidents currently have no political strategy, only a sense of grievance.

In the eyes of some older republicans who grew up in a world where republicanism was about pursuing realizable ends, this lack of strategy appears to rob the dissidents of legitimacy. But has republicanism really ever offered up a distinction between strategic struggle and ad hoc resistance? According to McIntyre, the republican physical-force tradition has always held 'that while there is a British presence in any part of Ireland, republicans will have an inalienable right to carry out armed attacks on Britain's forces and its interests'. If that can be considered the IRA's operational benchmark, then the killing of a British soldier carried out by the Real IRA in 2009 is morally indistinguishable from the same act carried out by the Provisional IRA twenty years earlier.

It is one thing, of course, to consider IRA operations in strategic and broad moral terms. It is quite another to relate them to the individuals affected. We met Jo Berry, the daughter of Sir Anthony Berry – one of Magee's victims – in the previous chapter. My conversation with her did not end with her description of her first meeting with Magee. In the anonymous railway hotel where we met, she spoke about the effect of that meeting, of the ebbing and flowing friendship that the pair has struck up, and of the work they have carried out together in the name of conflict resolution: 'Pat sort of felt in awe of me as soon as he saw me, and he was certainly very respectful. He was a very sensitive person, and I had a really strong feeling that he wasn't like other people I've met in the IRA. He wasn't all "I don't want to hear any of this" and I think he's really unusual. His capacity to listen and engage – he gets real lows after meeting me, yet he comes back and he's so committed to working with me. I don't think he always understands why he is so happy to do it – but he is.'

Magee tells me that dealing with the legacy of his actions is something that must be done: 'I came out at the end of the struggle, provided myself with some sort of space to look back and deal with it – and that's what I'm doing with Jo. It's just part of dealing with the legacy. And it's a necessary part – we have to sort it out.'

For Berry, 'sorting it out' is not a simple matter. When she meets up with Magee, her experience can vary, depending on how he is speaking: 'Sometimes Pat communicates more about how hard it is living with it, knowing what he's done. And at other times he will talk more about the fact that he had no other choice but to do what he did, and he talks about the strategy stuff. He can sometimes cut off from his feelings in order to talk about it – and it's much easier if you dehumanize the people involved. It's a bit like kids playing war games – you don't see the real people there. If he does that, I can get a bit wobbly, or a bit emotional, and I will say, "This is getting too much for me" and he will stop – which is really good.'

Magee accepts that there are contradictions in his attitude to his past: 'One of the things that I explore with Jo – and try to understand – is this big conflict that, on the one hand, you can justify – as I do – the taking of life and all the things that I've been involved in, while on the other hand, the fact remains that you hurt human beings – and that's a burden. It's like trying to square the circle. I mean, I haven't been a practising Catholic since I was 13, but that's the way I was brought up, and I do have a sense that there's going to be a reckoning at some time. I wish there had been another way. I wish I hadn't lived the life I did. But because, hopefully, I'm a moral person, I was in a situation that I couldn't have walked away from it. I felt I had to stay on the ground, make a decision, and stick with it.'

Weeks later I would listen as another ex-IRA man spoke of God and Jesus Christ, saying that at the Pearly Gates he was ready to make an account for himself. It would be a mistake to believe that the men and women who killed for Ireland are devoid of morality. I have no doubt that Magee is sincere when he tells me that he is a moral person. I asked him whether he has regrets about the things that he has done. 'I have many, many regrets,' he said. 'But I can stand over the actions that I thought was necessary. I thought Brighton was necessary. I *do* regret the outcome – like killing Jo's father and killing those three women. Of course I do. But you've got to think back to my view then, and it was an extremely reduced view. All I seen was the Tories, the people in power, and you hated them. These are the people responsible for the collusion and the murder gangs, the torture, and the suppression. I mean, why wouldn't you go for them, given the opportunity? We were taking a war to them – and I had no compunction about that. Absolutely none.'

Speaking about these matters is not easy for Magee, but his belief that they must be confronted is clear. I am given a vivid sense of his moral confusion when in one breath he distances himself from his past – 'it was an extremely reduced view' – and in the next he embraces it – 'why wouldn't you go for them, given the opportunity?' I asked whether it was acceptable to kill peripheral figures: 'I didn't make these distinctions between wives of Tories, of minor Tories, and higher Tories. They were all Tories, they were all the enemy. The only concern would have been about the staff in the hotel. We knew there was always a possibility that you could have ended up killing a chambermaid or something. But you timed all of it yourself, and I selected a moment when it was less likely to happen.' So is it possible to regret the fact that Berry's father was killed, while not regretting planting the bomb that killed him. 'That's the conflict! That's the conflict! I can't square that circle! My mind tells me that what we did was right – but I do feel regret.'

Berry has asked Magee what right he had to take her father's life. His reply has clearly caused her pain, but she is pragmatic nonetheless: 'It's what we are always going to disagree on. He actually believes that he had no choice. I guess he will live with the consequences of that. I know some people say it would be better if he renounced everything, and just said that what he did was wrong – but actually, I don't agree. The fact is that he's on a journey, and I'm on a journey, and we're dealing with a really difficult area to communicate about, and that's important. It shows the greyness of the area and the difficulty of resolution. It's a situation we can learn from, to make the world more peaceful. I would never try to change him.'

She believes that her discussions with Magee have given her an opportunity to bring into the open important issues concerning peace and conflict resolution: 'I have been in situations where it's not about me and Pat any more. It's about the people who are listening to us. I have been in prisons, in workshops, I've been to the Basque country, and everywhere people start sharing their own stories. Our journey is having an effect on other people.

These discussions have clearly had an effect on Magee too. 'I'm trying to understand more,' he says. 'I've come to the understanding that Jo's father wasn't just a Tory figurehead. You've met Jo; she's a wonderful person, and a lot of what's good in her came from him. He must have been a great guy – and I killed him. I carry that with me.' I asked what it means to 'carry it with him'. 'You carry this sense of loss, and you are the person who caused it, and it's got to be made up in some way. I can't bring Jo's father back to life, but I can try to understand him better, at least.' In the end, though, the circle cannot be squared: 'I feel sorry and I express sorrow. But that's a different matter from saying that what I did was wrong.'

Many times over the course of our meeting, Magee has stressed the fact that *he had no choice.* It is the recurrent theme of his conversation. But on a personal level, he must have had a choice about becoming involved. I asked him whether there were people around him who chose not to get involved. 'Yeah, of course there were. But there weren't many of them living in Unity Walk, I'll tell you that much.'

Magee has explained how the situation in Belfast in 1972 brought him into the fold. But what about the suggestion that the IRA had no choice but to wage its subsequent military campaign? Such a claim receives little sympathy outside of republican circles. Irish reunification was the primary goal of the Provisional IRA, but it was also a goal of John Hume's constitutional nationalists, a large body of people who were committed to following a non-violent path.

What of the argument that the armed struggle helped to achieve equality for Catholics once all peaceful methods had been exhausted? The fact is that the civil rights movement had achieved many of its demands before it was disbanded, but its potential had not yet been fully realized. Why could republicans not have continued to demand further peaceful change? Magee's view is that by the gerrymandered nature of the six-county state, democracy was impossible, and he could not work within the state to change it. But does it necessarily follow that because Northern Ireland was built on a system of political and social inequality – as it undoubtedly was – internal reform was therefore impossible and the only remedy was the violent destruction of the state?

Yet Magee is speaking sincerely when he says that there was no choice. As he suggests, most of those in Unity Walk, living in fear of their lives, felt the same way. He also says that he has never thought of himself as a victim: 'I've been shot, I've been blown up, I've been tortured, but all I can say is that when you have stood on your own two feet and struggled against it, you are no longer a victim.' This chimes with the words of Martin McGuinness, six months before the Brighton bomb exploded: 'Without the IRA we are on our knees. Without the IRA, we are slaves. For fifteen years this generation of republicans have been off their knees. We will never be slaves again.' The IRA provided its communities with self-respect – so while alternatives to the armed struggle existed, in the eyes of many republicans emotional and psychological alternatives did not. Magee says, 'I'm very, very proud of what our communities achieved against a very powerful enemy. And it was not part of my make-up to walk away – so it's not as if I had a hard decision to make when it came down to it.' So, for many years, for many republicans, the other choices did not seem like choices at all.

One man who cannot accept that the choice to use violence was ever acceptable is Peter Sheridan, a Catholic from County Fermanagh who joined the RUC in 1978 and rose to become the Assistant Chief Constable of Northern Ireland. 'People will never convince me that they *had* to do those things,' says Sheridan. Which is not to say that he doesn't understand why people joined paramilitary organizations. 'I often think that if I'd been born on these estates and grew up in that, I could have been sucked into it,' he says. 'If the Troubles hadn't been on, a lot of these people wouldn't have been involved in murdering.' But in his view unacceptable choices were made. 'It doesn't matter how difficult the society you live in. I don't think anything in Northern Ireland could justify making a deliberate choice to plant a bomb in a street, to take a sniper rifle out and wait to shoot somebody, to put a bomb under someone's car.'

Sheridan was the target of a number of IRA death threats, and two direct attacks. In 1981 his police Land Rover came under sniper fire, and in March 1987 he was injured by a bomb at Magee College in Derry that killed two of his colleagues. 'I was walking away from a car when it blew up. Had it been a couple of seconds earlier, I would have been standing next to it. I have a memory of officers further away than me being blown off their feet – but I wasn't.' He can remember the bright flash of the blast, then, a second later, the heat and pressure, and finally the debris. 'I stayed on my feet because I was at the thin edge of a mushroom cloud. The officers further away got hit by the shock waves more than I did.' He says that the experience didn't shake him psychologically. 'I'm pretty strong and I was able to deal with it – but I suppose it did shake me to see the remains of people. I knew that the two officers were dead within seconds of going over to them. They were badly burned and their clothes were ripped off.' Sheridan claims that the incident didn't make him angry. 'I was saddened more than anything. It was the pure futility of it. But people talk about enemies – and I've never thought of the people that did it as my enemies.'

I was rather awed by Sheridan's attitude to those who had tried to kill him. It was, I was fairly sure, more generous than mine could ever be. But he considers that, as time passes, there is a danger that the Troubles will be remembered as a fight between the paramilitaries and the police 'in a kind of equilibrium'. He argues that '95 per cent of police officers got out of bed in the morning thinking about how they could prevent the next bomb or shooting'. He accepts that there were rotten apples in the police force, but the vast majority of officers 'weren't thinking about who they could kill or maim. That wasn't in their mindset. But that's what the paramilitaries did every day. They got up thinking who their next target was. *It wasn't an equilibrium.'*

I remembered these words of Peter Sheridan as Patrick Magee got his things together and prepared to leave my hotel room. I felt very bleak as I tried to reconcile these two men – both now committed to peace – in my mind. I said goodbye to Magee and he made his own way downstairs. He is direct and honest but inscrutable, and quite a contrast to the open and playful Jo Berry. As I settled down on my hotel bed and let the conversation of the past few hours wash over me, I thought about Magee and Berry giving talks and working towards conflict resolution, even as issues remain unresolved between them. But then, perhaps, as Berry suggested, that is a reflection of real life, and therefore more helpful to others than a neatly resolved happy ever after.

Berry had told me that she does not have the right to forgive Magee. She says that true reconciliation is not about forgiveness, it is about understanding him as a person. As I considered the contrast between them, I started to wonder whether her drive isn't – at least partly – fuelled by a desire to hear Magee apologize for the act that killed her father. Then perhaps she would forgive Magee – and maybe achieve some kind of closure. But would an apology really make anything better? And wasn't I just imposing my own feelings on her? Just as I was awed by Peter Sheridan's attitude to those who had tried to kill him, I found it difficult to imagine spending time with someone who had killed a member of my family – particularly a man who won't apologise for doing it. But I am not Jo Berry. I do not have her generosity of spirit. And as I was discovering, there is something about Northern Ireland that has a way of bringing out the best in people. As well as the worst.

9

THE PRISON

Adrian Callan lives in Derry. I met him in the café at Austins Department Store in the centre of the city. Austins is housed in a rather fine Edwardian building and it claims to be the oldest independent department store in the world, older than Harrods by fifteen years. As daytime shoppers sat around us, comparing their purchases over cups of tea, Adrian Callan and I had a different sort of discussion; he told me about his time in the Provisional IRA, his murder conviction, and his time spent in prison during the hunger strikes.

He is a warm, intelligent man. I felt immediately at ease with him, even as he expressed reservations about our meeting: 'Over here you're always suspicious of everyone and everything. Ten years ago it would have been very hard to be having this conversation with you, because I would have been very suspicious. There was a time when I wouldn't talk about my past.'

Callan's past began in the Bogside. As a boy at the time of the Battle of the Bogside he can remember his grandfather placing buckets of water around his house, with wet blankets beside them. He believed that the RUC and loyalists would throw petrol bombs into the house, and the blankets could be used to douse them. It is the sort of precaution that was commonly taken by those who lived through the London Blitz. Callan remembers that one of his aunts, who was a nun living in Twickenham, was staying with the family at the time. In a lull in the fighting Callan's grandfather walked him and his aunt around the Bogside. As they were walking, Callan had his first encounter with CS gas: 'I remember seeing a piles of canisters, in a pyramid shape, stacked together. I lifted one of the canisters and looked at it and I shook it. I could hear stuff inside – the granules of gas – and the next thing I knew, I had red eyes and I was choking. I thought it was funny at the time.'

In 1970 Callan's family moved to the Waterside. At that time his was one of only three or four Catholic families on their street, yet within a short time, after what he calls the 'switchabout', the street was exclusively Catholic. Carol Lynn Toland explained to me how a switchabout might take place: 'My best friend lived on the east bank for the first bit of the Troubles but their house was petrol-bombed and her brothers were beaten up going to school, so they swapped houses with a Protestant family who lived in our street. No money changed hands. They just swapped.'

People were forced out of their homes in Belfast too. I met a Catholic man who described his family's move: 'We were living in the Donegall Pass, it was mixed, and we were forced out. The loyalists came and banged on the door in the early hours, shouting, "All Fenian bastards out! Or we'll burn you out!" Basically we ran out of the house, went to my aunt's, and a couple of days later we were rehoused in the Lower Ormeau Road, where Protestants had been forced out. It happened on both sides, like. Don't get me wrong.'

Travelling around the Waterside area of Derry today, you are never in any doubt whose area you are in, and how comprehensively the switchabout was realized; orange kerbstones turn suddenly to green, as you cross borders unrecognized by the Ordnance Survey. If you carry on to the 'Top of the Hill', you will be confronted by a stunning view of the city and the sweep of the river. It is hard to reconcile this picture with the rage and hatred that once coloured, and still tinges, it.

Adrian Callan describes himself as 100 per cent Irish: 'I've never thought of myself in any other way.' He does not believe, however, that people in the Bogside hate the English: 'If you said that we hate the British government – yes, we do. But there have been so many ties with families moving to work in England, you can't say we hate the English.' An English army officer who served in Northern Ireland during the Nineties told me of the sorts of reactions he used to receive from local people. On an estate in Dungannon one of his soldiers began playing football with a 5-year-old boy. The kickabout didn't last long before a woman came flying out of a house, slapped the boy, and screamed, 'What have I told you about talking to these fucking Brit bastard soldiers?' The same officer remembers the banter sometimes shared between the Brits and known IRA men: 'We were strolling around one evening, and one of the local Provos was leaning out of his window, having a fag. We used to call them by their first names, and one of my lads shouted out, "All right, Brendan?" "All right, fellas?" he shouted back. "Give us a fag, Brendan!" "Aww, fuck off!" "Why? Smoking bad for my health, is it?" "No. Semtex is bad for *your* health." One of my soldiers, quick as a flash, shouted back, "Yeah, but I'm not fucking smoking it, am I?" It was very odd, this kind of mutually acknowledged relationship.'

Adrian Callan believes that a lot of what he became is down to the influence of his fervently republican grandfather. Yet despite this influence, two of Callan's uncles served with the British army. One of them came home on leave during the Battle of the Bogside: 'That was no problem at all, because he was down with the neighbourhood kids he'd grown up with, standing side by side, throwing stones at the RUC, defending the area.' But after the 1972 killing of Ranger William Best, a 19-year-old local boy who had joined the British army, both uncles stayed away. One of them died in 1974, after which Callan's family was visited by an unusually friendly army patrol: 'It was the chaplain from Ebrington Barracks, and he came over and offered his condolences to my granddad, and told him that we were entitled to a military funeral if we wished. My granddad said, "This is Bogside, it will just be a family funeral."' After that the IRA approached Callan's grandfather and told him that whatever type of funeral he chose, the IRA would make sure that there was 'no bother'. Callan's uncle was buried in the city cemetery, a few rows back from the republican plot, without mention of his British military rank.

Callan told me that when he had recently visited his uncle's grave, he had found a poppy placed on it. For a republican the Remembrance Day poppy is an enemy symbol, but Callan explained matter of factly – and poignantly – that another of his uncles had placed it there. He also told me that he had seen the other uncle, who is still 'involved with' the British army, at his mother's recent funeral, and that 'seeing him again was fantastic'.

Before joining the Provisional IRA Callan joined the Fianna Éireann, the IRA's youth branch. He remembers: 'A lot of the youngsters joined at 16. It's hard now to figure what the actual catalyst was. I hadn't lost members of my family to the RUC or the army – but I had been doing a lot of reading, books on the War of Independence and the Famine. I can remember reading my grandfather's book on Tom Barry. I even remember going into the local bookstore with one of my pals and buying Che Guevara's *Guerrilla Warfare*. We were trying to *find out*, and we wanted to *be something*. There was very little else to do. Some of the guys who were in the Fianna Éireann with me have good careers now. One is a professor in the university, another is senior in social services, some went into politics and kept the republican psyche alive – and others became alcoholics and went the other way.' When discussing his motives for joining, he talks about the legacy of the United Irishmen, the Fenians, the rebellions against the first plantations: 'There seems to be a constant need for Ireland to be able to prove itself. We're a young country but we don't need to be divided. We can run ourselves.'

When discussing attitudes in Northern Ireland, Callan returns to a theme I was familiar with from my talk with Patrick Magee. He ponders what would encourage unionists to join an Irish Republic: 'If you look at reunification in political terms, that's where there's a problem. They don't think they can be part of a united Ireland – but if you think of it in pure economic terms, they could tick all the boxes of having harmonized tax laws and so on, north and south, and they probably couldn't come up with a valid argument against it. It comes down to the sense, "I'm not Irish, I'm British."' He may be right, but he has just told me that he is 100 per cent Irish. If the scenario was reversed, and he were unable to come up with a valid economic argument for a united Ireland, it seems unlikely that he would be any more prepared to accept a new unionist identity than unionists are keen to become nationalists.

At 17 years of age Callan and other members of the Fianna Éireann were asked if they wanted to join the IRA. 'Most of us did. Nobody could have told me at 17 that they knew any better than me. I had the invincibility of youth.' In the short time that he was an active member of the IRA, Callan received training in weapons and bomb-making. 'But it was all very rudimentary and the guns were in very short supply. The guns were centrally held in the Bogside – and they were issued as and when. The first weapon I trained on was the Sten submachine gun.'

Middle-level members of the IRA came and talked to the new members. 'They warned us about things we should and shouldn't do. "Don't be going around with tattoos on your arm saying IRA." "If there's a checkpoint, don't talk back to the army." "Don't make yourself known." And at 17 you think there's no way the army or the RUC could know anything about you. But I know now they were watching everything.'

One day Callan and several others were told by the IRA to go to a particular spot in a mixed area. While they were there a car pulled up, and fearing a loyalist ambush, Callan and his group bolted. Callan threw himself under a barbed-wire fence. He was caught, thrown into the car, and taken to a house where he was spread-eagled against a wall and interrogated. At one point he turned round and punched his interrogator, and was told, 'Calm down! It's us! It's us!' He had been captured not by loyalists or by the security forces, but by the IRA, who were staging a practice interrogation. In retrospect Callan wishes that such interrogations had been carried out more frequently. 'It might have made a difference,' he says. An IRA document, found in the possession of the Provisionals' Chief of Staff when he was captured in Dublin in 1977, acknowledges that 'detention orders are breaking Volunteers, and it is the Republican Army's fault for not indoctrinating Volunteers with the psychological strength to resist interrogation'.

Callan was arrested after he had been a member of the IRA for just two months. He claims that he had not yet been involved in an operation: 'Apart from moving guns about, no. At that time I was in charge of the weapons. It was my responsibility to hide them, put them in dumps, and make sure they were safe.' On one occasion he was elsewhere when some weapons came across to the Waterside from the Bogside: 'One of the other lads met them and put them down a manhole. That night he told me where they were, so I went to get them and put them in my house. My family was away on holiday in Donegal.' At six the next morning somebody came to the door. 'Ah Jeez, I thought, that's the army. They searched the entire house, and I thought they weren't going to find them! But one frigging soldier had started searching up the stairs, and I was watching him like a hawk – and he didn't find them. Just as he was coming out, he looked up and found a little shelf … and that was me caught.'

Callan was taken to Strand Road Barracks, where he was interrogated: 'Oh yes, they beat us.' Strand Road was an RUC barracks, the Derry equivalent of Castlereagh; its use reflected the strategy of Ulsterization, which saw the police doing much of the work that had previously been done by the army. Callan says, 'I could stand the beating now without a problem. But at 17, when you don't realize what is going to happen next, and you're on your own …' He recalls what happened: 'At first I was sitting on a chair, facing two RUC interrogators, when the door opened, and the next thing I knew, I was flung off the chair. A detective had come in and smacked me across the head. That was my introduction. After that I was stripped to the waist and stood against a wall with my hands on top of my head. I knew I was going to get beat, and I tensed my muscles, waiting for the moment. I couldn't hold my muscles any more and I relaxed – and bang. Right in the side. And I flew into the corner. Two of them sat on either side of me, and they flexed my wrist back. They knew this wouldn't leave any marks. They yanked out my hair. I can remember the door of the interrogation room open-ing behind me, I had long hair in those days, and I could see almost a tumbleweed of my hair blowing along the ground.'

The detectives were trying to 'persuade' Callan to sign a confession admitting that he had been involved in the recent killing of a police officer. Callan is adamant that he had nothing to do with the killing. At one point the detectives took him to the manhole in the Waterside where he told them the guns had been placed: 'They lifted up the manhole and when two of the Special Branch men were on their knees looking down it, I thought, fuck this! I can run! So I ran like lightning down a school alley, but I was cursing myself up and down, because the pair of shoes I'd put on when the army lifted me was a pair of leather-soled shoes, and not my Dr Marten's. I kept hearing them shout, "Stop or we'll fire!" The next thing I heard a crack, and I ran on, then I heard another crack, and I was judging the distance between myself and the corner, and I was thinking I was never going to make it. When they caught me they took me back to the barracks, where they took my black blazer away, and came back and said, "You were lucky!"' The detectives had found a singe mark on the jacket where one of their bullets had struck a glancing blow. 'Or else,' says Callan, 'they'd just scored something on it, to frighten me.'

The detectives showed Callan photographs of IRA volunteers who had been killed; one of a woman whose own bomb had exploded, another of an informer lying dead in the Creggan with his hands tied behind his back, a third of two IRA men blown to pieces when their bomb was detonated prematurely by the sensor on a supermarket door. 'It was simple. It had a psychological effect on me.' After that the beatings continued. 'The main thing was to get me to sign a statement saying I was involved in the killing by looking after the guns. All they wanted was to get you off the road. None of the guns I was in charge of had been used in that killing; they never actually found the guns that were involved in it. But I signed after two and a half days. That was it. I couldn't take any more. I couldn't face another beating. They were coming and telling me, "We know you did this. We know you were here … We know you were there …" And I just signed. Jesus, it's hard to go back …'

At his trial Callan was tried by a 'Diplock Court'. This was an anti-terrorist criminal court, unique to Northern Ireland, where a single judge sat as the tribunal of fact. The logic behind jury-less courts was that it was difficult to find a jury in Northern Ireland that was both unbiased and free from the prospect of intimidation. In the days before DNA evidence, and in a society where witnesses were often threatened, confessions took on supreme importance in gaining convictions. As a result the common-law rules which stated that a confession must be voluntary were supplanted by an amendment to the Northern Ireland (Emergency Powers) Act, which stated that a confession should only be excluded if evidence was adduced that the accused was subjected to 'torture' or 'inhuman or degrading treatment'. The trial judge in each case had discretion to decide what amounted to inhuman or degrading treatment, and in one ruling Lord Justice McGonigal (the judge at Adrian Callan's trial) held that 'a certain roughness of treatment' such as 'slaps or blows of the hand to the head' would not rule out a confession. According to a 1979 report compiled by Mr Justice Bennett, this meant that police officers might be tempted 'to see how far they can go and what they can get away with'. As one local lawyer admits, 'there were examples of over-enthusiasm on the part of the police'. Another lawyer suggests that such over-enthusiasm was 'understandable'. Understandable or not, it was relatively easy to disguise in the days before the tape recording of interviews. Indeed the RUC fought hard to resist the eventual introduction of tape recording.

The effect of this state of affairs was that interviews which would today be excluded were routinely admitted. Adrian Callan's trial counsel adduced evidence that Callan had been beaten, and brought a medical expert to back up the claims. An RUC detective gave evidence, in rebuttal, that Callan had been within his sight at all times and had received no mistreatment – although he subsequently changed his testimony to say that Callan might have been out of his sight immediately after his arrest, at which time he could have been mistreated by the arresting soldiers. Lord Justice McGonigal decided that Callan might have been hit outside the interrogation room but he was satisfied that he had not been hit during the interrogation itself. Callan was convicted of murder, grievous bodily harm, possession of weapons, and membership of the IRA. As he was under 18, his sentence for murder was detention at the Secretary of State's pleasure.

He was taken to the recently completed Maze Prison, still referred to by republicans by its old name 'Long Kesh', to serve his sentence. By the time he arrived new paramilitary prisoners were no longer being granted special category status. The first IRA prisoner to be sentenced under the new rules was Kieran Nugent, who entered the prison in September 1976. He refused to wear a prison uniform in protest at the loss of special category status, and instead draped himself with the blanket from his cell. So began the 'blanket protest', which would escalate into other, more extreme forms of protest, intended to secure inmates the status of political prisoners. Adrian Callan arrived at the Maze in July 1977: 'I'd just turned 18, and Kieran Fleming [a fellow Derry IRA man who was to drown in 1984 while fleeing from the SAS] and I went "on the blanket" together. The screws give us a prison uniform and I remember looking at Kieran, and being told to wear the uniform, and saying to him, "No. Don't do it!" The two us were then marched round to D Wing, where the prisoners "on the blanket" had seen the minibus coming in. They made such an uproar that you just knew you were in safe hands. If there had been deadly silence you would have been, "Christ, what are we doing?" but the very fact that they were all yelling and cheering and banging the doors, you felt a hell of a lot better. It was amazing – we had a sense of being *right*, and although we'd been sentenced to life imprisonment, it didn't matter. You were there with the rest of your boys and that's what mattered.'

Prisoners "on the blanket" remained locked in their cells for twenty-four hours a day. According to Callan, 'The only time you got out was if you went to Mass on a Sunday morning – other than that you were in your cell. You were allowed to go and wash and shower and then come back to your cell. But that changed and it triggered off a new protest. You had been allowed to walk up the wing in a towel to wash and have a shower. Gradually they adopted the policy of only allowing you out if you were wearing a uniform, and they started bringing two bowls of tepid water into the cell. We refused to use them. Why couldn't we walk five or six yards with a towel around the waist? The instruction came in to destroy the stuff in our cell, one or two chairs, a small wooden table, the metal bedstead. And that's when the "dirty protest" came on.'

The dirty, or 'no wash', protest, as it was more commonly known by republicans, started when prisoners began using chamber pots in their cells. The prison officers would come round each cell with a bin. The prisoners started refusing to fill the bin with the contents of their pots, and a stand-off developed. Eventually the prisoners were ordered by their commanding officer, Brendan Hughes, to cover the walls of their cells with their own waste. 'You can get used to anything,' says Callan. 'There were people taken out to the hospital, and worms were rampant. But apart from worms and diarrhoea, I never got ill. The option was to leave the protest, but I didn't want to "squeaky boot".' A prisoner who came off the protest was known as a 'squeaky booter' because the prison authorities would issue him with new boots, which could be heard squeaking as he walked down the corridor on his way to new and clean accommodation.

The situation in the prison was revealed to a wider public by Cardinal Tomas O'Fiaich, the Catholic Primate of All Ireland, who was shocked at the 'inhuman conditions' in the cells, declaring that 'one would hardly allow an animal to remain in such conditions, let alone a human being'. His words quickly attracted support for the protest from around the Irish diaspora, and raised awareness elsewhere.

One of the problems faced by the prisoners was communication, both with one another and with the outside world. They could shout between cells, often in Irish, or they could pass 'comms' to one another and to visitors to the prison. Comms (an abbreviation of 'communiqués') were messages written in tiny writing on squares of toilet paper or cigarette paper. Callan remembers a number of ways that they could be passed. They could be swung on the end of a pair of prison-issue trousers between windows, they could be pushed through gaps around heating pipes, or forced through a small vulnerable area in each cell wall. They could also be handed to men in other wings during Mass. Visits from those in the outside world were crucial, as not only could comms be passed out of the prison and on to the IRA leadership, but important items such as pens and tiny crystal radios could be smuggled in.

Callan remembers: 'I was once coming back from a visit with smuggled contraband: two Papermate [ballpen] refills and an ounce of tobacco. I'd told my mum to cut off the tops of the refills with pliers, to wrap tobacco around them, and to cover the whole thing with clingfilm. But she'd placed the refills on the outside, which left a jagged edge. I had to insert them up my rectum, and as we were walking back from the visiting block to H5 it was cutting the backside off me. I told the prison officer with me that I had a "parcel" on me. I said that I was going to test him. He said, "You'll be caught!" So I pushed the "parcel" right up, and we walked along side by side. We got to the mirror placed on the ground, and I had to straddle the mirror, while other officers pushed you down, so they could look up to see if anything was there. They couldn't see anything. When we got back to the cell I thanked the officer, and he said, "What you can't see, you can't say." He was a nice man.'

Callan does not remember all the prison officers, or 'screws', with such equanimity, however. A lot of the warders, he says, used to pick on him because he had been convicted of murder. 'I remember coming back from a visit, a half-hour every month with the family. I was in a foul mood because it hadn't been a good visit – and one screw made a remark to me and he tried to trip me up. I stood on his foot and carried on walking. I went to the room where they had all the prison uniforms and I took off the uniform and wrapped the towel round me. I was chatting away to the screws and they were taking me back to the cell, when there was this massive clang as one of the grilles was flung open, and the screw whose foot I'd trodden on came in and he was shouting, "Get him back in there!" So they pushed me back and said, "What have you done to Sammy now?" He come flying in through the door and grabbed me and pushed me up against the locker. He was saying, "Who the hell do you think you are?"

As soon as I felt him coming off me, I flew forward and punched him. I got flung by the hair into the corner and the screws were on me like a shot, taking punches. I got a quick beating and I was dragged out and put in the punishment cells in another part of the Kesh.'

After being taken to the punishment cells Callan was given 'the most methodical beating' he has ever had. 'They were wearing Chelsea boots with dreaded leather soles. They kicked me up and down the ribs and legs, and I was bruised left, right and centre. There were a few other blanket men in the punishment block, and we weren't allowed to speak, but we came up to the door that night, and they said it scared the hell out of them how badly I was being beaten. Next morning the screws in charge of the punishment wing came back in and I could hear them going round the cells, opening the doors and saying, "Were you talking last night?" The guys were saying yes, because they were so afraid of saying no. All I could hear was the thump of punches in the guts. Bang. And they came round to me, and all this screw said was, "I'm surprised at you!" That was it. I couldn't understand why he didn't punch me.'

Yet for all the filth, the rough treatment, and the monotony, Callan's memories are not all negative. One of his cell mates was Laurence McKeown, a man who would later spend seventy days on hunger strike. Callan recalls: 'There was so much fun I had in the cell with "Lorny". There we was, stuck in a small cell, 24 hours a day, it's got shit on the walls and shit on the ceiling, and we'd sit and talk about how we're going to go on a motorbike to the south of France, all over Europe, how we'd do this and that. Other times we'd have serious discussions about where the whole blanket protest was going – what could we do?'

At the beginning of 1980 the prisoners set out 'Five Demands' which explained what they meant by 'political status'. They were:

1. The right not to wear a prison uniform.
2. The right not to do prison work.

3. The right of free association with other prisoners, and to organize educational and recreational pursuits.

4. The right to one visit, one letter, and one parcel a week.

5. The full restoration of remission lost through the protest.

These demands were expressed in dispassionate language, in an attempt to play down the protest's political nature and play up its civil liberties aspect. Further demands regarding the reform of the Diplock Court system and the rules relating to evidence were considered but discarded.

Initially the British government announced that it would cede the first demand. But the government's offer to allow the wearing of 'civilian type' clothing would not satisfy the prisoners who insisted on the right to wear their own clothes. Both sides stood entrenched in what was to become a struggle of principle. At the head of the British government was Margaret Thatcher, the 'Iron Lady', renowned for holding her ground on matters of principle. A bitter stand-off loomed, particularly as the prisoners were about to raise the stakes by announcing a hunger strike. No act suggests greater adherence to principle than dying slowly through an act of self-denial.

The hunger strike has a long tradition in Ireland. It was a pre-Christian custom that a victim of a debt or injustice could fast outside the house of the wrongdoer, in order to induce a settlement. If the faster died, the wrongdoer would be held responsible for his death. The self-sacrifice of the hunger strike chimed with Catholic ideas of the redemptive power of abstinence: St Patrick himself is supposed to have staged a hunger strike against God – and won. So far as the IRA was concerned, such redemptive power might publicly legitimize the actions of men who had killed in the name of a cause. If those men were seen to be willing to die for their cause, then the cause would be greatly strengthened. If, however, they were not willing to die, the cause would be weakened. A hunger strike could only be effective if the strikers were willing to see it through to the death. The scene was set for a dark battle of wills.

The pressure for a hunger strike came from the prisoners themselves. The IRA leadership was not initially in favour, nervous that, should it fail, the IRA would be irreversibly damaged. But the determination of the prisoners to go ahead was such that the leadership was forced to give its consent. A start date in October was chosen so that the critical period of failing health would fall over Christmas. This, it was felt, would give the strike an emotional edge. Seven men, including one member of the INLA, began fasting simultaneously. They were led by Brendan 'The Dark' Hughes. One of these men was Tommy McKearney, who explained to Bobbie Hanvey that 'the prison leadership asked for volunteers. I submitted my name, and then about three to four weeks before the actual event, I was told that I had been selected'.

McKearney did not consult his family about embarking on the fast; he merely informed them that he had decided to do it. He felt that: 'The major battle was to retain the steely firm resolve to see the hunger strike through, rather than think about how precious life is. But the thing that struck me most was that it would have been easy to die if it hadn't been so physically painful. I was actually more concerned about the pain of dying than the passing away.' McKearney was not a religious man: 'I was convinced that there was nothing there to meet, that death is the end, but having said that, others of my colleagues believed passionately that they would meet with their God.'

As the weeks went by, McKearney became weaker but he did not lose hope that the issue would be politically resolved: 'You have to keep in mind that our hunger strike wasn't by any means a suicide pact. The battle always continued, and under those circumstances, I don't believe that any of us ever gave up hope. There was always a lingering belief that victory may be achieved at the very last. But in physical terms, I felt the major deterioration in my health came after forty-five days. Up to the forty-fifth day, I was able to move about. I could walk to the toilet the few times that I would go, and put on my dressing gown and slippers. But on the forty-fifth day, I fainted. I was unable, thereafter, to leave the bed on my own, and within hours, my eyesight deteriorated rapidly. I went blind in one eye, I lost control over the optic motor nerve in the other eye, and the internal organs started to deteriorate quite rapidly. By the fiftieth day, I was in a state of flux, drifting in and out of coma. And I remember hearing – or I thought I heard – incessant ceilidh music. It was only after the hunger strike was over that I was told that it was a hallucination …'

McKearney remembers being well treated in the prison hospital: 'I'm not a soft liner on prison authorities, but in this circumstance, I have to be honest and say that we were treated humanely, decently and on several occasions very kindly by the prison medics.' At the point when the hunger strike was called off, on its fifty-third day, McKearney was not informed for an hour and a half. Isolated in his hospital ward, he at first refused medical treatment, 'so they then sent for the man in charge, Brendan Hughes, and Brendan come over and said to me, "It's over, take whatever help you can!"'

One man, a member of a hunger striker's family, remembers that his relative had lodged an appeal against his sentence before the hunger strike began. 'That would allow us a fifteen-minute visit every day with him,' he told me, 'but it also meant that *we were only allowed to talk about the appeal.*' So the two men communicated in code: 'For example, I would ask him whether his barrister had been in touch, and that would mean, "Have the Brits been in touch?" Or if I wanted to know if the Catholic church had been in touch, I would ask, "Was your solicitor in?" But on one day, I was searched and warned, as usual, that I could only talk about the appeal, and then the cell door opened, and he was in bed with bed sores, he was very physically weak, and I made a mistake. Where we come from, we wouldn't normally say, "Hello", we would say, "How are you doing?", and I walked into the cell, and I said, "How are you doing?" And the screw says, "Visit over!" I said, "What?" and he said, "Get the fuck out!"'

The same man told me how the hunger strike was called off: 'On 18 December an agreement was reached. A document was drawn up allowing prisoners to wear their own clothes, allowing education to become prison work, and we were telling them to call it off as soon as the document arrived in prison. The next day one of the hunger strikers, Sean McKenna, collapsed into a coma. They argued it out among themselves, and they ended it, and saved Sean's life.'

The document came about as a result of the secret link between the British government and the IRA, that had last been used during the 1975 IRA truce. Brendan Duddy, the Derry businessman codenamed the 'Mountain Climber' by the IRA, telephoned his usual contact in the British secret services, Michael Oatley, and they spoke at length about how the situation might be resolved. Oatley drew up the document, which he then brought to Belfast with government clearance. It was taken to an IRA safe house in west Belfast, where it was scrutinized and found to be vague. In the meantime Sean McKenna lay at the point of death, and the IRA prison leadership, believing that the document would grant them the substance of their five demands, called off the hunger strike.

Sinn Féin subsequently put out a statement declaring, 'We are satisfied that the implementation of these proposals meets the requirements of our five basic demands', but within the prison Bobby Sands, who had succeeded Brendan Hughes as the IRA commanding officer after the first hunger strike, was sceptical as to whether the document would form an agreement, now that the prisoners had lost their bargaining power by ending the strike. According to Brendan Duddy, however, the document could have worked. He told me, 'The Provisionals made serious efforts – they ordered Bobby Sands to work the agreement. And I was working with an excellent person in the Northern Ireland

Office who was doing everything within *his* power. But among the prison authorities there was a belief that the prisoners deserved no hearing. So the prisoners' own clothes were brought in, but then after three, four, five days nothing had happened.'

In effect the prison authorities failed to implement an already vague document, and a second hunger strike was immediately planned. The external IRA leadership was still not in favour, but once again it had to give its consent. This time, however, the hunger strikers, a combination of IRA and INLA men, would start their fasts at staggered intervals, beginning with Bobby Sands on 1 March 1981, the fifth anniversary of the ending of special category status.

Sands has, not unnaturally, come to polarize opinion down the years. Of all of the republicans who died during the Troubles, he has achieved the most revered status among sympathizers. He is venerated by republicans, respected by nationalists, and often vilified by opponents. He has streets named after him in France, and memorials to him in the United States, Cuba, and Iran. Margaret Thatcher declared his death to be suicide, while Glasgow Rangers supporters chant, 'Could you go a chicken supper, Bobby Sands?'

The man seems sometimes to become lost in the haze of legend. One purportedly serious biography claims to record his childhood: 'In those long summer days of youth, all nature began to open up to him, the soft sunshine falling on the earth, the clear blue sky, the long green grass, the trees and hedges alive with the hue of flowers, the humming of bees, and the music of birds.' Are you *sure*? I spoke to an acquaintance of Sands, who spoke of him as 'a very intelligent, articulate human being, very full of life, and politically aware. He knew the chance that he was taking [by leading the second hunger strike], but he was always optimistic of achieving success up until the end.'

Sands was born in north Belfast, in a predominantly Protestant area, from which his parents moved when it was discovered locally that they were Catholics. They went to another Protestant area, where they experienced similar difficulties; Sands's sister Bernadette remembers a hostile unionist neighbour standing outside their house, unashamedly offering it to a newly married Protestant couple. Shortly afterwards, she recalls, the family were intimidated: 'A rubbish bin was put through the living room window, stones were thrown, and there was a couple of shots fired. My mother went down to the Housing Executive the next morning and told them that we'd have to get out there and then.' Days later, she says, Bobby was waiting for the removal lorry to arrive, when the same neighbour came over to him and said, 'Get your furniture out! I've a young couple to go into that house!'

After leaving school Sands began work at a local coach building firm. He was twice convicted of possession of firearms. His first spell in prison, between 1973 and 1976, found him sharing a cage with Gerry Adams and experiencing the political education remembered by Patrick Magee. His second spell, beginning in 1977, followed the bombing of a furniture showroom. He joined the blanket protest and went on to become the prisoners' public relations officer. As an avid reader and a spirited poet, he was a logical choice for the role. He wrote frequent articles for *Republican News* while in prison, using the *nom de plume* Marcella, the name of another sister. He wrote the lyrics to 'Back Home in Derry', a song made famous by singer Christy Moore. And he set down the dirty protest in comic verse:

> *To dance and prance to love's romance*
> *Is elegant and neat.*
> *To wine and dine on red port wine*
> *Is such a tasty treat.*
> *To eat and sit where you've just shit*
> *Is not so bloody sweet.*

As the second hunger strike was about to begin, Sands was visited by Father Denis Faul, a Dungannon priest who came regularly to the prison to say Mass. Father Faul was a critic of both the prison authorities and the IRA, and he attempted to dissuade Sands from his course of action. It was now clear that the hunger strike, if embarked upon, would have to be carried through to a definite conclusion: the five demands, or death. The conversation between the prisoner and the priest ended when Sands quoted, 'Greater love hath no man than this, that a man lay down his life for his friends.' Struck by Sands's determination, Faul decided against further discussion.

Adrian Callan tells me that he considered joining the hunger strike, 'but I didn't think I could do it. It's a phenomenal thing to be asked to do.' He says that anybody who wanted to join the protest was asked to contact the officer commanding his wing: 'You would be asked whether you realized the consequences of what you were doing. That you might die. I was amazed at how many men were prepared to put their names down.' He remembers a man with whom he shared a cell who wanted to join the strike: 'I immediately wrote a comm to our commanding officer, saying that you can't put his name forward – he's suffering serious mental problems.' Every day Callan would watch as this man walked up and down their tiny cell, before stopping in the corner to argue and throw punches at an imaginary being. He would also throw a blanket over his own head and start talking to himself in different accents.

One day the cell mate attacked Callan: 'We started fighting, and the other prisoners were shouting to me, "Are you all right?" because I was a skinny runt. But I had got him down on the ground and got his head on the concrete floor, and I said, "I'm going to let you up now, but don't try anything – or I'll hit you." I eased off him, but as I did, he went to have a go, and I put his head down and I punched him four or five times. It was the emotion and frustration coming out of me. I lay off him then and he got up – and he never made a move towards me. I felt relief that I'd finally got it all out of me. But I felt disgust at myself too.'

After their fight the man's worrying behaviour continued: 'He told me one morning that Michael Collins had appeared to him, and told him that the key to the war in the north lay along the border. "All right," I said. 'No problem.' Later that day he got up and pushed the emergency buzzer in the cell. I said, "What's wrong?" and he said, "I need to see a medical officer!" I didn't see him again until I got out of jail. They took him to the hospital wing, and for the next couple of years they kept him sedated. Then he was transferred down to Magilligan Jail, where I was told he would sit alone in the canteen on a plastic chair, rocking backwards and forwards until the chair broke. He went through years of hell. But I've seen him since, and he's right as rain now. I've not spoken to him about it, though – I couldn't. It's probably something that he wouldn't want to be reminded of.'

Two weeks after Bobby Sands began the second round of hunger strikes, he was joined by Francis Hughes. Adrian Callan was a couple of cells away from Hughes at the time: 'We were sitting there with our food in front of us, thinking, how can we eat this, with him next door? and Frank comes up to his cell door, and he starts calling us all bastards, saying, "You're all sitting there, eating! Here am I, starving with hunger!" And what he done, he broke the atmosphere; he took the bad feeling away. It was an unbelievable thing to do.'

Whatever the mood inside the prison, on the outside it appeared as though the second hunger strike would receive less attention than the first. The British government seemed to have outwitted the republican movement. In the House of Commons the Northern Ireland Secretary, Humphrey Atkins, was urged not to refer to events in the Maze, in the hope that they would fade into obscurity. But on 5 March the Independent republican member of Parliament for Fermanagh-South Tyrone, Frank Maguire, died. A chain of events was set in motion which would give the hunger strikers, and the IRA, more publicity than they or the British government could have believed possible. The first link in the chain was the proposal that Bobby Sands should stand as a candidate in the by-election to replace Maguire.

At first other republican and nationalist candidates put themselves forward to contest the seat, but they all agreed to step aside to leave a direct contest between Sands and the Ulster Unionist Party candidate, Harry West. West had been such a fierce critic of Terence O'Neill's reforms that in 1967 he had been sacked from the cabinet. O'Neill later wrote, 'So long as Ulster was cosy and unreformed, Harry was well suited to office.' West, an archconservative keen to preserve untrammelled unionist power, was about to engage in an unthinkable political fight with a member of the IRA.

In the meantime a republican campaign had been mounted to disrupt the 1981 United Kingdom census, by encouraging supporters to destroy their census forms. Joanne Mathers was a 29-year-old Protestant woman who had taken a part-time job with the census, going from house to house collecting forms. As she arrived at a door in a Catholic area of the Waterside in Derry she was shot in the head by a masked gunman. The IRA and the INLA both denied responsibility for the killing; the IRA's Derry brigade issued a statement alleging that Mathers had been killed by people 'frantically attempting to discredit the election campaign of hunger striker Bobby Sands'. It is certainly difficult to understand how the murder of a young woman, at such a delicate time, could have assisted the republican cause. Yet the RUC alleged that the gun used to kill Mathers was traceable to two IRA punishment shootings. Whether this killing was carried out by the IRA or not, it acted as a reminder to the Fermanagh electorate, and to the watching world, of the activities for which the organization was known.

When the result of the election was announced, Adrian Callan heard it inside the prison on a radio that had been smuggled in.

He remembers: 'This young guy across the wing from me was in charge of the radio, a little crystal set they had made outside. Sean whispered to me, "When they read the news, don't be shouting! Don't be making a lot of noise!" But when they announced on the BBC that Bobby had been elected, Sean got up and he whispered in Irish, "Bobby won!" There was two or three seconds' quiet – then everyone was cheering and banging. There was a fantastic sense of elation. The jubilation went round the whole H block. There was an uproar.'

Sands had received 30,942 votes to West's 29,046. Sands was now a member of Parliament. Many years later Bobbie Hanvey asked Harry West about his reaction to the result. West told him, 'It was something that disappointed me very much. It destroyed the confidence that I had in the nationalist people that I regarded as my friends, because Bobby Sands at that stage had been convicted as a felon. I didn't expect them to vote for me, but I expected them to at least abstain from voting. But to my surprise, and to my disappointment, those people, almost to a man, voted for him.' With regard to the hunger strikes, West told Hanvey, 'It's a pity it happened, but if these people decide to take their own lives, there's nothing much we can do about.'

In Long Kesh, Adrian Callan and the his fellow IRA men were convinced that the fasts could now come to an end: 'We thought instantly, that's it! It's finished now! We thought there was no way Bobby could die in this prison. There was no way the British government could let it happen. It was a fantastic feeling.' But less than a month later their elation was confounded when Bobby Sands died on the sixty-sixth day of his hunger strike. Margaret Thatcher was apparently not for turning. In the aftermath of his death she told the House of Commons, 'Mr Sands was a convicted criminal. He chose to take his own life. It was a choice his organization did not allow to many of its victims.' Adrian Callan is spare in his description of the mood in his H block: 'The devastation. It was total.'

Once Sands had died, three other hunger strikers, Francis Hughes, Raymond McCreesh, and Patsy O'Hara, died within the next fortnight. Patsy O'Hara was the first man to die from Derry; a British officer stationed there recalls that on the night he died large crowds came down from the Bogside and the Creggan and attacked shops in the centre of the city. The officer's platoon base came under attack from a mob with petrol bombs. At one stage it seemed to the officer as though the crowd would force its way into the base.

Just as internment and Bloody Sunday had before, the hunger strikes radicalized Catholics in Northern Ireland, bringing support from nationalists who would otherwise have had had little time for republicanism. But as some were hardening their attitudes, so others were being convinced of the need to compromise their principles. The joint military and political strategy conceived by Gerry Adams and his colleagues in the cages of Long Kesh, and articulated by Danny Morrison in his 'Armalite and ballot box' speech, was boosted immeasurably by Sands's election success. In the H blocks, Adrian Callan was encountering this new way of thinking: 'It was laid on the line – the difference between being a pragmatist and the dogmatic approach. The dogmatic approach is for a united Ireland or nothing. The pragmatic approach, and this is what we were told in some of the discussions we had in jail at this time, was that you can move about an object. If you've got a wall in front of you that's blocking you from where you want to be, what's the point in battering your head against it? You find alternative ways to get around the wall. There's many paths to the one goal.' The hunger strikes were fuelling the political strategy that would ultimately lead to the signing of the Good Friday Agreement. Callan says, 'If you look at the modern republican movement, if you look at the Sinn Féiners who are up in Stormont now, many have been through Long Kesh, and they were shaped by the political discussions that took place there. And we have ministers there, now, who have taken the Queen's shilling. Is that what Bobby Sands and the others died for? No, it's not. They died for something better. But we hope that what we have now will take us forward – on a path that won't cause as much loss of life. I think this is the only way it could have happened.'

In June other prisoners had begun joining the protest, replacing the four dead men. In a general election held in the Irish Republic, two prisoners, one of them a hunger striker, won seats in Parliament. And a further by-election was scheduled in Fermanagh-South Tyrone to elect a replacement for Bobby Sands; Owen Carron, who had previously acted as Sands's election agent was nominated to stand as his successor. In the meantime moves were being made to mediate between the British government and the IRA, in the hope of ending the hunger strikes. These moves were taking place at two distinct levels, one public, the other secret. Publicly a Dublin-based body, the Irish Commission for Justice and Peace, was negotiating with the Northern Ireland Office. Secretly Brendan Duddy was once again speaking by telephone to a London contact, and then in person to the IRA. On 4 July the prisoners made a considerable concession and announced that they would accept the introduction of the Five Demands for *all* prisoners; in other words, by not demanding to be distinguished from 'ordinary' prisoners, they were no longer insisting on political status. But the commonly held understanding of what happened next has been thrown into doubt by recent allegations.

The previously understood version of events was that the British government made an extremely vague approach to end the protest. Brendan 'Bik' McFarlane was now the IRA's commanding officer in the prison and Richard O'Rawe was his public relations officer. McFarlane wrote a comm to Gerry Adams saying that 'more clarification and confirmation was needed to establish exactly what the Brits were on about'. An official from the Northern Ireland Office then agreed to come to the prison to clarify the situation, but he did not arrive, and Joe McDonnell passed away, the fifth hunger striker to die. In the wake of McDonnell's death an effort was made to renew the secret contact, but the initiative fell away as the IRA prison leadership rejected the British approach. They considered it a vague proposal, similar to that which ended the first hunger strike, and to accept it would be an affront to the memory of the men who had already died.

However, on 23 May 2009 I attended a meeting in a converted gas yard in the Bogside at which this version of events was contested by some of those involved. The speakers at this meeting were Richard O'Rawe, Gerard Hodgkins (an ex-hunger striker), Willie Gallagher (of the Irish Republican Socialist Party), Liam Clarke (of the *Sunday Times*), and Brendan Duddy. Gerry Adams and Danny Morrison had been invited to take part, but they did attend. I had already spoken to Brendan Duddy at his home, where he had said, in reference to the second hunger strike: 'Basically, everything that sorted it out was on the table … This thing could have been sorted …'

His meaning became clearer as I listened to the speakers, and to the comments from members of the large audience, crammed into a strange, spherical room as high as it was wide. People had come from Belfast and elsewhere to be present. There was a nervous mood in the room, with families of deceased hunger strikers present, but it occasionally became aggressive, as those who had lived through the period struggled to make sense of the disturbing nature of what they were hearing.

The basic facts were set out by Willie Gallagher. He said that Bik McFarlane and Richard O'Rawe, on behalf of the IRA prison leadership, had accepted a British offer made on 5 July 1981 which, in effect, conceded four of their five demands. This offer had come initially from Brendan Duddy's contact. O'Rawe studied the offer for some time before calling to McFarlane in the next cell, saying it should be accepted. McFarlane agreed and called back, saying that he would send a comm to that effect to the external leadership. The following day a comm was received in the prison stating that the external leadership had rejected the offer. The prisoners' acceptance was never transmitted to the British.

After Gallagher's précis Gerard Hopkins spoke. He declared that while he supported the peace process, the truth about the past, and about this issue, had to come out. Then Brendan Duddy confirmed that he had delivered an offer from the British government. His previous words to me, 'This thing could have been sorted', now made sense. Liam Clarke spoke next. 'These were good terms,' he said. 'The question is whether they were discussed by Richard O'Rawe and Bik McFarlane.' Richard O'Rawe answered his question straight away: he confirmed that he and Bik McFarlane had accepted the offer. He ran through the elements of the offer and asked a grimly rhetorical question: 'How could we play brinkmanship with our comrades' lives? Joe McDonnell was within days of death. It would have been insanity not to take this offer.'

After this a member of the audience, an ex-IRA man, Gerard Clarke, stood up and corroborated Richard O'Rawe's version of events. He had been in a cell beside O'Rawe and McFarlane, and he had listened to their shouted conversation. He had, he said, kept quiet for years, but he was now confirming that Bik McFarlane had accepted the deal. He stated that, as a blanket man, he felt that the British offer had been 'enough for a deal', and he wondered why the deal had not been accepted by those on the outside. Brendan Duddy added that the offer was genuine, but 'whether it would ultimately been carried through – who knows?' Somebody then observed to tumultuous applause, 'Anybody who trusts the Brits needs their heads examined!' As the applause turned to cheers I squirmed slightly in my seat. I made a promise to myself that I would not open my mouth, or emit any Brit-sounding noise while in the room.

A while later, away from the room, I spoke to Richard O'Rawe. I put it to him that the offer made by the British government did not actually amount to acceptance of 'four of the five demands' as Willie Gallagher had stated. What it actually proposed was the wearing of the prisoners' own clothes, the restoration of letter, parcel, and visiting privileges, the restoration of a fifth of lost remission, the concession that education and domestic tasks (cleaning, washing, and cooking) could constitute prison work, and the possibility of segregation – but not of free association. O'Rawe agrees: 'I don't accept that this was equal to four demands. People seeing it that way are being extravagant. But it was sufficient. Once we had our own clothes, we could have stood up and said, "We've defeated criminalization!" The rest of the stuff could have been granted at the discretion of the governor.' For O'Rawe the bottom line was that he and McFarlane – the prison leadership – had accepted a solid offer, the outside leadership had rejected it, and the hunger strikers were never informed. From then on the hunger strikers were no longer in control of their own destinies.

What became clear from listening to the speakers and the audience members at the meeting was that these allegations were not intended to discredit republicanism or to destabilize the peace process; they were intended to expose the fact that the lives of six hunger strikers could have been saved. O'Rawe is strongly in favour of the peace process and he does not believe that dissidents would be in a position to take advantage of the allegations. 'If they tried,' he says, 'I wouldn't let them!' Yet while the search for truth surrounding the hunger strikes might be a worthwhile quest, past truths in Northern Ireland can sometimes threaten to jeopardize the present. I asked O'Rawe whether he would agree that the best way forward might be to cast a veil over the past: 'The people who say that are those with something to hide. On the big issues that shaped the war, and that now shape the peace, like the hunger strikes, the important thing is that the truth is recorded.'

O'Rawe's allegations have not gone unchallenged. They have been denied by Bik McFarlane. In a 2005 interview he was adamant that there had been no offer from the British and that the conversation referred to by O'Rawe never took place. But in an interview conducted four years later he remembered a conversation with O'Rawe about an offer, in which he said, 'This is amazing, this is a huge opportunity, and I feel there is potential here.' In June 2009 McFarlane, Gerry Adams, and Danny Morrison met with relatives of the hunger strikers. At the meeting it was announced that the British 'had made no deal with the hunger strikers or their representatives in 1981'. This statement is undeniably true – but it does not reject the possibility that the British *made an offer*, or that the prison leadership accepted that offer. A statement was subsequently issued on behalf of the families declaring that 'Our loved ones made the supreme sacrifice on hunger strike for their comrades. They were not dupes. They were dedicated and committed republicans. We are clear that it was the British government which refused to negotiate and refused to concede their just demands.'

However, two letters recently made available under the Freedom of Information Act suggest that the British government *did* make efforts to end the hunger strike. In the first letter, sent from 10 Downing Street to the Northern Ireland Office on 8 July, it is recorded that Margaret Thatcher had met Humphrey Atkins to 'discuss the latest developments in the efforts to bring the hunger strike … to an end'. The letter states that a message, approved by Thatcher, had been sent to the IRA, but that the message had not been regarded as satisfactory by the IRA, owing to its 'tone' rather than its 'content'. As a result a draft statement had been sent to the IRA 'enlarging upon the message'. In the second document, a letter sent ten days later from Downing Street to the Northern Ireland Office, it is recorded that the IRA had asked that a British official go to the prison to meet the hunger strikers.

These letters support the contention that an offer of substance was communicated to the IRA. Perhaps Margaret Thatcher *was* for turning. I asked O'Rawe why he believes the offer was rejected by the external leadership. He gives me two possible explanations. The first is straightforward: the leadership believed that the British could improve on the offer. The second is more controversial. Owen Carron's election in Fermanagh-South Tyrone was crucial to the future of the movement. It promised to pave the way for Sinn Féin's political expansion, and the eventual eradication of the armed struggle. It was therefore important to maintain the hunger strike, and the support it engendered, until the election was won. Once victory had been achieved the militants in the IRA would be unable to resist the onslaught of electoralism.

The corollary of this is that if one accepts that the Good Friday Agreement was made possible by the republican shift from violence to electoral politics, then the current peace can be traced back to the rejection of the offer and the subsequent deaths of six hunger strikers.

I asked O'Rawe why he had not raised his concerns with those around him at the time. 'It's hard to explain to an outsider what it was like. In the IRA we were trained in a Teutonic manner. You did what you were ordered to do. I was convinced that Adams was speaking on behalf of the Army Council, and once they had rejected the offer I was comfortable that they were attempting to get an agreement.'

In the end the hunger strikes were broken – *after* Carron's victory in the by-election – by clerical pressure. Father Denis Faul, the priest who had sat with Bobby Sands discussing his actions, brought the families of the remaining hunger strikers together on 28 July. He told them that the IRA had the power to call off the strike and that pressure ought to be brought to bear on Gerry Adams. The families set off for Belfast to meet with Adams. The next morning Adams telephoned Father Faul, telling him that he would speak with the hunger strikers to pass on the families' concerns. Once at the prison he met eight of the ten hunger strikers. Two others, Kevin Lynch and Kieran

Doherty, were too weak to be present. After a discussion the hunger strikers chose to continue their fasts, but shortly afterwards the mother of Paddy Quinn, who had been without food for forty-seven days, brought him off the strike. He had been having fits and his mother was told by the prison doctor that his chances of survival were 50/50, if he received immediate treatment. She authorized the doctor to save her son and Quinn was rushed to the Royal Victoria Hospital, where he was placed on a drip. He is alive today.

Over the following weeks hunger strikers continued to die, while others joined the protest. Father Faul carried on meeting family members; five strikers were taken off the protest after the families intervened. At the time Richard O'Rawe believed that Father Faul was undermining his comrade's struggle. He drafted a statement on behalf of the prisoners that described Father Faul as a 'treacherous, conniving man'. But he came to review his opinion: 'Looking back, Father Faul was much maligned. We had very fixed ideas. Before he died [in 2005] I apologized to him in person. And he was magnanimous.' Adrian Callan echoes O'Rawe's sentiments: 'Father Faul got criticized very heavily for his intervention in the second hunger strike. I can say now, thank God he did intervene, because if he hadn't, Laurence McKeown, and God knows how many other hunger strikers, would have died. Men are alive now who can contribute more to the peace process through being alive than through being six feet under.' Shortly after Callan's release from prison in 1987, he saw Father Faul in the street. 'I walked straight past him because I was so angry with what he had done. But now I can look back with hindsight, and say thank God another mother didn't have to go through what so many did.'

On 3 October 1981, once the families of nearly all of the remaining hunger strikers had expressed their intention to save their relatives, and once the new Secretary of State, the ambitious Tory 'wet' James Prior, had spoken publicly of 'prison reform', the hunger strikes were called off. According to O'Rawe, a comm arrived in the prison from 'the Big Lad' (Gerry Adams) saying that he would end it. 'Two days later,' remembers O'Rawe, 'we had our own clothes.' Adrian Callan recalls: 'I wrote a letter to my mother, telling her what clothes I wanted brought up, and when I got them, they were all the style that we had in 1976. We were allowed outside into the exercise yard to walk around, but we all had to take our shoes off, because they were cutting our feet up. For four and a half years we'd been in our bare feet, and we couldn't handle a pair of shoes.'

Other concessions were quickly granted concerning remission, visits, letters, and parcels, and freedom of association. But, says O'Rawe, 'These concessions were watered down. They weren't the original offer [the offer that O'Rawe had accepted] made flesh. Education and segregation were not implemented.' Nevertheless, within a few years, and in the wake of a mass escape of IRA men (including Brendan McFarlane) from the prison, republican and loyalist prisoners were both being left to run their own wings, as they had done in the days of the cages. Not only did prisoners eventually receive their five demands, but the hunger strikes brought renewed support for the IRA. Yet they also fuelled the rise of the political movement that would ultimately overshadow the armed struggle, and enable the peace process. Republicanism was changed at many levels by the events of 1981 in Long Kesh.

Adrian Callan returned home to Derry for Christmas 1986 as part of a pre-release scheme. He told his mother that he was coming home during a visit, and he remembers her 'trembling like a bird'. As he got out of the car and walked along the street to his parents' house he received a shock: 'For ten years, I'd been walking on flat ground, and the street was on a slight slope. As I took those first steps, I thought, what the hell? I just wasn't used to walking down a slope.' A party had been organized for him, 'with people coming from everywhere'. When the time came to return to prison he tried to control his emotions, but as he climbed into the car with his parents 'everything went and the floodgates opened, and I just cried and cried'. When he arrived back at the prison he wrote an account of his experience and it was passed around the inmates: 'I was trying to give them an idea of what was ahead of them when they were released.'

When he was finally released for good Callan was given 'a bit of trouble' by the local RUC: 'A few of them pulled me out of a car and threatened to shoot me.' He never had a similar problem with the army, he says. He also faced problems coming to terms with ordinary civilian life: 'Believe you me, the opposite sex was one of the hardest things. It was down to age. I went into jail at 17, and I wasn't widely experienced. But coming out at 28 … On my second night out I was taken to a nightclub in the town. My brother-in-law was pushing me to talk to these girls, who said, "Come on ahead!" but, Jesus Christ, I didn't know what to say! I still had the mannerisms and expectations of a 17-year-old. I didn't know what age I was! But I came up to speed, and then I met my wife …'

Today Callan is a family man with children. He is making efforts to bring them up to be open-minded: 'I really think the only hope is to teach them to break down the barriers, that's where the future will come from. It's too late for us, but not for them.' But no matter how hard he tries, he accepts that negative influences are all around: 'My wee boy, if you walk into his bedroom now, it's like an IRA arms dump; there's guns everywhere. The teachers at school say he's got an amazing knowledge of the Second World War, and I don't know where he's getting it from. There was the influence my uncles had on me, and there's a bit of me in there somewhere.' Callan is heartened that nowadays, in Derry city centre, he sees girls in Thornhill College [a Catholic school] uniforms walking with girls in Foyle and Londonderry College [a Protestant school] uniforms. 'It wouldn't have happened twenty years ago.' But he believes that 'identifiable tags like names and school uniforms are the things that have to be dealt with if we are going to get people mixing'.

Callan finishes by telling me of two experiences that he had while abroad. On both occasions he and his wife met couples from Northern Ireland. On one occasion a Catholic bar owner decided that Callan must have been a policeman. 'You don't know how wrong you are!' Callan told him. The other occasion was on his honeymoon: 'We were chatting with this couple, and having a great time. I said to the husband, "What do you work at yourself?" He said, "I'm a prison officer." I said, "That must be a good job." He said, 'You have to be very careful who you talk to." So I turned to my wife, and said, "He's a screw!" She said, "Don't be doing anything!" I never let on, and by the end of the night we had our arms round each other, having our photographs taken.'

A while after I had spoken to Callan I thought about this last story. It was funny, but it was also sad, and it tallied with my impression of Northern Ireland as a place full of like-minded people who can only appreciate one another on a terrace in the Canary Islands. I decided that having spoken to Adrian Callan and Richard O'Rawe, I would meet a man whose experiences covered the same ground, but from a completely different vantage point: a prison officer.

I drove to Belfast to meet William McKee, who had been a governor of the Maze Prison. The prison did not have a single governor; it had many, in charge of different departments or areas. By the time he left the Maze, McKee was Governor IV, in charge of inmate services. I had met prison warders during my previous life as a lawyer. I had been into prisons across England, and spent many hours in court cells, chatting to pleasant enough men and women with large bunches of keys dangling from their waists. I think I expected Northern Ireland prison officers to be more dread-inspiring than those I had met in England. A ridiculous assumption, of course, but within five minutes of meeting

William McKee such a lazy notion was blown away. McKee is a sensitive man, nervous almost, touchingly eager to please, with a sadness about him. He is very easy to like.

McKee is from a working-class Protestant background. He was raised just outside Killyleagh by his father, a part-time farmer and bus driver, his mother having died when he was 12. He describes himself as a late developer; he failed his eleven-plus and suffered from a stammer that would sometimes leave him speechless. But he overcame his insecurities and received 'solid Presbyterian values' from his father: 'He was always preaching about being decent and honest. Those values helped me in my career, especially in dealing with the paramilitaries – just be honest with them. Don't tell lies.'

Before becoming a prison officer he worked briefly in the Harland and Wolff shipyard and then in a factory in Down-patrick that was '99 per cent Catholic'. The factory made belts and braces – and webbing for the British army. He left the factory, where he was earning £35 a week, to join the prison serv-ice, where he started on £80 a week. On his leaving, the factory girls clubbed together to buy him a St Christopher medal. They were worried for him in his new job, and hoped that St Christo-pher would protect him. 'Who's to say that's not the reason I'm still here today?' he asks. The poignancy of this aside escaped me so early in our conversation.

He began at Crumlin Road jail in Belfast in 1977. 'Prison offi-cers were being murdered. I would sometimes think, what on earth possessed me to join an organization that was losing members to the IRA? but I decided to stick it out. £80 was the tip of the financial iceberg. With the extra hours I ended up with £100 in my hand. You bought a flash car, a nice house, the craic was mighty, as they say in Ireland.' I asked him whether the job attracted a good standard of people. 'A mixture of people, as in any walk of life. But if you could walk and talk, you couldn't really fail to get the job. They were so keen to get people in and keep them.' In his opinion the major problem was a lack of recruits with 'people skills'. 'You were looking after prisoners, and you had to interact with them. But relations would often be fine until something went wrong in the prison, or a prison officer was murdered outside. Then you came into work and relations would be very strained, and there was no interaction at all.'

I asked McKee about the behaviour of prison officers. 'In my experience the majority of men were decent. I worked among them.' McKee is a friend of playwright Martin Lynch, who wrote a play, *The Chronicles of Long Kesh*, based on interviews with prisoners and officers. One scene depicts a warder beating a prisoner mercilessly, and McKee accepts that that incident occurred, but he is adamant that he personally never saw a prison officer beat a prisoner. I put to him what Adrian Callan had told me and he said, 'During the protests, there were allegations of brutality, and members of the prison staff may know about it, but I suppose they won't shit on their colleagues. If I had seen it, I would have taken the officer to be dealt with. I would never have tolerated it.'

McKee argues that mistreatment did not happen on a large scale because Northern Ireland is a small place, and if word came out that a particular officer was abusing his position, revenge would be exacted outside. 'There was a big fear factor.' He points out that over the period of the hunger strikes sixteen prison officers were killed. 'And yet our hospital staff were prison officers who, while their colleagues were being murdered outside, were 100 per cent professional in how they treated these hunger strikers. In fact the second hunger striker that died – Francis Hughes – actually sent for them when he was on his last legs, to thank them for the way they took care of him and his colleagues.'

McKee was working in the prison administration section during the hunger strikes. He remembers a dark atmosphere: 'The whole place was silent, eerie.' He was astonished when Bobby Sands died; he had never expected that Margaret

Thatcher would allow any of the men to die. He says that the hunger strikes brought home to him the dedication of many members of the IRA, 'that they would die for an all-Ireland'. He was also amazed that within a short time of the protest ending, the prisoners were granted their demands: 'It was like giving them an injection of adrenalin. It told them that they'd won. The fact was that they were committing criminal acts, and they shouldn't have been given recognition. But the other side of the coin was that it wouldn't have improved the situation for us. Things would have escalated again. They felt that they had won, and people are magnanimous in victory – and they were certainly easier to work with.'

From then on, McKee says, the prisoners had a say in everything that happened within the prison. 'The tail was wagging the dog,' as he puts it. 'You couldn't change anything without their agreement. They were unlocked twenty-four hours a day, they became very comfortable, and we gave them an input, so they could say, "The fish on Friday wasn't fresh, we didn't like it."' McKee was able to employ his people skills to keep the prison quiet: 'For example, I thought the rights to visit were abysmal in the Maze, so I sorted them out, building crèches for them, and giving them free milk and coffee. I just tidied the whole place up and got the system fixed. I was able to keep their letters coming in properly, and the food was good, and that kept the place quiet. And if the Maze was quiet, the staff had a fairly relaxed time. Because if things weren't working, the prisoners took it out on the staff. Whoever broke bad news got it in the neck.'

According to McKee, 'The IRA would be all nice and friendly, but they lulled the staff into a false sense of security, and the next thing you knew, they had escaped out the gate. So I played them at their own game; I conditioned *them*. I would say, "That's great the way your men have stopped swearing so much at the staff, and great the way we're solving problems together." And one of them said to me, "Hold on! We're the ones who do the conditioning!" But he said it with a laugh.' McKee's approach was successful. His handling of the problem of visits, and of a subsequent dispute over prison catering, led to his being given an award by the Butler Trust during a ceremony at Buckingham Palace.

Working in an unconventional prison like the Maze, however, meant that he was confronted with unconventional problems. In March 1997 an escape tunnel was discovered in one of the IRA blocks. The prison was locked down and a search was begun. It was found that prisoners had used washing-machine motors to power drills to cut through the concrete floor; they had used wood from chairs to reinforce their tunnel; they had even installed electric lighting inside it. The prisoners' commanding officer demanded a meeting with McKee, and insisted that his men should not be searched by the black-suited and helmeted officers of the prison's Immediate Reaction Force. McKee told him that so long as prisoners agreed to be searched by ordinary officers, the IRF would not be called in. The commanding officer glared at McKee and said, 'You have been warned!' The search was duly carried out – but one prisoner in each wing refused to comply, so McKee called in the IRF. The commanding officer confronted McKee, screaming, 'You are a dead man walking! Whether it happens this year or next year, you remember why it happened!' 'That's all right,' McKee replied mildly. It was not much of a reply, he tells me, but he was too terrified to say any more. For hours he could only sit and contemplate the threat to his life.

It was actually the second threat that he had received within a short space of time. Just before the tunnel was discovered a 'tail-wagging-the-dog' problem had arisen when all of the other paramilitaries refused to allow the Loyalist Volunteer Force, a breakaway group from the UVF, to have their visits in the main visitors' complex. As a result the LVF prisoners began taking their visits in a small, dilapidated room, and when better facilities were not quickly provided they rioted and wrecked their wing. McKee recalls: 'We had a pitched battle with them. They had snooker cues and whatever else they could get hold of. We had to ask permission to use batons. Eventually the block was secured, and the prisoners were relocated to an empty H block.' The following day, McKee was sent by the senior governor to tell the LVF prisoners that they would not be having their annual families party. Shortly afterwards, LVF prisoners were overheard planning an attempt on McKee's life, and McKee and his family were forced to move to a securely protected house.

McKee was anxious and uncomfortable as he described these events, and it was uncomfortable listening to him. But anxious experiences do not mark William McKee out from other 'participants' in the Troubles. One ex-IRA man with whom I spent time has never properly recovered from his experiences both inside and outside prison. A difference between them is that while McKee may have chosen to become a prison officer, he had no ideology, no belief in a cause to sustain him. He was not involved in a struggle. He was just a man doing a job for a wage – whose most disturbing experience was still ahead of him. In December 1997 LVF leader Billy Wright was shot dead inside the Maze while McKee was the senior member of staff on duty. The consequences of the murder affect him still.

On the day of the killing a number of staff had not reported for work. McKee insists that as a result he issued an order that all the prison towers should be unmanned, except for H6 tower. H6 tower had *always* to be manned, as H6 was the only mixed H block, housing loyalist LVF prisoners and republican INLA prisoners in adjacent wings. Later that morning an officer burst into McKee's office asking why H6 had been stood down. McKee claims that he said, 'It's not stood down, and if it is, get it back on again!' But before the designated officer had returned to H6 tower, two members of the INLA had made their way through a fence, into the area where LVF men were waiting to be taken to meet their visitors. The INLA men, led by Christopher 'Crip' McWilliams, opened fire with smuggled guns, killing Billy Wright.

The murder of Billy Wright very nearly derailed the peace process. It triggered a spate of retaliatory killings and caused the leaders of the UDA to briefly withdraw their support for the process. Only a visit to the Maze by British Secretary of State Mo Mowlam secured their support once more. In the meantime allegations circulated that H6 tower had been unmanned owing to collusion between the INLA and the prison authorities. McKee, himself, has many unanswered questions. How did guns and wire-cutters enter the prison? Why were Wright and two of his killers transferred to the Maze from Maghaberry Prison at the same time? Why did the INLA receive a visitors' list telling them where Wright would be at an exact time? *Did* somebody order the tower to be unmanned? An inquiry into the killing was established in 2004. McKee appeared as a witness, and the tribunal retired to draft its report in the summer of 2009.

When loyalists received the information that McKee had been in charge of the prison on the day that Wright was killed, he became an immediate target for assassination. In 2003 information was received that the LVF was about to make an attempt on his life. His wife went to stay with her parents, taking the children, while McKee stayed in a different hotel each night under a different name. Before long he was off work and on medication. Soon afterwards his name was also discovered on an IRA hit list; clearly the IRA had not forgotten the promise it had made six years earlier. As anxiety overwhelmed him his marriage fell apart, and he went to live at his brother's house. While he was there, police received a tip-off that a joint team of hit men from the LVF and UFF (Ulster Freedom Fighters) were on their way to kill him. He left the house before they arrived. Before long his condition deteriorated: 'I was taken away in an ambulance one day. I thought it was a heart attack, but it was a panic attack. That was my last day in the prison service. I lost my wife, my kids, my home, my career, my health. I was diagnosed with post-traumatic stress disorder, and I was suicidal.'

A few years on William McKee tells me that he still doesn't feel his life is safe, and will not be until the inquiry is over and he receives what he calls 'clearance'. He speaks of his marriage: 'I know it's not my fault, but my wife's life was ruined because of me. In town I bump into her and she will look at me with so much hatred.' At his son's wedding he and his wife 'went through the whole day without looking at each other and without speaking'. But if this interview gives the impression that McKee pities himself, then it fails to record his spirit. He smiles broadly and tells me that his life is back together. I believe him – I certainly want to believe him – when he tells me that he is full of hope for the future.

There is less hope for the future of his old workplace, the Maze Prison. Its prisoners are long gone: it was closed as a jail in 2000. There is much discussion about what to do with the place. Unionists want it razed to the ground. Republicans want it to remain as a memorial to the hunger strikers. In Northern Ireland rival sides will often take contrary stances on arbitrary issues – but the Maze/Long Kesh is not an arbitrary issue. It is a red-hot symbol of the Troubles; it stands for death inside its walls, death outside its walls, the political destiny of the state. And it also stands for the stories of men such as Adrian Callan and William McKee. Whatever becomes of the old H blocks, the lessons that these men can teach future generations, and the truth about what once happened inside – those are the things that are really worth preserving.

10

THE TRUTH

It may not be very surprising that the most effective persuader for peace in Northern Ireland was Tony Blair. During his time as Prime Minister his demonstrations of conviction were not always supported by evidence. Rather than engaging with the history of an issue, he would often view it as an immediate problem which could be solved with a demonstration of missionary-type zeal. As Blair justified the war in Iraq in 2003, the journalist and former Tory MP Matthew Parris was alarmed by the Prime Minister's level of conviction without evidence. 'Are we witnessing the madness of Tony Blair?' Parris asked. Yet in Northern Ireland such 'madness' reaped rewards. For years commentators had looked at the history, studied the evidence, and decided that peace was not yet possible. Beliefs were unbridgeable, people were unyielding. This did not deter Blair, however. John Major's government had built a framework for talks, leaders were in power with whom deals could be done, and he proceeded to sell shares in his own conviction: that history was there to be made. For people preoccupied with history, this was a tantalizing prospect. Even Ian Paisley eventually succumbed.

By placing the emphasis on peace at all costs, rather than on challenging prejudices and changing mindsets, Blair found himself engaging with the pragmatists on both sides. For any kind of a deal to be agreed, the pragmatists had to convince their people that they had won. And so a peace was created where little common ground existed between the sides, other than an agreement not to return to violence. Methods have changed, but attitudes have not. 'Whataboutery' will continue to exist for years to come.

Yet for all the accusation slinging that occurs, there sometimes seems to be an implied understanding in Northern Ireland that the truth about the past should remain hidden. As Peter Oborne noted in the *Spectator* in 2002, most people accept that 'the only way forward is by casting a veil of obscurity over the past'. Two years later Andrew Mueller, a *Guardian* journalist, interviewed Gerry Adams, a man who has cast something heavier than a veil over his past. Mueller commented that Adams's denial of IRA membership sounded as plausible as Paul McCartney insisting that he had never joined the Beatles, but rather than ask him *whether* he had been in the IRA, Mueller decided to take Adams at his word, and ask him *why* he had never joined. Adams's first response was: 'Well, I think the question is ... hmm.' He eventually replied that he had become involved in republican activism at a time when the IRA was just a skeletal organization.

In South Africa a Truth and Reconciliation Committee was set up in the wake of the apartheid era, in order to investigate political crimes. Chaired by Archbishop Desmond Tutu, the committee took over 20,000 statements and received more than 7,000 applications for amnesties, in its attempt to uncover the past, understand what had caused it, and ensure that it was not to be repeated. But despite there being so much that is dark and unresolved about the Troubles, no such inquiry into truth and reconciliation has been attempted in Northern Ireland. The Bloody Sunday Inquiry comes closest – but that is an investigation into one event, in one place, on one day.

Of course, there are many who would like the past to remain dark and unresolved. There are people who informed on their organizations and communities, whose actions have never been exposed. There are people who have never been held account-able for sanctioning and carrying out attacks and killings. And the role of the police and the army in providing information to loyalist killers remains a contentious issue. A recent attempt by the police ombudsman to investigate one such allegation encountered uncooperative police witnesses and large amounts of destroyed evidence.

The meeting at the Gasyard in Derry set me thinking about the merits of scrutinizing the past. Is the peace process strong enough to handle the truth, whatever it may be? Should we investigate and face the consequences, or tread lightly and trust in a rosy future? In the wake of the meeting I was surprised, as were others, by the scant exposure it received in the press, despite the fact that it was attended by a large number of reporters. I asked a leading journalist – who has been covering Northern Ireland for many years – why this might be. He told me that there is a reluctance to cover stories that could jeopardize the peace process. He compared the lack of coverage to a compara-ble dearth of stories in the late Sixties concerning inequalities in Northern Ireland society. In both cases newspapers displayed a marked reluctance to 'rock the boat'. He also noted that by cover-ing controversial issues reporters risked being 'cut out of the loop' by the political parties.

In the journalist's own opinion, however, the peace process is strong. It is conceivable, he says, that something could be revealed about one of the 'top men' that could cause the other party to pull out of Stormont, but that this would not mean the end of peace. If, for example, Sinn Féin was damaged by a reve-lation, the SDLP would be strengthened, but the province would not be plunged back into conflict. 'The things that got the IRA going were grievances, not problems with the leadership,' he says. 'We are too far in, to be honest. The peace process can take the scrutiny.'

This is not the end of the story, however. One republican I met at the Derry Gasyard told me that the past must be examined because 'it is crucial that decisions in the new Northern Ireland are based on truth and not on lies'. But is it really so crucial to the future of Northern Ireland that the past is revealed? I asked many people how they felt on seeing Ian Paisley and Martin McGuinness being sworn in at Stormont as First Minister and Deputy First Minister. The majority replied with variations on two themes: surprise and hope. The two men were nicknamed the 'Chuckle Brothers', as they laughed their way to shared power. The knowledge that they both had controversial pasts did not seem to suppress a public surge of hope that their double act would cement peace. Time has passed, and the initial surge has subsided, but should hope now be sacrificed for truth? Even if the peace process can handle it?

One young woman I met, Caitlin, might argue that hope and truth cannot be separated. I met her in north Belfast, at a group organized by the WAVE Trauma Centre. The group is attended by people of both communities who have been affected by the Troubles. Caitlin, whose father was shot dead in 1993, told the group – and me – of a visit from a policeman a few days after the funeral: 'The policeman came in through the front door and he said to my mummy, "There was three people at the funeral that were the murderers of your husband." And my mummy said, "Who were they?" and he goes, "We can't tell you at this minute." They couldn't arrest them, or touch them, or do nothing. And we never got answers. Never.'

Caitlin's family fell apart in the months that followed and she was taken into care. She says, 'You know you can't bring back the dead or nothing, but when people have been murdered, we need to know why they were murdered. And when people were getting released from prison [after the Good Friday Agreement] that didn't give us any answers. I would love to know why they done it. I know it sounds really stupid, but they didn't just kill my father, they killed my relationship with everyone in my family. They took everything away. They took me away as well. It's not really, you know, a big thing to ask – why?' For Caitlin the truth is not an abstract ideal. It is an answer to a question that can help her to make sense of her life. A while ago, while at WAVE, she met two politicians. She remembers: 'They come over to me, and they were, "What happened to you? Oh, your poor family." *No!* That's not what it's about! I don't want pity! I want answers and justice! Don't let my daddy have died for no reason!'

Tricia Magee works for WAVE as the head of Youth Services. She says that it is not just those directly affected who need answers. She tells me about meeting a group of young teenagers, too young to remember the Troubles but profoundly influenced by them. 'Some of them had tears in their eyes because for the first time they were able to understand, and ask questions, and process what's been going on around them. They were saying, "I'm referred to as so-and-so's niece, and so-and-so was killed thirty years ago. Who is he? I can't ask my mum. I don't know what happened. What's that about?" There's a whole generation of young people with big question marks saying, "I have no idea. I don't understand why."' For some people, at least, it appears as though a rosy future depends on light being shed on the past.

In 1977 the American psychologist Carl Rogers worked with a mixed Catholic and Protestant group, and described a 'sensitive young Catholic teacher' who 'had been forced to pull down a "steel shutter" between his functioning self and the seething feelings within. Otherwise he would go berserk.' The young man told Rogers, in a soft voice: 'it is violent and emotional and daft ... I take long walks and let this thing inside of me talk. It isn't quite the same as human feelings – it isn't quite the same as having a beast inside of you – some sort of animal feelings, you know.' This man does not stand alone in Northern Ireland. He is not a direct victim of the Troubles, but he is representative of that stifled world beyond belief and self-importance which has been forced to repress so much of what was going on.

Another member of this world was Jim Campbell, a quiet, thoughtful university lecturer, who told me that twenty years ago he was invigilating an exam in Belfast, when he heard a gunshot in the next room. Running through the door, he found that one of his students had been shot in the head. Campbell says that he rationalized what he had just seen by telling himself that the student was being taken away by ambulance and would be looked after. He goes on to recount other memories. In one breath he tells me of seeing bomb victims shovelled into black bin bags in Belfast city centre; in the next he tells me that he was never caught up in anything too explicit. He says that if people living in Northern Ireland during the Troubles had taken onboard everything that they saw, they would have gone mad. They had to try to make the abnormal normal. 'Things were happening all the time and you tried not to think about it too much. We became experts at doing that in Northern Ireland.' Campbell believes that the past should not be off limits: 'We have to understand that the past is always with us, and it will eventually have to be dealt with in some way. And it's better to do it in a thoughtful, reparative way than in an attacking, angry way – which is what we've always done.'

Dr Raman Kapur is a clinical psychologist in Belfast. He has spent many years working with victims, perpetrators, and those more indirectly affected by the Troubles. He describes Northern Ireland as a place where 'your level of trust in the world is significantly less because you live in a society where people have done damage to each other. In England people talk about the recession and they think the world's gone a bit shaky, but here people have lived in a shaky, persecuting, damaged world for years, and there's been a lack of belief in goodness in society.'

As a result Dr Kapur identifies a 'narcissistic rage' that runs across whole swathes of the community: 'I am special, my suffering is special, and if you don't make it special, I'm going to knock your block off!' These feelings, he says, are a defence against damage and loss in a society that has lacked plurality. His work involves stressing the universality of suffering in Northern Ireland, and encouraging patients to move beyond their rage. 'But a lot of people don't want a way out. They're fixated on it. It's their absolute identity, and it reflects the old discourses.'

Dr Kapur also gives me his views on the perpetrators of violence: 'The paramilitaries are ordinary people who have been tipped over the edge. We all have the capacity to be a terrorist. If the political environment plus a lot of other things are going against you, then you or I could become a terrorist very easily.' Brendan Duddy agrees: 'I think it's very easy to be one of these young men – or alternatively one of the victims of this level of living. The brutality of it is just an advanced mode of the brutality that we're all capable of doing to each other.' At the beginning of my journey such comments might have surprised me. How could men and women willing to kill soldiers, civilians, prison officers, policemen, and one another be the same as you or me? Spending a lot of time with ex-terrorists – a description, incidentally, that most would take great exception to – was like spending time with anyone else. They were people, and like people, they were not all the same. Some were funny, some were serious, some had an air of sadness, not many were dull, and a few had a charm that masked a chilly core. I soon learnt not to bother having preconceptions before I met them. Flicking randomly through my diary shows that I spent a Wednesday in a house off the Falls Road with an old IRA man and his adorable grandchildren, the next day in east Belfast with an ex-member of the UDA who made me take home a large box of scones because they were going to go stale, and the following evening in a bar in the Bogside, drinking too much and trying to convince an ex-IRA man that Jesus Christ *really wasn't* a prophet in the Jewish faith.

Brendan Duddy told me of the sorts of people who rise up the ranks: 'The guys who move up in terrorism are either the exuberant "Outside, put the fucking bomb in, and let it go off!" type of people, or the natural leaders – and there's much less of them.' Of course, some members would have had psychopathic or sociopathic tendencies, but as Raman Kapur pointed out, these people would have existed in any society. Kevin, a man in his early fifties, told me a story highlighting such behaviour within a paramilitary organization. Kevin remembers being told of screams coming from inside a republican club. 'I went in, and there was a man in his sixties with no shirt on, tied to a chair. I knew the three guys standing over him and I said, "What the fuck's going on?" One of them said, "It's none of your fucking business." I said, "It *is* my business!" He said, "You've got nothing to do with this fucking area!" The poor man was crying uncontrollably, but I wasn't getting nowhere with these boys.'

Kevin went round to the house of the local OC (Officer Commanding), and together they came back to the club and kicked the door in. They were told that the man in the chair was a spy, but the man was crying and screaming that he had just been walking through the area. 'These guys had picked him up, and they were burning him with cigarettes, punching him in the mouth.' Kevin and the OC got him off the chair, the latter warned the men there'd be more said about the matter, and they took him outside to the car. But the man was so terrified that he wouldn't get inside. 'He thought we were taking him away to do him in. I said, "Where do you live?" He told me and we said, "We'll walk you there." So we set off with one of us either side of him, trying to stop him crying.' The man started to calm down, but then they came to a dark lane. 'Looking back, he must have thought we were taking him into the darkness to kill him. He suddenly bolted.'

The man ran into the doorway of a house. The front door was open and he crashed through the glass inner door. He landed on the floor in the hallway, and lay there screaming. Inside the house were three old women, all of whom knew Kevin. 'They looked at the man on the floor, and said to me, "What's wrong?" I said, "Honestly, it's OK. Somebody knocked hell out of him down the road and he's scared, and we're going to leave him up there safe." One of the women said, "Are you sure? You're not going to hurt him?" I said, "No way!"' Just at that moment the OC, a man with a reputation, walked into the house behind Kevin. 'It was like the devil walking in, and the three women looked at him and screamed. They were convinced the man was going to be killed. In the end the women walked him home themselves.'

Kevin makes it plain that the behaviour of all three men in the republican club had been unacceptable – but his particular distaste is reserved for one of the three. 'I was once in a car with that bastard,' he says, 'and it was a lovely evening, and just coming up on our left-hand side were two innocent kids, about 15, with their fishing rods. This man reaches in and pulls it [a gun] out. I said, "What are you doing?" He said, "Two Jaffas!" ['Jaffa' is a slang term for a Protestant, derived from 'Orangeman'.] I said, "For real? You idiot!" Why he would have done that, I don't know, but I went straight to report him. He was shot dead not long afterwards as he was going to work. The Protestants came up alongside him and shot him. I had no feeling for him. None whatsoever.' Kevin leaves me in no doubt that this man, whether a psychopath or simply dehumanized by his experiences, is to be considered the exception rather than the rule within his organization. But the fact is clear: such people did exist.

Of course, psychopaths may not always be easy to spot. William McKee told me that Michael Stone seemed very 'normal' in person, yet this was a man who carried out a near-suicidal attack on an IRA funeral, and whose defence to a charge of attempted murder was that he was enacting a piece of performance art, intended to reflect 'the spectre of our troubled past'.

None of the ex-prisoners that I met attempted a Stone-like explanation for their past actions. Almost all of them considered the use of violence to have been a morally justifiable weapon against injustice and a feared enemy. Very few of them, even those who regret the pain that they caused, believe that what they did was wrong, or are prepared to see themselves as criminals. As I listened to them I tried to watch for clues that they were rewriting the past and cynically claiming a morally justifiable position. I kept in mind the plight of those like Caitlin, who are still looking to them for answers that can help to make sense of their lives. But if I found the vast majority of my ex-paramilitary acquaintances to be decent people – as I did – then can I conclude that Dr Kapur is right? Did most of the masks worn during the Troubles conceal ordinary human beings responding to fear and perceived injustice?

The fact that people are decent does not mean that they are being honest, however. The veil of obscurity encourages them to withhold what they know, and to rewrite the past without fear of informed contradiction. A 'party line' is encouraged, which is not to be disputed – as Richard O'Rawe has discovered – and a received wisdom is created. One such received wisdom concerns the issue of sectarianism during the Troubles. It is commonly repeated that while loyalist groups operated as sectarian assassination squads, attacking ordinary Catholics, republicans rarely targeted ordinary Protestants, concentrating instead on attacking soldiers, policemen, UDR men, and loyalist paramilitaries. The statistics seem to bear this out; between 1969 and 1989 less than a quarter of the victims of republican paramilitary attacks were Protestant civilians, whereas over 70 per cent of the victims of loyalist paramilitary attacks were Catholic civilians.

The 'official' republican stance was outlined by a man who told me, 'Kill a man because he's a cop. Kill a man because he's a UDR man. But do not kill Protestant people! Catholics would never kill a Prod!' Republicans did not consider attacks on policemen and soldiers to be sectarian, because these people were seen as the representatives of a foreign occupying power – but it could be argued that the availability of these 'legitimate' targets allowed the IRA to mount regular attacks that were sectarian in all but name. And there is no mistaking the attitudes of some republicans. I was told of a young man in prison for the killing of a British soldier. When he was informed that Wolfe Tone had been a Protestant, the young man was startled: 'Wolfe Tone? A Protestant? Dirty fucking bastard!'

For loyalist groups, republicans may have been the enemy, but active republicans were difficult targets to locate. A solution was found. According to a loyalist, 'If we couldn't get the IRA, we would have to slaughter members of the Catholic community who, after all, seemed to support them.' But the fact is that republicans did carry out attacks on Protestants simply because they were Protestant. In January 1976 a bus full of textile workers was stopped at a fake security checkpoint near Kingsmill in County Armagh. The men on the bus were each asked for their religion. The one Catholic on board was told to run away, and gunmen opened fire on the remainder of the passengers. Ten Protestants were killed. One man survived, despite being hit by eighteen bullets. Years later he told a newspaper, 'I was semi-conscious and passed out several times with the deadly pain and the cold.' Other republican attacks that appear to have had a sectarian motive include an attack on the Bayardo Bar on the Shankill Road in August 1975 which killed five people and injured forty, and an attack on a Remembrance Day ceremony in Enniskillen in November 1987 which killed eleven people and injured over sixty. The IRA subsequently claimed that the timer had failed on the Enniskillen bomb; it was intended to kill soldiers and policemen sweeping the area in advance of the ceremony. Whether this is true or not, ten years after the attack

Gerry Adams, speaking as the President of Sinn Féin, said, 'I am deeply sorry about what happened at Enniskillen.'

When I spoke to Richard O'Rawe I asked him whether the IRA had carried out sectarian killings. 'Of course there was sectarianism. It's just denial to say that there wasn't. Kingsmill, Bayardo, and there were Protestants shot by Catholics because they were Protestant. In retaliation. It's disingenuous to say otherwise. It's another example of people just blanking out the nasty bits.' Other 'nasty bits' which are sometimes blanked out include the punishment beatings and kneecappings administered by the paramilitaries of both sides to antisocial members of their own communities. Sean, a man from Belfast in his forties, told me, 'They made it quite clear that you weren't allowed to break into houses in your own area. That was totally breaking the code of conduct. You were dealt with severely; that would probably have entailed kneecapping. So being that way inclined, and smart, you would have said to yourself, "Right, if I'm going to do a job, I'm going to do it in the city centre." But that was still classified as antisocial behaviour, so your punishment was different, not as severely done, but still, you got dealt with.'

Sean was 'dealt with' for travelling in a stolen car. 'I didn't steal the car. I was just in it. It was one of these fucking things you get easily talked into. My mate was driving it, and he crashed into the Orange Hall on the Ormeau Road. There was a girl sitting on the wall, and he broke both her legs. There was police and army all over the place, and we got out and run – but somebody must have recognized us. News in Belfast doesn't take long to travel. After that, you was seen in the street, and told to be at such-and-such a place at such-and-such a time. When you went there, there was six or seven masked people waiting for you. One or two of them might have been important people, and the rest would have been volunteers coming up the ranks, put in there to prove themselves. I was batted with hurley sticks, and I just rolled up in a ball and took it, and hoped I walked away. I was bruised, I had cuts, my head was cut, and I had a broken wrist, but nothing to cry about.'

Shortly after his beating Sean was approached by a man in the street. 'He came up to me and says to me, "Would you consider joining the Provisional IRA?" There's a right "no" and a wrong "no" and I gave the wrong "no". I says, "Go and fuck yourself!" and I got a dig in the mouth. I think they would have been waiting on me going, "What's in it for me?" and their attitude back would have been, "Well, you were beat last week for antisocial behaviour. Now, you'll be giving out this sort of punishment, instead of receiving it." They knew that my brother had been killed, and they saw that I was going down the wrong track, becoming a wee thug and a runabout, and the only conclusion I can come to is that they could see I was in a bit of a dilemma, and they were preying on it.'

For those less fortunate than Sean, a more severe beating, or a kneecapping, could be administered. Kneecapping was normally carried out with a bullet – but not always. A British soldier witnessed a gruesome scene at the bottom of the Falls Road in 1980: 'On patrol, we came across a man. He had been kneecapped with a Black & Decker drill with a wood bit in. You can imagine the mess. My God, his knees just didn't exist. He was almost unconscious in pain – in utter agony. They'd stood on his legs to hold him down, one man had a gun, threatening to kill him, and another man had the drill and drilled right through his kneecaps. He wouldn't tell us why they'd done it. There was blood everywhere. We grabbed him and dragged him into the back of an armoured Land Rover, and took him to the hospital.'

It is worth noting that these stories come from two men – one who refused to join the IRA and the other a retired soldier – who are not cloaked by the veil and are willing to illuminate the past. I met two other men, both ex-paramilitaries, who have taken a considered view on Northern Ireland's recent past and agree that it must be illuminated. On the face of it, they are unlikely friends – Gerry Foster, a Catholic ex-member of the INLA, convicted of planting a bomb, and Alistair Little, a Protestant ex-member of the UVF, convicted of murder – but they share strong feelings about the rationalization, denial, and hypocrisy which, they believe, infect Northern Ireland's relationship with its past.

Louis MacNeice wrote of the men of action 'who sleep and wake, murder and intrigue without being doubtful, without being haunted'. Throughout their years in the INLA and UVF, neither Foster nor Little was doubtful or haunted, but this changed for both men when they had time to reflect on their lives; Little while in prison, and Foster after his release. Both are from working-class backgrounds, Foster's in Andersonstown, west Belfast, and Little's in Lurgan.

Little tells me that by the time he became involved in the conflict, at the age of 14, he had a 'very human sense that we [Protestants] were better, and superior, and that God was on our side. You had a sense of Britishness, and of being an Ulsterman, but no well-defined political ideology. Intellectually, all you knew was that you were special, and that God was a Protestant. In Lurgan we had a sense that this is our town, this is our country, our flags, our security forces, our army, our police; this belongs to us, if you don't like it, leave. In terms of rights, it was our rights that were supreme overall.' Little became friendly with the soldiers attached to an army camp beside his school: 'Our most favoured army unit was the Black Watch, because they had all the Ulster badges on their lapels. We were on personal-name terms with some of the soldiers, and we would have done anything for them. During the riots we stood back, because we knew they were going to get into the nationalists.'

At school the Christian Brothers taught Foster that 'the likes of Patrick Pearse and the other leaders of the 1916 rising were close to sainthood, and everything British had to be disdained'.

He feels that although the church condemned violence, it played a quiet and effective role in cultivating republicanism. When the British army arrived he 'could feel the fear and the apprehension. There was a cloud hanging and you could feel that something was going to burst.' He remembers the army searching the houses in Andersonstown. 'It was quite severe. Our house was getting wrecked all the time. You could hear their vehicles coming from miles away, and people used to bang bin lids to warn, and there were mad gun battles going on. My dad got a ball, and half put it in the door, so it would just open when they kicked it because the frame was getting beat every time they came in.'

Two of Foster's brothers were interned: 'As a kid, you were watching your brothers shooting at the British army, and there's no doubt they were role models. I looked up to them. When I was about 16 I was involved in the H block protest, and two of my brothers tried to talk me out of getting involved. They said, "Don't be going down that road. Don't do it. It's not worth it." They came quite close to convincing me.'

Both men point out that it was not a single incident that led to their involvement in violence. Nevertheless, they can isolate incidents that hardened their attitudes. For Foster, it occurred when 'myself and a friend were walking home one night, and the RUC drove by, there was a bit of banter and they drove by again, opened the back door of their car and started shooting live bullets at us'. He has a memory of bullets hitting the ground in front of him and splattering mud on his trousers. His friend shouted, 'Get down! That's real shots!' Afterwards, he remembers, a Belfast newspaper carried a story on its front page that the RUC had opened fire on a mob of forty petrol bombers: 'I started reading it and wondering where that was, and then I realized it was about us! But there weren't forty people, it was just the two of us, and we didn't have petrol bombs. I started realizing that the media just took the RUC's word for it, there was no investigative journalists, and they can kill people and get away with it. I thought, well, fuck it! I'm going to use violence to try and break the state.'

Little recalls: 'My best friend's father, a member of the Ulster Defence Regiment, was shot dead. I went to the funeral, and his 11-year-old daughter, who had also been shot in the legs, was in a wheelchair screaming for her daddy, and at that point I vowed that if I ever got the chance to take revenge, I would. That's one thing that sticks in my mind, but there was loads of stuff. Lurgan town was twice blown to pieces by the IRA, and that was your home.' He stresses the motivations at play: 'For young men, at a very human level, you didn't try to work out the rights and wrongs. Once you had accepted who the enemy were, you didn't need to try and justify anything. I've talked to republicans who would say the same, that once they had accepted in their minds that the British army and the police were the enemy, they didn't need to work out the rights and wrongs. For me, it was very much republicans, nationalists, Catholics, they were either in it or they were supporting them, or they knew who they were, so they were all fair game.'

Foster says, 'There was no political ideology in what I did. There was a basic right and wrong; we were right and they were wrong, and that's what you done. But if you say that today, people would object because they are so hung up on politicizing every single thing that was done, and for someone to say it wasn't a political thing, that it was a human response, they would see that as a threat to their political position.' Foster points out that while republicanism did become more politicized, it does not follow that the young men who were active thought in terms of political theory: 'Yes, when I was in prison, there was people who were up on their politics, but first-timers coming in, mostly teenagers, weren't. I certainly wasn't, and most of my peers weren't. When I got involved it was not a big deal. You didn't need to justify it to yourself. There was no wrong in it. And when civilians were killed you knew in your mind it wasn't right, but it was an accident because they weren't deliberately targeted, and you weren't losing sleep over it.'

As he grew older Little gravitated towards people who felt the same way as he did: 'There were people that went to school with me, but that were never involved, and they wouldn't have been in our inner circle. You quickly surrounded yourself with like-minded people, and you felt that you were special. There were other people that we liked as guys, but they weren't privy to our wee secrets, and that gave you a real sense of belonging; you felt you were involved in something, and doing something that was really important. You had a sense that you were bulletproof. I have clear memories of having a gun in my hand, and thinking that I was bulletproof.' Foster says that most of his childhood friends did not get involved. 'I can't just say that I am a victim of circumstances, a victim of my environment. If I was, we'd all have been involved. It's hard to explain why I did and they didn't, hard to know what the "X Factor" was that made you get involved. I've spoken to people about it, and Alistair has said that maybe we are more passionate about things. Maybe we took things in deeper, and responded to them in a different sort of way than people who go with the flow.'

Loyalists found themselves in a strange tug of loyalties, according to Little: 'It was a schizophrenic sort of situation, because if a UDR man or a British army man, or a policeman was shot, we would have run out and took revenge, but at the same time the RUC was arresting us, and we had gun battles with the British army, so it didn't make sense intellectually. But we didn't operate from an intellectual perspective – friends' fathers were dying, UDR men you knew were dying, and we were responding to what we were seeing and feeling at a human level. There was a tradition in Protestant communities of standing back and letting the security forces deal with it, but that changed. More and more young men got involved with paramilitary organizations because they felt the UDR and the police weren't doing what they should have been doing – going out and killing.'

Little recalls another spur to getting involved that is nowadays played down: 'There were politicians holding rallies and saying things that we took literally. I have recordings of a leading figure talking about smuggling weapons in, and fighting to the last drop of blood, and saying that if we were forced into a united Ireland these weapons would be used, even against the police – but that's all denied now. At the time this person was your hero. He was a strong Protestant who hated Catholics, and you went along with all that. They would deny that now and say that's not what they meant, but as a young person listening to it, it was a green light to go … It's one example of the retrospective thinking that's applied to the conflict.'

Little's initial entry into the UVF came through the 'Tartan Gangs', groups of young loyalists who would wear a particular tartan to identify the area from which they came. 'You became loyal to that tartan, and you wanted to be the most feared. It was about identity and belonging, and the sense you were doing something for your community.' The Tartan Gangs rioted, just as young Catholics rioted in Derry and elsewhere. 'The older guys were watching us, to see who was game, and that was a recruiting ground for the UVF.' Little tried twice to join the UVF, but was told that he was too young, before he was eventually accepted: 'We were never forced to do anything. People who say they were forced into it and led astray by older men – not true. There were more than enough young lads lining up to join.'

While he was a member of the UVF, Little made a decision to join the British army. He travelled to England by ferry at around the time of the Birmingham and Guildford pub bombs, with a man from the Irish Republic, but when they arrived he was bemused by the reception they received: 'In the NAAFI the other guys were throwing full tins of Coke at us, and calling us Irish bastards. I was sitting, thinking, what are they calling me an Irish bastard for? I'm British! When me and the guy from the Republic walked about, officers would see us and stop us, and make us do press-ups in front of them. I hated the army because of that experience.' He left the army and when he arrived back in Northern Ireland all he wanted to do was to get involved again with the UVF.

Foster joined the Irish National Liberation Army, an organization that was formed in 1974 with Marxist principles. For Foster, however, the organization's political ideology was no attraction: 'I joined the INLA for one reason, and one reason only. It was a lot more active in Andersonstown. If the Provies [Provisional IRA] had been more active, I'd have joined them. I just wanted to do as much as possible, as quick as possible, before I died or got caught.' Foster disputes that the Provisional IRA was as disciplined as ex-volunteers sometimes claim: 'The idea that the Provies were an upstanding, structured, disciplined army is really far from the truth, but that's their propaganda, their revision, to this day.' When Foster joined the INLA in Andersonstown, however, he acknowledges that it had almost no organization whatsoever: 'It was just a group of us together, and we made our own choices on the spur of the moment as to what we were going to do. There was very little that was pre-planned – only when you had a specific target, an RUC man or a UDR man, but most of the time you were just on the estate having a dig at the British army and the RUC.'

One reason why Foster and his colleagues were left to their own devices was the fear caused by the evidence of 'supergrasses' in the early Eighties. Supergrasses, known as 'converted terrorists' by the Chief Constable of the RUC, and as 'paid perjurers' by the republican movement, were paramilitary members from either side who were granted immunity from prosecution and a new identity in return for giving evidence against former colleagues. The first supergrass trial, that of IRA man Christopher Black, ended in August 1983 with the convictions of thirty-five IRA suspects, although eighteen of these convictions were overturned three years later. The use of supergrasses promised to overcome a problem faced by the security forces – that of turning intelligence into evidence, but judges began to question the uncorroborated word of witnesses with a personal motive for giving evidence, and the system became discredited and was discontinued.

During the period of these supergrass trials many members of the INLA (and other organizations) were on the run or in prison, and the organization in Andersonstown found itself leaderless. 'It gave me what I wanted,' says Foster, 'guns and explosives, and a free hand to have a dig at the British. All of a sudden you had armed teenagers running around Andersonstown, and no one to tell them what to do.' When Foster's father became aware of his son's activities he was furious: 'My dad wasn't in agreement with violence at any level. The only time I ever remember him hitting me was when I was 18; he had seen me in the area shooting at the British. When I came home he came down the stairs and he threw a kick at me. He had never lifted a hand to any of us. He said, "What are you doing? Are you trying to get killed?" I go, "No, of course not!" He said, "If they kill you, I'll bury you, but if you go to prison, I'll not be up to see you." He gave me a choice to get out of the house or get out of the organization, and I just walked out of the house.'

The limited training that Foster received consisted of getting used to weapons on the local estate. During the summer he trained in the local school: 'The Christian Brothers were there, they heard the shooting, and they knew what was going on, but they didn't let on. We could be quite open about it.' Foster did not see his role – as it might have been viewed a decade earlier – as one of defending the community: 'It was offence: the only thing you were trying to do was kill British soldiers and RUC men.' The advantages that Foster and his colleagues had over the soldiers were that they knew the area well, they knew where to snipe from, they knew where to hide, and they could escape through back gardens, whereas the soldiers needed maps and kept to the roads. 'We got cocky; we knew that once we started firing, their vehicles would be away, and their foot patrols would get down on the ground. If you hadn't hit something with your first two shots, they hit the ground, and you weren't likely to hit anything with the next twenty or thirty.'

He tells me of a typical action at the time: 'It was the summer and we were playing football, and a British patrol came in. And we thought, will we or won't we?, and some days we'd just carry on playing, and other days three or three or four of us would break off and we went and lifted a couple of rifles from a garden or a coal bunker, and had a couple of magazines at the patrol, and then took the rifles back and carried on playing football with the others. If it was still even numbers on the team, they'd have carried on playing. If not, they'd have sat down and waited ten minutes for us to come back.' Foster says that the British never came after the snipers: 'We used to think it was just cowardice, but looking back, their tactic was to get out of the firing zone and seal off the area.'

Over time Foster and his colleagues began mounting operations in other parts of Belfast, and planting bombs. 'We had no training in bombs. You were just hoping that whoever had made it up knew what they were doing. I think it was probably the most fearful time of my life, when I was carrying explosives made by somebody else. It was all commercial explosives – sticks of gelignite or dynamite from County Clare, stolen from the mines, and we used to carry it around in plastic shopping bags. Someone would have a bit of knowledge, and we would sit in a kitchen or bedroom learning about the stuff. I did it a few times, but in the end I said, "Look, you make them, and I'll plant them."'

He tells me how he would go about planting them: 'To make booby traps, we'd use command wires; there was a strong belief that the British had jamming devices for our remote controls, so we went back to the very basics. Sometimes the wee taps would work by movement, for example when a gate was opened, and then the contact would be made, but usually a command wire was preferred, so then you had total control of when to let the bomb off, and when not to. You would place the bomb and run the wire to the nearest place where you could be concealed. Obviously a wire running across the street was not the done thing, because even the dumbest soldiers would work it out, so you had to make it to run through gardens, or keep it out of sight. So if the army patrol was coming up the estate, you would run the command wire back from it, so they would come to the bomb before the wire. Simple things, commonsense things. Sometimes you wouldn't see the soldier till the last couple of feet, so you would need other people around to warn you. The bombs were probably no more than a pound of explosives, and then nuts and bolts, made of iron and steel, were put in for shrapnel. Overall there were soldiers and policemen killed, but also civilians. Common sense wasn't always so common.'

I asked Foster whether there had been a 'glamorous' element to what he was doing. He answers quickly, 'It certainly wasn't glamorous in any shape or form,' but he then says, 'Sometimes it would be good to be seen out doing stuff – a teenage ego thing. A mask can hide a face, but it doesn't hide the person. People would know you by your clothes, by your walk. Maybe within your peer group, some people thought you were more manly than others who weren't doing it. And maybe that stroked your ego. But other times you were worried about the repercussions of being seen, of the British finding out. And I know that people looked down on me; my parents, and neighbours who'd known you as a toddler, who would say, "Look, Gerard, you would want to wise up!" But I didn't pay any attention.'

Foster says that while he was aware of the dangers of what he was doing, 'you always thought someone else would get killed, and someone else would get caught. You thought about death a few times, but you dismissed it very quick.' But on one occasion he was struck by the reality of what he was doing: 'There was a time I remember lying there, thinking about it, taking in the enormity of it, and, Christ, it swept over me. There was no getting out now; I had gone beyond the pale.' Nowadays he goes to the graveyard to visit the graves of friends from those days: 'Some were killed with explosives, others were killed by the British and the RUC, some have committed suicide since it's been over. I look at the graves and I realize how young they were. That always sticks with me, so it does.'

One night Foster was told to bring a car from Andersonstown to the Lower Falls. Having delivered the car, he was taken into Divis Flats and ushered into a room containing a large bomb, with cans of petrol attached to it. Foster was told that he would be driving it to the headquarters of the Ulster Unionist Party, where the leadership was meeting, and could be finished off in one go. 'It sounded good to me,' he says. He drove to Glengall Street, to the party headquarters, with the bomb in the footwell of the passenger seat and a man in the seat over it. When they arrived the passenger got out of the car and attached the bomb to a security grille on one of the building's windows. The bomb was on a timer – it was to be a no-warning attack. 'A number of things happened then. I saw a homeless person, and thought, Christ! He doesn't deserve to die! So I got out of the car, and was about to say, "Back up, lad! We are putting in a bomb! Get away!" but I wondered, what if he runs shouting and screaming? So I thought, fuck it, if he dies it will be worth it, if we get them ones inside. So then we went to drive off, and an RUC jeep came up behind us in the street. My first thought was, we are dead, and my second thought was, well, you've had a good enough run at it. I was thinking we had been set up by an informer, that the RUC were pre-warned. The other guy said, "Let's get out of here!" but I said, "No! No! We will let them pass!" I was waiting for them to shoot us through the hatch; they wouldn't arrest you, they had you where they wanted you, and no one was going to question them killing two people with guns and a bomb. But there was no sense getting out with our hand guns, because our bullets wouldn't have got through the jeep.'

In fact the police jeep passed by. It was not a set-up, and Foster drove away. 'You had all them emotions at once. From playing God with someone's life, to being about to be killed yourself, to the jubilation of realizing you weren't about to die. And it shows the enormity of it, how you were willing to weigh it up in your head, and let some person die. We drove away and I never heard the bomb go off. I've spoken to the other guy about it and he cannot believe that I didn't hear it, because it was so quick. I have no memory of it. But what happened was the homeless guy rapped on the door of the headquarters and said to security, "I don't want to worry you, but two young lads have just left something here." The building was evacuated and the lives were saved of James Molineaux, Harold McClusker, the whole leadership, the cream of the unionist political system.' Nobody was killed in the blast, but when the news reports first came through, 'I was sitting, tense, waiting and hoping that there was a lot of casualties, a lot of deaths. When I was later taken to Castlereagh the cops were jumping all over me, shouting, "Were you trying to start a civil war?"'

Within hours the police were searching for Foster: 'They were up in the house, wrecking it, so that gave you an indication that they knew who was involved in it.' He remained in the Andersonstown area, moving around, between friends and family. He was eventually caught at his mother's house: 'Maybe I should have been more disciplined, more thoughtful, but there is a bit of cockiness and over-confidence. At the time it's a bit strange, but there was also a small amount of relief. Maybe it was all the ducking and diving, and running, not having a steady life, it was mentally wearing you down.' Foster was taken to Castlereagh, and from there to Crumlin Road Prison, where he served two and a half years on remand, and then, after sentence, he was sent to the Maze.

Alistair Little was convicted of the murder of 20-year-old James Griffen in Lurgan in 1975. Griffen was alone in his house when Little and three other men pulled up in a car. Little got out, walked to the front window, and fired six shots into the living room, killing Griffen, whose 11-year-old brother watched from the street. Little returned to the car and was driven away. He was later sentenced to detention at the pleasure of the Secretary of State, and to twelve years' imprisonment for possession of a revolver and ammunition. Nowadays he is determined to use his experience to shed light on the truth of Northern Ireland's past, and to try to prevent others – in Northern Ireland and elsewhere – from doing what he did. He has run workshops for people affected by violence, believing that by spending time together and sharing their life stories with one another they can build relationships and foster an understanding that will discourage violence.

He is clear about why he killed. 'When I done what I done, it was because I believed it was the right thing. Someone gave me a gun, and said, "Go and do it!" I went and did it.' He understands why people try to rewrite the past. 'Every group, and every organization,' he says, 'wants to be seen as the good guys. They want to have right on their side. And whether that "right" comes from political analysis, or whether it comes from the faith basis, everyone wants it. And in order to have it, you have to tell lies. You have to mix truth and falsehood. And myth and history. It may not even be a conscious thing they're doing. So these loyalists and republicans who talk about their involvement, they'll give you a history lesson. But the truth is, that's not what they were thinking when they were involved. That came afterwards. There was an indirect political motivation behind what I done, but I had no well-defined ideology. *They were the fucking enemy, they're killing us, we'll kill them.* When you go into prison you start to read history and you construct a political analysis. You come out, and someone asks you why you got involved and all this analysis comes out. So the guy that you killed – he was involved or he had threatened a Protestant. And you hold onto it. It makes you political. But when you start to question it – it starts to hurt. You're thinking, maybe I did kill an innocent person.'

Little tells me of a meeting he attended where a loyalist ex-paramilitary announced that he had been fighting republicans. Little describes his reaction: 'I'm sitting there, from my loyalist background, thinking, please! Somebody in the group ask what he means by that! Nobody did. I had to say something. "When you make a statement like that, what does that mean?" "Just what I said. I was fighting republicans." "So, everybody you killed was a republican?" "I'm not saying that." "How many were republicans?" "I don't know the numbers. A whole lot." He knew what I was getting at. He didn't like it. I said, "If you're going to sit here and say that you were fighting republicans, then everything that you did would have been going out to kill a republican, and that's not true. There's a wee lad across the road there, 18 years old, never involved in anything, how come he got killed? You went down his house to kill him and there's nobody but you saying he's a republican. And you know he wasn't a republican. So why don't you say, there were times when you killed Catholics?" I'm not supposed to say things like this – but why paint a picture that's based on lies? What's the point? Where's it going to get us? What are we going to learn from it? But it's much easier to say, "I was fighting republicans" – because it's easier to live with.'

He is alert to the difficulties that flow from dealing with the past: 'A gap exists between the intellect and the heart. Someone will say, "I don't regret killing someone." But then you ask, "Do you regret that your own brother was killed?" and he will say, "Of course I do." "Why?" "He died as a result of the conflict."

"But if you can't regret the death of the person you killed as a result of the conflict, then you can't regret your brother's death." "But he's family ..." That's inconsistent. It's selfish and hypocritical. It doesn't square.' This has shades of the inconsistency that Patrick Magee acknowledges – but cannot resolve. Magee regrets killing Sir Anthony Berry but does not regret carrying out the act that killed him. Alistair Little accepts that what *he* did was wrong; but such acceptance has come at a cost: 'I came to that realization after years of mental torture. Of trying to be true to myself. But you realize that there were things you were involved in, and beliefs that you had, that were given to you by other people. And there were lies around some of them.'

Little considers the culpability of society: 'In South Africa the ANC would have said that a young white girl growing up in a privileged position at the expense of black children wasn't innocent, even if she didn't fully understand the politics of South Africa. But if she was killed her parents would say that she was just an innocent young girl growing up. The problem is that one denies the other.' Little questions whether, when living in a regime that is built immorally, people can really claim to be innocent. And if they are not innocent, should they be prepared to pay the price? He points out that in South Africa society's responsibility is acknowledged, whereas it is not in Northern Ireland: 'If I was injured letting a bomb off, I can't complain, because I was going out to kill people. I have to accept that. It's why I don't complain about being in prison. But it goes beyond that. Why was I in prison? Without denying personal responsibility, I'm not going to take all the blame. I wasn't the teacher that showed us UVF badges when we were 13 years old. I wasn't the politician standing up talking about fighting down to the last drop of your blood.'

The difficulty for those who used violence comes when they are forced to question what they have been told by society, by teachers and politicians, by colleagues in prison, by their own need for vindication. Little says, 'If you go any way at all with some people, to question that, they will resist you, because they fear that everything will come crashing down. They will resist you, even when their resistance defies common sense. Leonard Cohen says, "There's a crack in everything, that's how the light gets in ..." But some people have such a shell around them that there's no light. And I didn't realize the heartache, the emotional turmoil, the torture, the loss of friends, the isolation, the loneliness that this sort of thinking was going to take me into.'

Perhaps it is small wonder that relatively few people are willing to engage truthfully with the past. According to Foster: 'Alistair questioned himself in prison. I didn't. I saw prison as a continuation of the struggle. If I wasn't fighting on the street, I was fighting in prison. Defiance, blah, blah, blah. And I came out totally disillusioned because the ceasefire had kicked in. People were saying to me, "Come on back!" I said, "It's a waste of time, it's over!"' But Foster discovered that he was not being asked to return to the struggle; he was being asked to deal with political issues, and reluctantly he agreed to attend the Peace and Reconciliation Centre in Glencree, in County Wicklow. It was where he met Little. 'The third time I was there, Alistair and myself got talking. Coming back on the motorway, after we'd met a few times, I suddenly felt like someone had slapped me in the face. I thought, what the fuck am I doing? I'm sitting in a car with a UVF lifer! Why aren't I trying to kill this cunt? It was as blatant and blunt as that.' At Glencree Foster met the victims of republican violence: 'It's the first time I've seen the pain. You would obviously have seen grieving families in the past, but you wouldn't have given a damn. At Glencree there was a coachload of families of soldiers who had been killed, and I was talking to them, and God, it all went pear-shaped. To see men and women crying at what I was saying, seeing it was you who was causing the pain and hurt. That brought it home to me, you can't be so dismissive.'

Foster has had to overcome the sense that he is betraying dead comrades: 'At Glencree I felt a sense of injustice at first. There should have been *more* soldiers killed. *More* loyalists. You go to graveyards, and think that you're betraying dead people, and then you think, perhaps its not them you're betraying, but yourself. You start questioning what you believe in – so now I can sit quite comfortably with Alistair. Not long ago we would have taken great insult at what the other was saying. Nowadays I try to be truthful. You meet people who still want the conflict to go on, and you find yourself agreeing because you feel that sense of injustice, but then a part of you says, "It didn't work *then*. Why should it work *now*?" I've said to these people, "All right, you want to kill people? You've got a bloodlust? Go away over to London, kill Gordon Brown, there's no sense in shooting the foot soldiers! Better still, go and stuff Adams and McGuinness." But you know they won't do it. These are people in their teens and early twenties who feel they've lost out on the sense of adventure of the struggle. They just want to kill a cop, and there'll be nothing achieved except more hurt and pain.'

Little points out that these young people want to be part of something exciting that would give them significance. He believes that they need to hear voices like his own who can tell them that killing is wrong. There were no such voices on his side stopping him from becoming involved, and once he was involved it was too late. He is discouraged by the shallowness of what often passes for discourse: 'When people say, "I regret all the deaths", that's just words to cover them politically. People are comfortable with the party line, and there is a lack of real honesty. A lot of our political settlement is built on deceit.'

Peace in Northern Ireland owes much to the missionary zeal of Tony Blair, and to the pragmatism of a handful of politicians. Pragmatism pushed truth aside and, a decade on, the past remains covered. Alistair Little believes that reconciliation must be built on truth, and that if it isn't it will fail. In the aftermath of the dissident shootings of 2009, he wonders how politicians were able to say that '*these* killings' could not be justified, as though *past* killings somehow could. He listened to Gerry Adams and Martin McGuinness calling on the dissidents to stop, when violence appeared to have worked for them. And for Caitlin, and for many of those who have never come to terms with their own pasts, the veil continues to cloud their search for understanding.

Yet the fact is that peace is holding, and once bitter enemies are now trying to work together for some sort of a future. Many will argue that there is no purpose in scrutinizing the past if it threatens to jeopardize the future. Given peace, passions will cool, leaving future generations little incentive to take up arms. But others will ask how a better society can evolve if the truth is swept aside. If peace offers anything, it surely offers an opportunity to re-examine old discourses, identities, and truths. But it is debatable whether that opportunity is being taken. If the motivations of those who once did the killing are veiled, then they can become heroes to one side, villains to the other, but never human beings from whom lessons can be drawn. And if nobody is willing to accept responsibility for what they did, then subjective experience can continue to pass for truth, and the age-old intensities of belief will stay solid. To go straight from a black world of violence to a veiled world of politics, without pausing to engage with honesty, threatens to leave people like Caitlin, and all those who have repressed their feelings, crying into a void.

It would be nice and cosy to conclude that Northern Ireland will achieve some form of true reconciliation, but it is a brave visitor to Northern Ireland, and a foolish one, who offers opinions too freely. A decade ago the Dalai Lama came to Derry and was interviewed on local radio. He was asked, 'Your Holiness, have you some advice to offer us?' His answer was measured, succinct, and wise. 'No.'

11

THE PEACE

In June 2009 I sat in the lobby of the Da Vinci Hotel in Derry, eavesdropping on a conversation. An English woman behind me was yelling into a phone: 'Four and a half million people in Ireland! Sixty-one per cent are overweight! We work out that's at least three thousand … no … no … no … three million! *There are three million overweight people in Ireland*!' She was almost screaming. Her excitement was explained, a couple of calls later, when she introduced herself as the editor of a slimming magazine. Now that the people of Derry had stopped hating one another, this lady had arrived to help them to hate themselves. During the Troubles she would probably not have come within a cannon's roar of the city walls. But with peace comes business in all its forms.

A Catholic businessman I met in Belfast assured me that Catholics like himself have put a lot of pressure on Sinn Féin to maintain the peace. Over the past decade there has been a surge of Catholic enterprise and success, and good relationships have been fostered between Catholic and Protestant business people. Catholics have a lot more to lose than they once had. Yet while business opportunities have improved and town centres have homogenized, it can sometimes appear as though little has fundamentally changed. On the evening of 26 May 2009 I switched on BBC Radio Foyle. The first item on the news consisted of an interview with the wife of a Catholic man who had recently been murdered by loyalists in Coleraine. She was requesting that nobody seek revenge for her husband's death. Next was a report that a Belfast solicitor had pleaded guilty to a charge of incitement to murder. He had encouraged paramilitary members to kill a man who was recovering in hospital from a previous attempt on his life. Eleven years into the era of peace in Northern Ireland, and the headlines could have come from 1985. The next item explained that the unionist Tourism Minister was vetoing the commentary of a podcast intended to guide tourists around Belfast, because it displayed republican bias. This story, at least, showed *some* progress. The introduction of tourism was giving old adversaries something new to argue about – but the bulletin hardly suggested a Brave New World beyond the Troubles.

Yet so much *has* changed. One of the most striking changes has been Ian Paisley's metamorphosis from stubborn belligerent to laughing democrat. But perhaps, in truth, this transformation contained an element of predictability. Paisley's outspoken loyalism had been a significant factor in the outbreak of the Troubles, and in the years that followed he and the IRA became yoked together, as though one gave the other a reason to be. They represented the poles between which everybody else existed, and theirs were the words and deeds that dominated the English media during the Troubles, blocking genuine discussion of motives and resolution. If true peace was to be achieved, they would either have to come closer together or become an irrelevance.

When the Good Friday Agreement was signed in April 1998, driven to a positive conclusion by Tony Blair's missionary zeal, Paisley and his Democratic Unionist Party wanted no part in it, refusing to involve themselves in talks that included Sinn Féin. David Trimble, the bold and progressive leader of the Ulster Unionist Party, who signed the Agreement on unionism's behalf, claimed that the DUP's absence had actually made an agreement possible. 'Had Paisley been there,' Trimble said, 'we would have been forced to raise our terms too high for Sinn Féin or either government to accept.' Paisley and the DUP objected to the proposed release of IRA prisoners, to the fact that the IRA had not yet decommissioned its arms, and to the prospect of IRA men in government. In fact the Agreement forced considerable concessions on both sides. Republicans had to accept the principle of consent, a huge compromise that seemed to contradict the IRA's very reason for being, and it forced unionists to accept a shared power executive and a cross-border ministerial council. An all-Ireland referendum followed: 71 per cent of voters in Northern Ireland and 94 per cent of voters in the Republic voted to ratify the Agreement. This affected both sides: it meant that republicans could no longer look to the 1918 General Election as an all-Ireland mandate for a united Ireland, and it meant that unionists had to accept that the majority of the population of Northern Ireland favoured shared government and ties with the south.

In the aftermath of the Agreement a power-sharing administration was set up, headed by the moderate parties: the Ulster Unionists and the SDLP. Trimble became Northern Ireland's first First Minister, but the administration was soon to fail and support began to migrate to the parties at the poles: Sinn Féin and the DUP. Sinn Féin was the party closest to the IRA, to say the very least, and it moved centre stage as the British and Irish governments made concerted efforts to ensure that the IRA decommissioned its arms and refrained from violence that might jeopardize the Agreement. The SDLP could do little but support Sinn Féin's position and it was duly eclipsed in terms of influence and support. In the meantime something similar was happening on the other side. Many unionists came to believe that Trimble and the UUP were not protecting their interests: decommissioning was delayed, a radical overhaul of their beloved RUC was recommended, and IRA prisoners were being released. UUP politicians, as well as voters, began to defect to the DUP, who could be relied upon not to surrender to the enemy; there were no Lundys in the DUP. In the Assembly elections of 2003 the DUP became the largest unionist/loyalist party and Sinn Féin became the largest nationalist/republican party. It was now up to the extremes to cement the Good Friday Agreement – or else destroy it.

Over the following months Paisley and the DUP refused to speak to Sinn Féin until the IRA had fully decommissioned its arms, and disbanded, while Sinn Féin was adamant that an agreement on power sharing had to be struck first. Deadlock seemed inevitable, particularly when a number of setbacks hit the process, including a multi-million-pound Belfast bank robbery that was attributed to the IRA. Nevertheless, those who had once stood at the bellicose edges of the Troubles were now in control of the province's political destiny, and they began to demonstrate a genuine determination to reach a workable agreement. Following pressure from influential Irish Americans, including Senator Edward Kennedy, the Provisional IRA declared a formal end to its armed struggle in July 2005, and two months later it was announced that all IRA weapons had been decommissioned. Old habits died hard for Ian Paisley, however, at least when speaking to his traditional supporters. On the 2006 anniversary of the Battle of the Boyne, he said, 'No unionist who is a unionist will go into partnership with IRA – Sinn Féin. They are not fit to be in partnership with decent people. They are not fit to be in the government of Northern Ireland. And it will be over our dead bodies that they ever get there.'

Such words were familiar from Paisley. The events that followed were not. At multi-party talks in St Andrews in October 2006 a timetable was approved for an agreement that would lead to power being shared between Sinn Féin and the DUP. The talks were problematic; the main sticking point was Sinn Féin's failure to pledge support for the Police Service of Northern Ireland and the criminal justice system. But pressure was brought to bear on all parties by the British, Irish, and United States governments, and Sinn Féin promptly held an Ard Fheis which ratified the policing and criminal justice institutions. An Assembly election was held in March 2007; the DUP and Sinn Féin were returned as the largest parties, and on 26 March 2007 the world witnessed an extraordinary scene: Ian Paisley, the man who four decades earlier had accused Terence O'Neill of declaring war on loyalists, sat at a table with Gerry Adams, the man who had formulated the 'long war' strategy in Long Kesh, and together they announced an agreement to form a shared government. The Big Man and the Big Lad, the bookends of Northern Ireland politics, had finally come together. Paisley duly became First Minister of Northern Ireland, while Martin McGuinness became the Deputy First Minister. Paisley and McGuinness began laughing, joking, and working well together, to the delight of most, but to the dismay of some supporters who believed that too many concessions had been made, and to the dismay of some observers who wondered why, if such a relationship was possible, so many thousands of people had to die before it could be achieved.

And then, of course, there is *the* question – why did Ian Paisley change his position so utterly, so suddenly? How, in a matter of months, did he go from warning that Sinn Féin would be in government 'over our dead bodies', to sitting with Adams announcing a shared administration? There have been many theories. In August 2004 the 78-year-old Ian Paisley became ill. Some have suggested that his illness, for which he was hospitalized, was responsible for a relaxing of his stubborn resolve, and for the realization that, if he was to reach the political summit, he would have to make swift and unaccustomed concessions. Others have postulated that his wife Eileen, the woman who had once been startled by Joe Graham, was urging him to fulfil what they both considered to be his destiny. At the St Andrews talks

Tony Blair made a point of isolating and talking directly to Paisley. The two men had already spent a great deal of private time together, discussing Blair's theological troubles as he contemplated converting from the Church of England to Catholicism. On the face of it, the Protestant fundamentalist was an unlikely counsellor for the Catholic convert. Was Blair stroking Paisley's ego in a – successful – attempt to secure a deal?

In March 2009 Bobbie Hanvey interviewed Paisley, who claimed that *he* had not changed: 'It wasn't my change. It was really the change that the Sinn Féiners made. I never talked to them directly, but every time I had talks through the British government, I said, "We must only have those in government who will absolutely and totally give their allegiance to that government. You can't have people who are undermining it and destroying it. And it must be proved by support of the police. These things must be honoured.' And the British government wasn't on my side. The British government held out to Sinn Féin that there was a hope that I would change. I didn't. The Prime Minister rang me seven times in one day to change a sentence, and I said, "You want this sentence changed so that you can tell the people that Sinn Féin will agree with this, and Paisley will agree with this, and that's it." I said, "There's no agreement, Prime Minister! Why build another rotten building in Belfast? We've had two forms of government, and they've both failed! They were built on sinking sand! We're not going to build on sinking sand!" And so he saw that I was adamant, there was no change in me, I wasn't another Trimble! And immediately we were there. I never met Sinn Féin until we both sat down in the room, and signed the thing. The deal was made – but at the last minute, Sinn Féin said, "We will support the police, but not the *Northern Ireland Police Service*." And I said, "Do you mean you will support the *New York police*?" And everybody laughed! I said, "Aye, come off it! Let's get this straight!" And eventually, they signed it. And they have kept to it. They kept to it.'

Paisley told Hanvey that the happiest day of his life 'was when we saw the structures of our own government back again, in Stormont. That was a big step; the first step of a long journey, but we're making the journey. And I mean, you and I know, that never before have we seen the coming together of both sides. Both sides can meet, they can argue their cases, but there's no threats or anything like that. We're coming back to proper democracy. And that's a wonderful thing.' Hanvey suggested that Paisley could have taken all the people of Northern Ireland down a similar path in the late Sixties. 'I know, I know,' said Paisley, 'but I don't think the time was ripe. I think we had to go through the fire.' If you listen carefully you might just hear Terence O'Neill turning in his grave.

In March 2009 the fire was rekindled by republican dissidents who killed two soldiers – Sappers Mark Quinsey and Patrick Azimkar – in County Antrim, and a policeman – Stephen Carroll – in Craigavon. For fourteen hours after the Real IRA attack on the soldiers, there was no reaction from Sinn Féin. Finally Gerry Adams made a statement. He had taken his time, and he had chosen his words very, very carefully: 'Last night's attack was an attack on the peace process. It was wrong and counter-productive. Those responsible have no support, no strategy to achieve a united Ireland. They want to destroy the progress of recent times and to plunge Ireland back into conflict.'

Adams took his time because he was in a difficult position. He had to reassure two groups of people at once. First, his one-time unionist enemies, but now partners in government, needed to hear him speak out against the killings. And he did speak out – but only up to a point. To describe a double murder as 'counter-productive' is not to condemn it out of hand. His language was restrained because he had also to convince his core republican supporters that Sinn Féin had not lost touch with traditional 'Brits Out' thinking, and that the only way to achieve the goal that really matters, a united Ireland, was through his long-term strategy, once a mix of violence and politics, now politics alone. The underlying thrust of Adams's message to republicans was this: killing British soldiers used to make sense. It does not any longer. Stay with me and we will achieve our shared ambition. Support the dissidents and all will be lost.

When PC Carroll was subsequently shot dead by the Continuity IRA in Craigavon, Martin McGuinness made a statement. He was still in a difficult position, but this time his remarks were remarkably forthright. 'These people [the attackers] are traitors to the island of Ireland,' he said. 'They have betrayed the political desires, hopes, and aspirations of all of the people who live on this island.'

There are several possible explanations for the contrast in tone between the statements of Adams and McGuinness. Perhaps, having gauged republican opinion to the first statement, McGuinness felt that he could afford to react more strongly. Perhaps the killing of a policeman was now seen as a more serious matter in republican terms: the British army was still 'an army of occupation', whereas the police force now had Sinn Féin support. Or perhaps McGuinness simply said more than he had intended to in a tense and nervous moment. Whatever the case, the attacks did not succeed in driving a wedge between Sinn Féin and its unionist partners. The politicians demonstrated a united front.

So far as the Real and Continuity IRAs and their supporters are concerned, republican politicians who have entered government with unionists have committed an act of treachery. The handing over of IRA weapons and the support offered to the police force are betrayals of republican ideals. And most of all they reject the idea that a political solution will ever bring about a united Ireland. The union with Great Britain, they believe, is still strong. Only physical-force republicanism can hope to fracture it. Perhaps they have a point. By signing up to the Good Friday Agreement, Sinn Féin agreed to be bound by the principle of consent, which holds that Northern Ireland will remain a part of the United Kingdom until a majority of its people votes to become part of a united Ireland. In 2008 Adams stated: 'The economic and demographic dynamics in Ireland make Irish reunification a realistic objective within a reasonable timescale.' On the face of it, such optimism reflects a belief that when Catholics come to outnumber Protestants in the province, the Catholic majority will vote to end the union. In the 2001 census 43.8 per cent of the population had a 'Catholic community background', compared with 53.1 per cent from a 'Protestant community background'. So even if the Catholic birthrate continues to exceed the Protestant rate, it will still be a long time before Catholics are in the majority. But even then they will not necessarily vote along predictable 'religious' lines. Polls carried out at the time of the census suggested that a quarter of the Catholic population would not vote for reunification. And as time passes, and old prejudices subside, more Catholics will be living in good housing, working in responsible jobs, and far less anxious to challenge the status quo.

So it is by no means a foregone conclusion that, under the terms of the Good Friday Agreement, Ireland will ever unite. Unionists would not have signed up to the document had they thought it would send them into the arms of the Republic. Gerry Adams's 'realistic objective' might only be realized by a creeping symbiosis, a gradual merger of cross-border institutions and policies, as northerners and southerners, unionists and nationalists learn slowly to cooperate. There is no doubt that republican thinking on the meaning of a united Ireland has changed over recent years. Shortly before his death in 2004, Joe Cahill, the ex-IRA man who spent four and a half weeks in a British condemned cell in 1942, said, 'If you have the unity of the people, you'll have a united Ireland. *Borders don't count.*' These are extraordinary words from a man so steeped in republican tradition. Yet if enough republicans come to question the strategy on reunification, and conclude that borders *do* count, then perhaps Northern Ireland could return to the bad old days.

But is this really likely? By 1998 the people of Northern Ireland had been exhausted by three decades of bloodshed. The subsequent years of peace have seen a massive improvement in the lives of people of all communities. The vast majority of them have absolutely no desire to see the clock turned back. Most of the ex-prisoners that I came across in my time in the north have lost their taste for the fight. In the words of Adrian Callan, 'Now that we have a voice, and a share in power, it's not right that anybody should be killed.' In 1969 northern Catholics had legitimate grievances; Terence O'Neill's attempted reforms had failed, and Catholics were excluded from jobs and from civic life. This is no longer true, and there is little incentive to relight the revolutionary fire.

Whether this mood changes, whether the next generation will be induced to take up the struggle, whether a small number of people, acting sporadically, can reignite the Troubles, these are things that remain to be seen. The hope is that, so long as the dissident groups remain small, and so long as loyalists are not tempted to retaliate against them, we will not have to see, once again, British troops manning checkpoints across the province. After all, when the accumulated misery of thirty years of bombs and bullets is totted up and seen to amount to little more than stalemate, why would anyone believe that another ten, twenty, thirty years of violence could serve a useful political purpose? And now that something approaching consensus politics has been achieved, can killing still be excused by weighing it up against historical wrongs committed by Britain or by the Northern Ireland government? All the same, it is worth marking the words of Richard O'Rawe: 'A lot of rubbish has been spoken about the fact that they [the dissidents] don't have an infrastructure or wide support. They don't need a whole heap of support. All they need is somewhere to hide a few rifles and they could keep this going for years.'

Sinn Féin's ongoing struggle to reassure its core supporters of its loyalty to republican principles has contributed to the veil of obscurity, which is so abhorred by the likes of Alistair Little and Gerry Foster. Starting with his 'long-war' thinking in Long Kesh, through his negotiations with Father Reid and John Hume, and on into his support for the Good Friday Agreement, Gerry Adams has walked a tightrope. He has managed to bring most of his old comrades with him on the journey towards peace, towards equality for Catholics within a partitioned Ireland, towards an electoral struggle for reunification based on the principle of consent.

Brendan Duddy, for many years the secret negotiator between the British government and the IRA, offered me an insight into the change in republican thinking. 'People do not know the effort that has gone in,' he says. 'They've accepted a suitable narrative – that the Provos caught themselves on, that they were bad people, that morale had dropped, that they couldn't find enough troops to fight on. Rubbish! It was a very, very difficult task which McGuinness and Adams had. They found the possibility of a way forward and they worked on it. The biggest breakthrough I had was when I got McGuinness recognizing that "Brits Out" was a slogan and not an answer. This started in '86 or '87, and it was just a constant reiteration. Like a drip-feed. He used to sit on my settee and put his hands up to his head and his eyes would be closed, and I would say, "Martin, you know, go for the bigger picture!" He would look up and say, "My time's up. I have to go." That went on for years, until I started to hear sentences come out, and I knew that he *had* heard, and he was now influencing the Army Council. So what changed? When McGuinness was listening to me, he was focused on war – and then he changed and became focused on peace. He switched from A to B. My job was to make it clear that the Provisionals *would* negotiate. And when it was clear, it would have been a very foolish government who would say no.'

But as the journalist Johann Hari has written of Gerry Adams, 'If he admits what he did – skilfully manoeuvre the IRA into giving up its weapons and accepting peace, after so long fighting, with so little to show for it – he will lose his support.' If such sleight of hand is at the very heart of the peace process, it is hardly surprising that truth has become Northern Ireland's most prominent victim. The achievements of Adams and McGuinness have been very real – but it remains to be seen whether a new generation of leaders will emerge, free of the baggage of the previous generation, able to speak plainly and honestly.

As my journey was nearing its end I went to meet a man who, I had been told, would speak more plainly and honestly than any politician. Ken Bloomfield – or Sir Kenneth, to grant him his due – joined the Northern Ireland Civil Service in 1952. He became head of the Civil Service in 1984 and retired in 1991. Since then he has held a vast range of public and private sector appointments, ranging from the Northern Ireland National Governor of the BBC, to the co-commissioner of the Independent Commission for the Location of Victims' Remains. I visited him at his well-protected house in County Down. It is small wonder that it is so secure; in 1988 his home was bombed by the IRA. He remembers: 'My wife and son were in the house when it was bombed. My daughter, thank God, was at law college, because had she been there, she would have been killed: her room was completely devastated, lacerated with great shards of glass. Some of the ceiling fell on my son, but none of us was injured. It was not a pleasant thing.'

Shortly after the attack, Bloomfield spoke to Davy Hammond (a teacher, writer, singer, producer, and film-maker) at a book launch. 'Davy was very much involved in the cultural scene. He said it must have been awful, and I said, more than anything, I regretted the loss of so many of my books. One day, through the post, came a little postcard and a little parcel. Davy had written, "I was with my friend Seamus Heaney, and we were talking about the loss of your books, and we both thought it would be nice if you had this copy of his poem 'Sweeney Astray', in which we've both written a little message for you." I was very chuffed about that. And two or three years ago I found myself negotiating with Martin McGuinness – who was effectively in control of the IRA when the house was bombed – on the education issue at Belfast City Hall. It was a mock parliament, and I was across the dispatch box from McGuinness. One part of me thought, God, this is uncomfortable and the other part thought, well, it's a damn sight better than the relationship we had all those years ago when he and his colleagues were prepared to murder me for the cause they believed in! McGuinness may have left school at an early age but, listening to him, he's extremely eloquent. So – we have moved on.'

Bloomfield is an engaging man to spend time with. He is as comfortable comparing rival football managers Arsène Wenger and Alex Ferguson as he is describing the eloquence of Martin McGuinness. He speaks openly, without bitterness, and is willing to admit to his own lapses and misunderstandings. As I listened to him I become aware of how pivotal his own role has been in the history of the province. I had long been impressed by a speech made in 1991, by a more than usually thoughtful Secretary of State for Northern Ireland, Peter Brooke, which marked a shift away from the familiar British government apathy towards Northern Ireland. Brook declared that Britain had no 'selfish strategic or economic interest in Northern Ireland: our role is to help, enable and encourage'. This speech was a genuine sign that Britain was prepared to seek a solution to its problem – and Bloomfield wrote it. Was the speech intended as a signal to the IRA? 'Yes, probably it was. But I thought it really rather important to make as wide an audience as possible understand what the fundamental British presence here actually was. And the fundamental nature of the British presence was simply defending the electorate. That people should not be forced to do what they won't decide to do by vote.'

In other words, Bloomfield's words were intended to communicate the fact that Britain was a neutral presence, defending the democratic right of the majority not be bombed into a united Ireland. Bloomfield was highlighting the same issue that John Hume was stressing to Gerry Adams in their talks. The speech was a crucial step towards peace. Politicians came and went, but so much of the credit for real change must rest with people behind the scenes, people like Ken Bloomfield.

Before we delved into the specifics of war, peace, and the future, I asked Bloomfield whether religion could be blamed for modern attitudes. 'People's political and public attitudes are often formed by their religious background and affiliation. On the Catholic side, there is a great belief in authority. When I was working with Tom King [Northern Ireland Secretary 1985–9] he would periodically invite the SDLP MPs to meet him, and it became clear that the others had no idea what their policy was until John Hume spoke. Whatever he said was their policy. But it was completely different on the Protestant side. It was more difficult to manage the Protestant population because the Presbyterian ethos which dominates here is the individual conscience – "Nobody is telling me what to do. I am guided by God, and I will listen to the voice of conscience within me." And that makes them particularly immovable. These are traits that run through the cultures.'

Bloomfield notes other differences: 'When I was Cabinet Secretary to the power-sharing executive of 1974 a certain cultural difference was evident. The unionist ministers would arrive for an 11.30 meeting at 11.25; the SDLP ministers might drift in at any time up to 12 o'clock. The unionist ministers had probably gone to bed early after a round of golf, while the SDLP ministers had sat up half the night drinking with a visiting Irish American congressman, singing "The Town I Loved So Well". And who did the congressman come away thinking were the most agreeable people to deal with? Who were the more congenial and the more outgoing? Unionism and loyalism have a problem with public relations. When is the Cannes film festival going to screen a movie in which the RUC are regarded favourably? Or even as a force that suffered, most of whom behaved pretty decently? Nobody will ever make one. It has no market.'

I asked Bloomfield what Britain's interest in Northern Ireland has really been over the years. 'Northern Ireland was set up by statute, and it was a constitutional novelty. It was a devolved entity within the United Kingdom – but there was a false analogy in people's minds with the British Commonwealth: there was this idea that we should just let them get on with it, that we shouldn't interfere. But that flies in the face of what the statute actually said, which was that the sovereign authority of the United Kingdom Parliament remained over all persons, matters, and things in Ireland. Yet that ultimate authority was never used, and think how irresponsible that's been! An entity was set up in which one lot was never going to be in charge. It was a recipe for disaster from the start! It really was!'

Bloomfield explains that the British attitude was that the Catholics had their Free State in the south, the Protestants had their state in the north, and they should all get on with it. 'But of course there was a hell of a difference between Northern Ireland and the Free State. There was a Protestant unionist minority in the Free State, relatively small, and most of them accommodated themselves very rapidly to the new realities. But that was not the position in the north. From the word go, a very major element of the population was entirely apathetic, and it was just an explosive substance. What happened had a horrible inevitability about it. I ultimately blame British governments for not taking an interest in the whole situation. A lot of people have died because there was such a reluctance to get mixed up in it. One can't just shrug off a sovereign responsibility.'

It is fascinating to hear such condemnation of successive British administrations – but nor does Bloomfield spare himself.

I asked him how discrimination could have been eliminated within the state, and he tells me a personal story: 'I think one of the worst things about Northern Ireland is that everybody endlessly justifies everything that they've ever done. They've always been bloody perfect – it's always the others' fault! Well, *mea culpa*. I was a young guy in my thirties, in the cabinet, and some leading Catholic lay people came along, and they had a list of all the main public bodies in Northern Ireland, and they said, "We'd like you to look at these lists, and just think about how many Catholics there are in these bodies!" And I'm afraid my reaction was, "Why are these people always moaning?" That was the mindset – and it needed some external influence, and that didn't happen until very late in the day. The old Northern Ireland Labour Party had an honourable record in this. In the early Sixties they did a lot to alert their counterparts at Westminster to the reality of life here. At the time I was probably one of those they regarded as a bloody nuisance.'

Bloomfield is adamant that Britain has not had any recent interest in Northern Ireland other than its democratic responsibility: 'Enoch Powell used to peddle notions about the strategic importance of Northern Ireland, which in the modern world was absolute balls. And the idea that Britain was making money out of Northern Ireland was demonstrably nonsense – the place existed on a substantial subsidy. In recent times the interest has been no more than protecting the democratic rights of its people.'

I asked him what he feels have been the most significant factors in the move towards peace. 'What dawned on the conflicting parties was that neither of them was going to win in a conventional sense. I think it was the emerging logic of the situation, rather than the influence of any particular individual, that mattered. But in many ways the most significant transformation was that of Ian Paisley. It was extraordinary because I had regarded his contribution to our affairs up to then as almost wholly negative and malign. Was it Eileen saying to him, "Ian, do you want to go down in history as the man who always said 'No'? Would you not rather go down in history as the man who made the brave jump?" He never wanted to sit down with these people – but perhaps he saw there was no alternative. The alternative was indefinite direct rule, and movement to a condominium form of government, and Paisley understood that – eventually.'

There were other factors, he believes, in the move towards peace: 'Nobody but a lunatic doesn't want violence to end. This is a place where there's virtually nobody who doesn't personally know somebody who's been murdered. And there is a real sense that sacrifices *had* to be made if it meant fewer people were going to be murdered. And another factor was the attraction of power to the politicians. Office has a great charm, doesn't it? Why would anybody be a politician, other than to get a share of power, to be able to get something done? Otherwise, it's all bloody hot air!' And Sinn Féin, he believes, came under powerful pressure from Dublin and America to move towards peace: 'I think the Irish American influence on this has been quite profound. I think, eventually, people like Teddy Kennedy were persuaded to wrap it all up. It wasn't doing anyone any good. I think they've always been pretty keen in the republican movement to keep their links with Irish America as fresh and strong as they can.' It was as a result of this influence that the events of September 11 came to have such an effect on Northern Ireland and, in particular, on the decommissioning of IRA weapons; Irish American politicians could no longer be seen to display ambivalence towards terrorism, and northern republicans had to accept a new international perception.

Bloomfield has mixed feelings about Tony Blair's role in the creation of peace: 'I think it's greatly to his credit that he did something that, arguably, predecessors should have done, which was to recognize that the Northern Ireland problem was a major national issue. Belfast was the first place he came to, after he'd been elected, so from the beginning he showed a determination to get stuck in, and he deserves great credit for that. On the other hand, his determination to keep the process going, no matter what, meant that the British government had bargaining cards they could have used much more skilfully. A major issue in this was the prisoners. The republican prisoners were very important to the wider republican movement. If I had been involved in this, I would have said, "Begin by making a gesture; let out either someone convicted for a lesser offence, or someone who is getting quite near the end of their sentence. And beyond that, it will depend what the republicans do." I think the British government was prepared to make too many unilateral sacrifices, and failed to put pressure on the republican movement. You can say, yes, it worked out in the end, but it took a hell of a long time, and it should have been quicker. I had a sense that Blair was determined to feed the republicans almost anything they wanted, so long as it kept the process going.'

I asked Bloomfield whether he feels that one side has benefited more from the peace deal than the other. 'No. Each side *says* they have. But I think it's the only outcome you could expect – a kind of trade. Of course, the republicans present it as a significant move to accelerate the process towards a united Ireland. But I don't believe it has. On the other hand, it does entrench the republican movement very firmly in the seats of power, which is not an insignificant thing. They tell the faithful that they expect a united Ireland to happen fairly rapidly, but I think they're too intelligent to believe that. It will be a very slow process – but something that could have speeded it up was the feeling, until quite recently, that the Irish Republic had totally bypassed us economically. When you went to Dublin you saw this rich, flashy, developing place. But a lot's changed recently. Belfast has been developing at quite a rate and the Republic's been in serious economic trouble. That makes unity less attractive.'

What does he make of the theory that the reality of the Good Friday Agreement has been that republicans and nationalists have given up the claim to unity, in return for equal rights within Northern Ireland? 'There's something in that. Republicans have to go on saying to their supporters that a brilliant future is just over the horizon – but I think it's well over the horizon. Yes, we are clearly into a more equal Northern Ireland, and that's a thoroughly good thing. One sees more members of the Catholic community in positions of great influence in business and the public sector. We've had a Catholic head of the Northern Ireland Civil Service. I would hope that people feel more comfortable – and that's not a small gain.'

Bloomfield regrets that the political centre has, as he sees it, been fatally eroded: 'The people who are artificially conjoined in government have deep reserves, and mutual antipathy, and they find it very difficult to observe the principle of collective responsibility. I just hope that our fragile structure lasts long enough for a generation to emerge who are not so directly associated with the unhappy past.' But surely a fragile structure is better than no structure – and had the political centre not been eclipsed by those at the 'extremes', the peace process might well have failed. A process that seeks to bring an end to conflict has to include those fighting the conflict. Unless they have been comprehensively defeated, the warmakers must become the peacemakers. The generations to come may, one day, applaud this fragile structure, aware that it contained the foundations of something permanent.

But does Bloomfield believe that the foundations are strong enough? Will peace last? 'I hope so. The recession has been unhelpful. One sees youths with few opportunities in terms of employment and leisure getting up to things. I'm concerned about more unemployment in areas that are already run-down. Idle hands looking for something to do. At the moment there's not a vast number of people involved in the dissidents, but how many people were ever in the Baader-Meinhof gang? There are going to be these episodes – and the important question is – can you control the reaction?'

It occurred to me that so much of our conversation has focused on the relationship between Britain and the republicans, Britain and the unionists, Britain and Ireland, so I asked him whether Irish history has been entirely defined by Ireland's relations with Britain. 'That's very interesting. One of the least satisfying things I've done since I retired was a spell as president of the European Movement of Northern Ireland, and we'd practically no members at all. There's very little interest in Europe here despite the fact we've got a lot of money out of it. But European membership has had an enormous impact on the Republic. When I joined the civil service in 1952 we would have thought that we were metropolitans, affiliates of the big British Civil Service, and there were all these peasants down in the south. But the situation changed. Your colleague from the Irish Department of Transport would tell you about a very interesting conference he'd attended in Stuttgart, and suddenly the Irish psyche was leaping over Great Britain, which had been like a big boundary wall, into the European environment. They had always had access to the United States, but now Britain was bypassed, and it made an enormous difference to the Irish psyche, and it has meant that Irish policy is no longer fixated on Britain, and what Britain does. That's very important. Eastern Ireland, the great Dublin conurbation, is now a big European metropolitan centre. But here in the north, people still can't see beyond Britain.'

So would it be fair to say that Northern Ireland now consists of two groups, each identifying with a nation that no longer identifies with them? 'Yes. I sometimes feel like somebody conjoined in marriage with a partner who no longer has any great affection for me. It's not very comfortable. I have relatives in England who say – in a very friendly way – "We wouldn't much mind if you guys floated off into the middle of the Atlantic and sank." That's why I personally wouldn't mind a united Ireland – if it were the kind of united Ireland that I would regard as a better option. But how many people in the Republic, other than in terms of a ritual declaration, really want a united Ireland? If you ask the question, "Do you want a united Ireland?", they'll all say "yes", but when you really explore it, what enthusiasm is there within Irish political parties and organizations?'

I asked Bloomfield to place a bet on the future. In fifty years' time, would the room in which we were sitting, in County Down, be situated within Ireland or within the United Kingdom? 'I think where we are sitting now may have a very different relationship both to Great Britain and to what is now the Irish Republic. I don't know what it will be. But it will be different.'

One person who believes that Ireland will eventually unite is Anna Lo, an Alliance Party Member of the Legislative Assembly (MLA) of Northern Ireland. She is a liberal, a woman, a Daoist – by birth, at least – and Chinese. Surely these factors make her an unlikely political representative in socially and religiously conservative Northern Ireland? 'Yes, but I am seen as someone without an axe to grind,' she says.

Anna Lo is originally from Hong Kong. She married a man from Northern Ireland and came to live in Belfast in 1974, at the height of the Troubles. She intended to stay for six months, but is still here thirty-five years later. In her memorable accent, a soft, almost hypnotic blend of Hong Kong and Belfast, she told me that her parents were not happy about her choice of domicile. They would have been much happier if she had moved to London. But when she arrived there were already over 1,000 Chinese people in Northern Ireland. 'Nearly all of them were in the catering trade,' she says. 'I met them sometimes in the street, and I'd say, "Oh, Chinese people! Hi! Hi!"' She started the first English class for Chinese residents on the island of Ireland. 'It was because they couldn't speak English! They were so isolated.

When they worked in the kitchen they only spoke Chinese, and they'd only travel from home to work and back again. They hadn't been to any of the places of interest, so weekends I started taking them out, to get a feel of the place and the beautiful countryside.'

Lo believes that Ireland will unite out of expediency. 'Maybe not in my lifetime,' she says, 'but it makes social and economic sense for such a small island to be united. Your business can have an office in Dublin, in Belfast, in Cork, and you wouldn't be bound by different laws, by different rates of corporation tax.' Lo's overview is as close to impartial as one is likely to hear in Northern Ireland, so perhaps it is worth paying attention when she offers comfort to supporters of Gerry Adams's strategy by saying, 'The Protestant community will have to be convinced to buy into this – but it *will* happen through negotiation.'

Negotiation – or at least genuine negotiation – is still a newish activity in Northern Ireland, and I asked Lo whether real issues are debated in the province. 'It's not *real politics* for the common good. No one takes risks. We are still very much a divided society with each side not trusting the other – each side thinking, "You're getting more than me! I'm not getting enough!"' I had already been told by a DUP politician that most elections in Northern Ireland are a straight sectarian head count, and that his constituents vote simply to keep the other side out. So does Lo feel that sectarian politics can die away? 'We've been so polarized that it will probably take two generations and a whole new lot of politicians for things to become diluted. Don't forget, we still have institutionalized sectarianism. We have separate public housing: 98 per cent of our public housing is one side or the other. We have different educational systems: Catholic schools and state schools which are really for Protestant children, so people don't have the chance to meet.' Her hope is that today's children, encouraged by peace and a more 'normalised' society, will become less sectarian. 'And things *are* slowly changing,' she says. 'More and more parents from both sides of the community are choosing to send their children to integrated schools – where they are seeing that the other side doesn't have green horns or an orange nose. And there is a policy to build more mixed housing, and to turn existing housing into mixed housing.' Her ingredients for change are peace plus time. But is peace assured? 'I think peace is here to stay. People have had enough.'

As Northern Ireland matures into a settled and peaceful society it will begin to experience more of a phenomenon familiar to the rest of Europe: immigration. I wanted to ask Anna Lo, as one of its – so far – few immigrants, about her experiences as an outsider. 'To me personally, people have been friendly. A lot of them would not have met any person from a Chinese background before, so there was curiosity. There were incidents; I was walking home from work a couple of years ago, and four young men walked towards me, chanting abusive language. I walked past them and the next thing I knew, one of them kicked me from behind. They all ran across the road, jumping up and down, screaming abuse and laughing. Actually my sons had worse. They had quite a lot of racist abuse, and they have been attacked.'

What has been the experience of the Chinese community as a whole? 'I think they would say that they have had racism against them from the start. Research was carried out in 1997, and 50 per cent of Chinese people claimed that they had had their properties damaged.' She thinks that there have been more racist incidents in Protestant areas than in Catholic areas, and that there are two reasons for this: 'A lot of Chinese people moved into Protestant areas, which tend to be more affluent than Catholic areas, so there has been more interaction with Protestants. But also the Catholic community feels that they have been the victims of oppression, and they don't want to be seen to oppress a minority.' Lo tells me of a current project to build a Chinese community centre in south Belfast: 'The plan has been to build it in a loyalist area. So someone has distributed full-page flyers saying, "We have successfully fought the Catholics, and now we have to face the Chinese. And they're worse!" We are seen as a threat to the loyalists' identity.'

Lo estimates that 60,000 migrant workers have come to Northern Ireland since 2004, most of them from central and eastern Europe, which means that about 5 per cent of Northern Ireland's population now comes from an ethnic background. Eastern Europeans have also come in large numbers to the Irish Republic – creating unusual problems. One Polish individual – 'Prawo Jazdy' – became notorious there for committing a remarkable number of traffic offences. Over fifty times Jazdy was stopped, and over fifty times the police took down the details on his licence – but his address was never the same twice. His crime spree was only halted when somebody pointed out that 'Prawo Jazdy' is not a name. It's the Polish for 'driving licence'. I asked Lo whether the arrival of large numbers of outsiders had diluted the traditional sectarian divide in the north. 'I don't think so. I think, if anything, sectarianism and racism are very much related. If people are sectarian, it's very easy for them to be racist as well. Both things are about a lack of tolerance and a lack of respect.'

Probably the oldest distinctive community in Northern Ireland outside of the traditional groups is the Jewish community. Despite being a non-believer – albeit one who doubts his doubts and berates God for anything that goes wrong – I spent several Saturday mornings in the Belfast synagogue on Somerton Road. I suppose I was taking a sort of refuge among familiar people carrying out a dimly remembered activity. But I was also interested to see how Jews function in a society in which they are so marginal, and to find out whether they have experienced racism from Catholics and Protestants so clearly preoccupied with each other. My questions were answered by members of the congregation who told me that there had once been a thriving, self-sufficient Jewish community in Northern Ireland, about 1,500 strong in 1945, but that numbers had recently dwindled. There had never been Jewish schools, so children had attended the local schools. According to one man, 'Some went to Christian Brothers schools, and they became little republicans, while most went to Protestant schools and became little unionists.' He stressed to me, however, that the community as a whole had been careful never to take sides. The exodus had occurred for various reasons. Some people had left during the Troubles, some had gone away to university and never returned, some had gone to find marriage partners, and some of the older people had gone to be near children who had already left. Of all the Jewish people I spoke to, very few had experienced anything approaching genuine anti-Semitism. But I heard plenty of lighter stories, like the one told to me by a young woman who remembered receiving a low mark at her Protestant school for an essay she had written about Jesus. When she protested about her grade, she was told, 'Sorry. It's not enough to write it. You've got to mean it ...'

Yet incidents did occur. I saw one myself. One Saturday afternoon I was walking away from the synagogue with the rabbi, a young man with an impressive beard, a Homburg hat, and an overall appearance that marked him out as unusual in Belfast. Suddenly a car full of shaven-headed young men pulled up alongside us, honking its horn. One of the young men leaned out of the window and with a grin on his face made a loud, guttural noise. It was the sort of noise that a child might make in a zoo, trying to get the attention of an exotic monkey, quite aggressive but not really meaning it. This continued for a few seconds before the car moved off again. 'What can you do?' shrugged the rabbi. He wasn't sure what to make of what had just happened. Had the men been angry? Intrigued? Scared? In a resigned voice the rabbi told me how a group of kids had recently thrown stones at him in the street, shouting, 'Jew!' The moral of all this, I suppose, is that Belfast Jews are unlikely to be bothered so long as they don't look different.

I had already been told by the cab driver bringing me into Belfast that Catholics are anti-Semitic – but I wasn't about to take his word for it. I had a strong suspicion that he had a vested interest in trying to turn me against the other side. Still, it is hard to ignore the fact that republicans fly Palestinian flags in their areas – to demonstrate solidarity with people whom they consider are engaged in a comparable nationalist struggle – while loyalists fly Israeli flags – to demonstrate solidarity with people whom they consider are under comparable siege from their enemies. Of course, support for the Palestinian cause does not amount to anti-Semitism – so long as the supporters in question appreciate that there is a distinction between Israel and Jewish people. But the fact is that, in Northern Ireland, when one side associates itself with 'Cause X' the other side will associate itself with 'Cause Y', and the result is that the associations became so devalued that they stand only for a local quarrel. As one member of the congregation said to me, 'They haven't got enough to fight about, they've got to find something else?'

Whatever the levels of racism in Northern Ireland, the problem has been ignored until very recently. The Race Relations Act was extended to the province only in 1997. One of the campaigners for its introduction was Anna Lo, who told me, 'There was a serious belief that we don't have racial discrimination here. The Act was seen as *not necessary*.' It seems astonishing that politicians could conclude that racial discrimination does not exist in a province with such a legacy of sectarianism. And it is not just in relation to race relations that Northern Ireland lags behind the rest of Europe. Abortion is still illegal in Northern Ireland. In 2008 a bill was placed before the House of Commons aimed at extending the 1967 Abortion Act to Northern Ireland, but both Sinn Féin and the DUP opposed the bill, and eventually it fell off the Parliamentary timetable. Only two

MLAs expressed support for the bill. One was Dawn Purvis, the leader of the PUP (Andy Park's party), and the other was Anna Lo. Lo told me, 'It's illegal to have an abortion here. Even victims of rape or incest can't have an abortion And every year some 2,000 women go to other parts of the UK, and to Europe, to get abortions. There's a lot of hypocrisy – because we all know these women go over in secrecy to England. And we also know that some women access the internet, and get hold of drugs to cause a miscarriage. For me it's an equality issue. A woman should have the right to choose. But here it's a religious issue, and a conservative issue.'

Another religious and conservative issue was raised by Ian Paisley Jr. in 2007. 'I am pretty repulsed by gay and lesbianism,' he said. 'I think it is wrong. I think that those people harm themselves and – without caring about it – harm society. That doesn't mean to say that I hate them. I mean, I hate what they do.' When he spoke these words, Paisley Jr. was a junior minister in the office of the First Minister and Deputy First Minister – the department responsible for promoting equality in Northern Ireland. He is not the first man in his family to hate what homosexuals do. His father launched a campaign in 1977 called 'Save Ulster from Sodomy'. This failed in its stated aim, for homosexuality was decriminalized in Northern Ireland later in the year. Since then, of course, Ulster has been dripping with sodomy. And this fact concerns at least one senior politician.

Jim Wells, the Democratic Unionist MLA, is a very interesting man. I met him at Stormont, in his Parliamentary office. He is utterly charming, self-deprecating, and genuine. He is deeply committed to various charitable foundations, at home and abroad. He is critical of Northern Ireland's lax planning laws and very serious on the subject of the environment. His is not a sentimental interest – it is a rational, practical, and progessive concern for the state of the planet. All of which makes his views on other matters disconcerting. He tells me that homosexuality is 'an abomination', and as he says it his whole manner changes from boyish enthusiasm to righteous anger. He glowers and raises his voice as though I am encouraging him to lie with mankind as with womankind. I am not sure that anyone has ever seriously used the word 'abomination' in my presence before, and I tried – and failed – to imagine an elected English politician taking a similar stance. But then Wells's party, the DUP, is not like any English party. Launched amid the bombed ruins of the Four Step Inn on Shankill Road, it is the biggest political party in Northern Ireland, and it is – and always has been – the party of Ian Paisley's Free Presbyterian Church. Jim Wells is actually a Baptist, but the vast majority of the party's politicians are Free Presbyterians and their brand of unionism is subtly different from that of the Ulster Unionist Party. Whereas an Ulster Union-ist might express total fidelity to the union with Britain, a member of the Free Presbyterian church will place his funda-mentalist Protestantism before his loyalty to his country. And since the Irish Republic is an expressly Catholic country, the surest means of protecting his Protestantism is through adher-ence to the union.

Such subtle difference in approach may explain why, in 1971, Ian Paisley was able to tell Irish journalists that, were the Irish Republic to scrap its constitution and change certain laws relat-ing to the influence of Catholicism, 'the Protestant people would take a different view' on unification. Northern Ireland's most notorious unionist was – briefly – willing to question the union. Northern Ireland is, indeed, a place of contradictions, and one in which religion rarely seems far from the surface. Which brings me back to my most surreal exchange with Jim Wells. As our discussion of human sexuality continued, he leant in to me and asked in a low voice, 'Do you know how many transsexuals there are in Northern Ireland?' 'No,' I replied. Wells paused for effect before dropping his bombshell. 'At least seven …'

12

THE SUNRISE

David Johnston looks like a great big bear. But unlike most of the other bears I met in this land of defiance and bravado, a lot of whom could find work on the professional wrestling circuit, his appearance isn't matched by his temperament. He is the gentle and reflective head of the School of Languages at Queen's University, Belfast. He is an award-winning translator of Spanish drama and his versions have been staged by the Royal Shakespeare Company and the Royal Court Theatre. He was raised in loyalist east Belfast, in a world of traditional beliefs, from which he has distanced himself. He is a man with a love for Belfast, who has thought deeply about his connection to the place. I met him in his office at the University. For one reason and another I had barely slept the night before, and I soon found out there was a mix-up over times; I thought I was on time, he thought I was an hour late. This did not make for an easy first few minutes – but it was not long before he was talking passionately about his favourite spot in his home city. 'To give you a feeling for Belfast,' he said, 'I would take you up to a place called Rocky Road. That was my stomping ground as a little boy. I lived on the outskirts of the city in a loyalist estate right on the edge of the countryside, beside the Cregagh Glen. The Rocky Road was somewhere that you could climb up, and look physically down on the city. And I could see how the areas that seem so far apart are actually right on top of each other – and that was a really important lesson. The separations and the differences and the distances in Belfast are actually psychological. Belfast is a city that is divided and apart – but it is a small city.'

Even when he was not looking down from the Rocky Road, Johnston was set apart from other young boys in east Belfast by his family. His mother was Welsh and his father was a merchant seaman who had spent time sailing between the Caribbean and Venezuela, where he had picked up some Spanish. And although Johnston's grandfather was a staunch supporter of Carson's UVF, he was also friendly with the local Catholic priest, and he sent Johnston's father to a Catholic school. 'As a result of his schooling, my father had a very dismissive sense of the petty smallnesses, the tribal communities of Northern Ireland. Even when the soldiers arrived in 1969, my father was absolutely hostile to the fact that they were on the street – not from an ideological point of view, but because it simply seemed wrong.' Johnston grew up on an estate that was partly UDA and partly UVF, and at 15 he found himself being asked to do guard duty, to defend the community: 'There was a very deeply rooted sensation that there was some sort of ethnic cleansing going on.' Many of his friends became active paramilitary members as they grew older: 'They were asked *to keep something*, to put it under their bed.'

Johnston did not follow that path. Why not? 'If I had been asked at 16 or 17 to keep something under the bed, I probably would have been enough of a herd animal to have done it. But there was some sort of serendipity, some sort of sense that I was a wee bit different to others because of my family, because I went to grammar school, because I liked going up into the hills, and I was never asked to do anything. So I never got involved.' In his A-level year Johnston made a discovery that would set him even further apart from his contemporaries: 'I went to the theatre. I was on a school trip, and I was dragged kicking and screaming. I didn't want to go. But while the rest of the class sat and giggled,

I just loved it. I can remember walking home on air through the dark curfew streets. It became obsessive with me.'

I asked him what it was about the theatre that gripped him: 'It was about feeling both individual and part of something. It made me realize that there are ways of relating to people other than through the traditional Belfast ways. It was about dreams other than the cheap dreams that are sold here so easily. And it's another reason why, unlike many other people as good as me or better, I didn't slide into the Belfast abyss.' Johnston studied at Queen's University, where he met Catholics for the first time. 'I was slightly a fish out of water, because here I was, a Belfast Protestant, studying Spanish in a department in which the students were mainly Catholic. So when Bloody Sunday happened I was immediately exposed to the shock and anger and horror of people that I'd grown to like very much.' At home in east Belfast people were painting 'Paras 13 IRA 0' onto walls, but at the university Johnston's friends were experiencing different emotions. 'So, for me, university was a place apart, a special place, like the hill. It was a continuation of the search for a separation from the city.'

Yet for all that Johnston stresses his separation from Belfast, his feelings for the place are very clear: 'I love this city. It's vibrant, and there are a lot of clever people here, people who question, think and talk. I think it was Padraic Fiacc who said you can love Belfast the way you love a beaten dog, but I also love the way the new Belfast is emerging. There's a refusal here to say we're beaten.' Johnston emphasizes that Belfast people have had to become 'good readers of situations'. 'In this city,' he says, 'we are very alive to the signals that people can give that speak to their allegiance. This is a very complex city. The way in which people relate is rural – they say hello, and they talk to you. But because of the Troubles they also became hard-nosed. So people are pretty friendly – but cautious.' He explains how he needs to keep a measure of separation between himself and the city: 'Every couple of months I need to get out of here. If I don't,

I go crazy. And I need to visit the theatre because when you go to the theatre you're leaving a physical place to go to an imaginary place.' He describes himself as a constant emigrant from Belfast: 'I'm in exodus. When I was younger my exodus was from the bullying nature of the kids who were the hard guys in the area. As I got older it was exodus from the way I saw the lives of the people in the area panning out, from the fear of never getting away. When I went to university it was exodus from the loyalism of the estate where I grew up. And now I'm in exodus from the two tribal communities; I detest so much the rhetoric of loyalism. I detest the smugness of unionist politics. And I detest the cynical dreams of nationalism and republicanism.'

This idea of exodus, of being committed to the place while maintaining a distance from it, helps to explain, believes Johnston, Northern Ireland's political situation: 'We've created a political culture in which the two tribes live in exodus from each other within a single political culture. It's a very interesting model. It's like the bi-national solution to the Israel–Palestine problem. I think we've done it already. We have two competing ideologies, living together, each with its back turned to the other.' Johnston recalls hearing Gerry Adams saying, 'Northern Ireland is no longer Orange. It's Orange and Green.' 'Adams,' he says, 'was referring to the bipartisan relationship that holds together, and it's the dynamic of pulling it apart that holds it together. By that I mean that people live in the division until there are extraterritorial pressures. Then we realize what we have in common – the fact that we're not English, we're not British, and we're not from the Republic. What we are is a group of people who have lived something together.' If you scratch beneath the proud identities, Johnston seems to be saying, you will find another, rarely acknowledged identity. Like a married couple who fight but cannot part, the sides share a connection that sets them apart from outsiders. This identity might be described as 'Northern Irish' but there are not many yet prepared to label it as such.

Perhaps this shared connection can, in time, develop into something proud and healthy. Johnston certainly seems to think that it will. He believes that attitudes among the young are already changing. While he accepts that some still live within the traditional mindsets, he stresses that, for others, the Troubles are little more than history. 'My generation,' he says, 'lived with a constant sense of an undead history. But it's not true any more. The majority of my students are not concerned about that. It's true that if a group is cross-community, people have a certain hesitation in talking about the past, but that isn't because they're scared of each other's histories; it's because we've licked our wounds in public for so long that licking wounds isn't high on the agenda any more.' He thinks that the influences within society have changed. His students see EasyJet bringing planeloads of stag and hen parties into Belfast, they have heard different languages spoken in their schools, and they have the chance to travel outside their own immediate areas. All of these are recent developments. And he points out that the mixed areas are expanding now: 'You have different people living in areas that would have been in the front line a few years ago. It's part of the housing boom, part of more ethnic diversity, part of an expanding lower middle class. All of these elements have come together to push the boundaries of the boundaries.' Johnston is a firm believer in what he calls 'intra history': how the lives of ordinary people bring about significant changes in society. 'Change comes from below. In the 1980s I could see the peace process starting to develop in the fact that each younger generation was more committed to going out. There were more restaurants opening, bars staying open late – and it was a powerful factor in forcing the political agenda. The determination to live a wee bit was absolutely key – and it still is.'

David Johnston has an unusual perspective on Northern Ireland. He is both an insider and an outsider, a man who once watched Belfast from the hills, and now observes it from the university. What particularly struck me about our morning together was his suggestion that it was serendipity that prevented him from becoming a member of the UVF or the UDA. His detachment from a traditional Belfast identity was the chance result of his upbringing. Gerry Foster suggests that those who became *involved* may have been 'more passionate about things' than those who did not. The young David Johnston *was* passionate – but his was a more eclectic passion than Gerry Foster's, and it has led him down an utterly different path.

We have already come across a young woman called Caitlin, whom I met at a group organized by the WAVE Trauma Centre in Belfast. While there I was introduced to a cross-community group of young people, in their teens and early twenties, who spoke to me about their lives and hopes and fears for the future. Dissident killings had taken place a fortnight before and, on one crucial point at least, these young Catholics and Protestants were all agreed: as Riona says, 'I don't know anybody who'd want all that trouble back again. It's affected so many people. The people that want it back are such a minority.'

We were talking in the front room of WAVE's headquarters, a spacious Edwardian house off the Antrim Road. There was an interesting atmosphere in the room; both tense and relaxed, as though the young people were eager to speak but nervous of revealing thoughts they had long been keeping to themselves. These were not old-timers taking stock of their lives. They were youngsters making their way in a province where new ways of relating will have to be found. As a mixed group of Catholics and Protestants in a place where such groups are still uncommon, they might even be considered pioneers. And though most were too young to have clear recollections of the Troubles, they had been directly affected by them, and I soon recognized that blend of friendliness and wariness that ran through my dealings in Northern Ireland.

I asked the group whether the paramilitaries still play a significant role in local communities. There was a general consensus that they do. 'There's things you don't hear on the news that's happening all the time,' says Caitlin. Such as? 'Punishment beatings.' 'Loads of places are run by the paramilitaries,' Darren adds. 'Up our way, it still is. Punishment beatings for joy-riders and drug dealers.' 'They're just not as forward about it,' says Curtis, 'because in the past it was men running around masked, whereas now, you know who they are, so they don't have to wear a mask to be intimidating.' Tricia, the WAVE coordinator, says, 'We've had six new referrals in the last couple of months, and they're all young men who've had punishment beatings or punishment shootings. Not all of them are related to criminal activity; some have said no to the paramilitaries, and the response is that they get their knees done. I don't see them here, because they won't leave their houses, they won't take taxis, you know? These are 18-, 19-year-olds. It just breaks your heart.' 'The paramilitaries will never give up,' says Caitlin, 'there's too much power and money in it.' 'Not necessarily,' says Emma Jane, 'because in the estate where I live, there's nothing. You've no paramilitaries, no community watch, no nothing. You have joy-riders, you have people getting stabbed, there's fights, there's the whole shebang.' So what causes these problems? 'Some of it's poverty,' says Caitlin, 'but I know that people go out and rob houses just because it's fun.' And what are the police doing? 'They refuse to come into my estate,' says Emma Jane, 'because they get bricks and stones thrown at them. There's maybe 12-, 13-year-olds falling over drunk on street corners, doped up to the eyeballs on God knows what drugs. People are scared to leave a window open.'

Now that Sinn Féin is advising its supporters to cooperate with the police, I asked whether these young people would go to the police if they had a problem. 'I wouldn't,' says Caitlin. Why not? 'Because of the repercussions.' Aidan says that he recently went to the police and got in trouble for it. 'I saw one of the policemen in town,' he explains, 'and he said, "Hello, how are you doing?" and then we started getting phone calls and someone came to our door and said, "Why was Aidan talking to a policeman?"' Caitlin says that the police don't do much, and need to prove themselves. But how, I asked, could they prove themselves when people don't want their help? 'The police don't try,' says Emma Jane. 'Just the other day a car was stolen. Nineteen people phoned the police before they'd come out, and they sent out thirty policemen in riot gear to arrest ten teenagers.'

So how do these young people view the old days when the paramilitaries had a greater hold on communities, and 'ordinary crime' was rarer? Riona says, 'My daddy would sometimes say that whenever the men in masks were around, there wasn't as much drugs, rape, all that kind of thing. These people were God! And that isn't something that I would ever want to see come back, because I don't think anybody has the right to do things to another person, but whenever you think of it like that … Especially now I've got my wee girl and I think about things like that, and I'm thinking, my goodness, they actually got things sorted! It might have been a bad thing to do, but places were maybe safer to live in!' Emma Jane says, 'Well, it would definitely be a much quieter place. People wouldn't be scared to leave a window open. They wouldn't panic that they'd come back and find their house raided.'

We started talking about the recent dissident attacks. 'It was murder, clean and simple,' says Riona. 'They're scumbags. There's no reason behind it.' 'It's just so they can make their presence felt,' believes Emma Jane. 'It's just to warn people.' 'Yeah, definitely,' agrees Riona, 'it's like "Don't forget about us!"' Are the dissidents powerful? 'No,' says Emma Jane, 'there's too many people against them.' 'I really don't think it's all going to kick off again,' adds Riona, 'because they don't have the same support they used to have.' 'Yeah,' cautions Caitlin, 'but one man can murder, it doesn't take ten men.'

Given that everybody in the room seemed keen to consign the Troubles to history – even if there was a certain amount of inherited nostalgia for the days before 'ordinary' crime became rife – I asked whether the old sectarian attitudes are likely to persist in the future. Aidan, from a Catholic estate, talks about a Protestant family who used to live next door to him: 'It was awful. We were friendly with them, but they would have got tyres lit and rolled down the hill to try and hit their front door, to get them to move out. And people just accepted it! People didn't think it was wrong at all, because they didn't know the Protestant family like we did, and it was just something that happened. But it was so strange! They weren't any different to us!' There is a general agreement that there is still very little interaction between the communities. Bessie moved to an integrated school at 14, and she says, 'It changed my point of view. You didn't want to talk to them or anything, but you ended up messing about with them, and we were all mates.' I asked her if there was any difference between her and her mates from 'the other lot'. 'No,' she said, 'none at all.'

Integrated schools currently make up about 6 per cent of all schools, and are attended by around 18,000 pupils. Even though only one of this group has attended an integrated school, they all seem to approve of the concept. 'It's about bringing the two sides together,' explains Emma Jane. Riona is in favour of integrated schooling, but she says, 'I don't see why people have to be put into school together to get on. My boyfriend's Protestant, I'm Catholic, and I don't think that it should have to be that you have to go to school together, or else you're never going to meet.' So how did Riona and her boyfriend come together? 'I was working in the bar of a nightclub, and I saw him there. It turned out one of my best friends was a friend of his. I didn't ask him what religion he was. We'd been together for two weeks before we even knew.'

I edged warily onto the topic of religion. Caitlin, a Catholic, talks about her recent visit to a Protestant church: 'There were two leaders, and they done everything they could, before and after the service, to convert me. You know, "You're going to hell", and all that. It didn't have any effect on me …' I asked what were the differences between Protestantism and Catholicism. Curtis, a Protestant, says, 'A Protestant church will refer to Christianity, not Protestantism, whereas in a Catholic church it's Catholicism, not Christianity. And a Protestant service is a lot simpler. You sit and listen to the pastor, whereas my girlfriend's a Catholic – we have a baby and she was christened in a Catholic church – and there's a lot more to it in a Catholic church. Lighting candles and processions. I was stumped. They kept mumbling something, and I couldn't make out a word of it. Everyone was saying something, except me and my family.' Riona tells how the priest who christened her daughter was very understanding about the fact that the baby's father and godfather were Protestants. 'I thought he was fantastic,' she says, 'because that wouldn't have happened years ago. The priests wouldn't have been as nice as they are now.'

What about politicians? Are they trusted? 'I think they've got what they wanted,' Bessie says, 'and they just don't care.' 'I don't really believe that,' says Aidan. 'My area is mainly Catholic, but if something is wrong, people don't go to Sinn Féin, they go to the DUP. You should see some of the things the DUP have done for people!' Curtis confirmed this from the other side: 'The area I'm in is really, really Protestant, and it's run by the UDA – but if something is wrong I go to Sinn Féin!' Why? 'Because they want to be seen to be doing something more for the other community. So they work that little bit harder for you.' I had once been told that Ian Paisley was an excellent constituency MP, who worked extremely hard on behalf of his Catholic constituents; this was not so difficult to believe, but I was now being told that the sectarian divide was encouraging democracy. It was an unexpected revelation.

There was a consensus among the group that politicians are genuinely in favour of peace. 'Yeah, they want peace as well,' says

Caitlin, "'cos they're all backing each other up. I think some of it's down to self-interest. Martin McGuinness knew he had to change his tune to get trips to America and a big wage packet.' Tricia, the coordinator, recalls a visit to WAVE by Gerry Kelly (a Sinn Féin MLA, who was imprisoned for the 1973 London bombings but escaped from the Maze in 1983) and Jeffrey Donaldson (an MP who defected from the UUP to the DUP in 2004 in protest at David Trimble's moves towards peace). She says, 'They were sitting with an injured group at a little table, and the guys in the group were saying, "You've been together for a year now, and what have you done? Show us what you've done!" And they said, "We're from opposing parties, and we've got a lot of stuff to work out, and it's difficult ..." And one of our management committee said, "Well, in the room you have people from communities who are responsible for each other's pain, and responsible for each other's loss, and *we* work together and *we* manage it, so why can't you?" It was powerful. Neither of them had an answer. They just sat in silence.'

I asked how these young people define themselves. What is their identity? 'I call myself Northern Irish,' says Riona. 'I'm British, maybe,' says Curtis, who explains, 'I've been brought up and told I was British, and I've looked into the politics, and that kind of confirmed I'm British. I don't want to be seen as one side or the other, but we have the same head of state as mainland Britain, and they still pass our laws.' 'I'd say I was Irish probably,' says Caitlin, 'but when I needed a house I would have been anything. I'd gone to Sinn Féin and they were dawdling for eight weeks, and then I went to the DUP and they got me a flat. So I'll be anything ...' 'It doesn't mean anything to me at all,' says Bessie.

So is there going to be a united Ireland? 'No,' says Curtis, 'I don't see it happening.' Riona agrees: 'It's been so long now, it's never going to happen.' 'I wouldn't want it to happen,' says Emma Jane, 'because at the end of the day, everything would go back to the way it was. They've only just got it settled, and it would start rocking again. It would sink ... like the *Titanic*.' Curtis says, 'If you look at how the whole confrontation started, there's Ireland as a whole, then the plantations, then partition, and then the people who wanted it back as a whole Ireland again. But now, when you look at it, it's Northern Ireland's individuality that has brought peace about. They've their own government now – not part of the Irish government, not part of the British government.' Curtis seems to be repeating what David Johnston had told me, that the bipartisan relationship between the sides is creating a new identity that is neither British nor Irish. It is why Riona is able to speak of herself as Northern Irish. Yet she tells me, 'I would love it if I lived to see the day when a united Ireland happened. What an amazing thing, you know? That all of this could be restored to the way it was.' Curtis believes that a united Ireland would offer little but renewed confrontation. 'Practically,' he says, 'the only thing that a united Ireland would bring about is the removal of a line between the two countries. It's not going to mean traditions changing, it's not going to mean Protestants all leaving so that things will be peaceful, it'll just mean there isn't a line on a map.' There is a pause after he speaks, which is filled by Caitlin. 'To be honest with you,' she says, 'I couldn't care less about a united Ireland so long as there's peace. I couldn't care less, like ...'

But some people still care a great deal about Irish unity, including many of those with whom Dominic Bonner has worked. Bonner is a bright and enthusiastic youth worker who spent many years working in Derry's Bogside. He tells me of his initial reaction to the area: 'Young people were so involved in politics, and a lot of them felt that the only way to move forward was to use violence; a number of them were quite happy to take a gun in their hand and use it to defend their area, their country, and I was angry and upset to hear so many young people coming out with so many negative comments.'

Bonner explains that a lot of older people in the Bogside were involved with the IRA in years gone by, and passed their views on to the next generation. 'The children have no choice in who they want to be, and what direction they're going in. Some young people would do quite well in education, but they decide not to continue into further education. Many young people would listen to their parents saying the Brits shouldn't be here, the Protestants shouldn't be here, and when the youth worker comes in and tries to talk about further education, confidence, self-esteem, it's a different kettle of fish. There's a lot of bitterness and sectarianism. You've got 12- and 13-year-olds involved, and the younger children watching. Even at 4 and 5 years old they'll be trying to make a petrol bomb, because they've seen their older brother doing it, and it's a hard cycle to break. There's a glamour about it. Sadly, one night I saw a parent who stood back and watched her son lighting a petrol bomb and throwing it at the police. She was shouting, "Watch yourself, son!" I challenged her, and she said, "God, it's like the old times, Dominic! Isn't it great?"'

Bonner says that the paramilitaries still have a real presence in the Bogside. He describes a recent problem of a couple of hundred young people congregating locally, drinking and causing bother, but that when residents complained, the police were unable to deal with the problem. The void was filled by the Irish Republican Socialist Party, which sent volunteers into the area. 'The IRSP gained support because they created peace and quiet – but they're linked with the INLA, that has no problem punishing anybody, and it's very hard to have discussions with them. The way a lot of people saw it was – "There's peace and quiet, and I don't care if there's twelve masked men walking about ..." Nowadays we don't have the fear of waking up every day with bombs at our front doors, but we need to have a proper police service. The police won't walk through the Bogside. In the centre of town you'll see the police patrolling on foot, or on bicycles, but not in the Bogside. If there's a car accident in the Bog, people will call the police, because they have to do that for the claim. If there's an unexpected death, people will ring the police, and young people will stand back, to give a bit of respect to the person who's died. But at other times young people will attach hoax bombs onto cars, set fire to cars, anything to draw the police in. Some of them think this is great craic – and sometimes the police will make matters worse. I've seen the police dressed in full riot gear snatching 6- and 7-year-olds who were throwing stones.'

It might be forty years since Free Derry was sealed off by barricades but, according to Bonner, less tangible barricades still exist: 'A lot of young people who have been brought up in the Bogside find that there's still a barrier, and they're afraid to step outside. This is their patch and they want to stay in it. But all they're faced with is negative images of their history. Every gable wall has some reminder of the past, and it's with them every single day.' So are the paramilitaries still attracting members? 'It's small numbers. They are looking to recruit young people. It's easier to bring them in young. I've experienced the befriending stage; they have kids handing out leaflets at doors, about community or voting issues, and they get friendly with them. That's how they get them through the door.'

Bonner now works in Shantallow, a mainly Catholic area of Derry, which he finds very different from the Bogside: 'Young people in Shantallow are a completely different mentality. I get young people coming to me, and saying, "Is the army going to come back? Is there going to be war again?" They are scared of it – completely different to the young people in the Bogside. Sectarianism is now mainly in the interface areas. If you work with young people outside of the interface areas, you won't find discussion about Catholics and Protestants, about the army and the police.'

I asked Bonner how the his job differs from that of a youth worker in England. He says, 'It's the same in that we all want young people to have positive and enjoyable lives and careers, but I suppose if you look at England, the problems are knife crime and racism; here we have a bit more complication with the fact that young people are fighting against the government and against Protestants. And we're starting to see racism here; there are Protestants fighting against the Polish and ethnic groups that are coming in. In the Catholic community we see Palestinian flags hanging off lamp posts, and we've even had young Palestinians here; in fact the Palestinians were upset that we were flying their flag; they couldn't understand why. They felt we were disrespecting their flag and their culture.' He tells me of a cross-community trip that he led to the Netherlands: 'The young people were all the best of friends for the simple reason that we took them out of their environments. One of the wee lads from the Bog had a relationship with a Protestant girl, and when we came back this girl was happily walking around the Bogside with him, hand in hand. People knew that she was a Protestant – but her family didn't accept it, and when he went to hers he was threatened and told to break off the relationship.'

Bonner believes the peace process will take a long time to bed down: 'We're still in a long process. It may take a long time to find real solutions, to integrate schools and communities, to create employment, and make towns more appealing to live in. I wouldn't be surprised if the peace walls are still there in fifteen years' time – but I don't think we're going back to the Troubles. I don't think anybody's going to let that happen.'

Dominic Bonner agreed to introduce me to a couple of young people from the Bogside, and so, on a grey summer's afternoon, I parked my car outside a Bogside youth centre and waited. In the event Bonner did not show up, and I was shown into the centre by two young men, both named Sean. We played pool and chatted about football, the universal male ice-breaker. I think they were surprised to find a middle-class Englishman interested in football rather than, say, showjumping, and perhaps this was why we were soon chatting easily. They were 20 and 21 years old, and both had been born and raised in the Bogside. The contrast between them and the WAVE group was marked. There were no chinks in their self-belief, no shades of grey in their understanding; despite their ages, their senses of identity were solidly formed. Neither of them was working, so I asked what they would like to do. 'Just a job,' says the first Sean. 'Something that brings money in. None of this lawyer crap. Just a normal working-class job. Bricklaying.' 'There is work available if you really want to get out there,' says the other Sean. They talk about jobs in call centres that they have applied for: 'People do that – just for the money. But that's all people work for: money. You get the odd person that works because they like their job. Like, do you enjoy your job?' Since my job involves spending the afternoon with them, and because I really do enjoy it, I say yes. 'Well, there you go,' says the second Sean, 'our people go out and work just 'cos it's money. It puts bread on the table. That's why. Nothing happy about it.'

Two or three times a year they both cross the sea to watch Celtic play at Parkhead. 'We watch Celtic 'cos they're 100 per cent Irish – like ourselves.' Do the Scottish fans make them welcome? 'Aye, we're very welcome, but they think they're Irish! The Scots think they're more Irish than us! When we went over last year a boy in the street goes, "I'm Irish!" He was drinking Magners Irish cider so he believes he's Irish!' 'Aye, anybody who drinks Guinness believes they're Irish. That's just the way it is. Americans are the same.'

What does it mean to them to be Irish? 'It means I was born Irish. It's like, you're born in Finland, you're Finnish. That's it. You're brought up in it. Loyalists here were born in Ireland, but they say they're British, which I don't understand. They're born underneath an Irish sky.' But the fact is that unionists and loyalists *do* consider themselves British, so how will violence persuade them to change their minds? 'We're stuck with this problem because of the British government. It's Britain who caused all this murder and mayhem. When people ask who created the IRA – the British invented the IRA.' These are the arguments that have been used by republicans for many, many years. And if Britain was suddenly to renounce its claim on Ireland, do the Seans believe that a civil war would ensue? 'Yes, I think the hard-core loyalists would start bombing and shooting innocent Gaelics and republicans.' How would republicans respond to that? 'Well, there's five and a half million Irish – as I am – and there's a million people calling themselves British. They won't have a chance.' And how would *you* respond? 'I would do the same thing. No question.' The boys may be right to conclude that – even today – a sudden British renunciation of claim would lead to civil war. And they do not seem averse to the prospect of taking up arms against their Protestant neighbours.

So what is their ultimate political goal? 'To see a united Ireland. For it to be a free country, run by Irish people. Nothing to do with Britain. A socialist republic with no king or queen.' 'You see, I'm sitting here, and just because the British troops have left the street, it doesn't mean that Ireland's free. Sinn Féin are trying to tell people that. But just because there's not a soldier out there with a gun, it doesn't mean Ireland's not under British rule. If we want to send a letter, it's the Queen's head on our stamps, our money's got her head on it, our postboxes have her crown, the phonebox is British Telecom. It's all British. And the fact is, I'm Irish.' 'You've people round here painting the post-boxes green because that's what they are down south.'

What was their reaction to the Massereene barracks shooting? 'Supported it,' say both young men in quick succession. ''Cos if they weren't in the country, they wouldn't have been killed.' 'See, Britain complained. Britain was, "Oh, why did this happen?" It's plain and simple. Take your troops and your government out of this country, and it won't happen.' 'All six of them should have died!' Even the Polish pizza delivery men? 'Aye.

'Cos they're serving the British. If they're going to live in this country, they need to learn what they're getting themselves into.' So do they support the Real IRA and the Continuity IRA? 'I support anybody that fights the war.' And are the Real and Continuity IRAs strong in the Bogside? 'You can see it! You can see what's written on the walls all around the Bogside!' I pointed out that while there was graffiti supporting the Real IRA, there was also graffiti that read, 'Fuck the Real IRA'. 'That's done by druggie scum. Because the Real IRA are sorting out drug dealers, killing them, chasing them out of the country. Which is right! They shouldn't be poisoning the community! It's like hoods that rob grannies and break windows. They're the ones saying, "Fuck the Real IRA!"' I asked how drug dealers are 'sorted out'. 'There's threats handed out, there's many been shot in the knees, many that's told to get out of the country, and one shot dead recently.' Why, I wondered, did people deal drugs in the Bogside if the danger was so great? 'That's what I don't understand. Because they always think they're one step better.' 'Aye, they think, they'll not get me, but three months down the line, they'll be got, no matter what.' Are mistakes ever made? Are the wrong people ever 'sorted out', because of a personal grudge, for example? 'No. No. The people you're going and telling aren't stupid. They would say, right, no bother, and they would keep an eye on them and see what's going on before they jump to conclusions and actually shoot them.'

The mood changed when I asked how somebody would go about joining the Real IRA. 'I wouldn't know.' I was paid back for the question almost immediately, with a description of what would have happened to me, had I wandered into the Bogside twenty years earlier: 'You would be kidnapped and interrogated.' 'If they heard your English accent, they would have said, "Round there!" and took you somewhere.' 'And then you might see daylight a couple of days later.' 'If you're lucky.' Between them the Seans have described an ordeal similar to that of John

Beresford-Ash, interviewed in an earlier chapter. And what about ten years ago? 'Probably still taken away and interrogated.' But I doubt I would have come into the Bogside ten years ago. I'd have faxed my questions through.

Do they have Protestant friends? 'No.' 'Don't bother.' Why not? 'I just wouldn't. I haven't had one for twenty-one years. I don't see why I need to change.' Would they go out with Protestant girls? 'Same again. It hasn't happened for twenty-one years.' We discussed the difference between a Protestant and a loyalist: 'There is a difference. A Protestant is someone who loves their life and gets on with everybody. A Protestant is someone who doesn't really care about their religion. You couldn't kill guys like that.' 'Wolfe Tone was a Protestant!' 'There's loads of Protestants fought for Ireland!' 'Bobby Sands was actually brought up in a Protestant area, in Rathcoole, and he was forced out. That's why he supposedly joined the IRA.' 'A loyalist is somebody that wants Britain to remain here.'

They talk about the sectarian trouble that exists between Catholics and Protestants in Derry, most blatantly at the interface area between the Bogside and the loyalist Fountain area, which is marked by a wall topped with a large wire-mesh fence: 'They're all talking about taking down the peace walls and the fencing. And that can't happen.' Why not? 'If that fence wasn't there, it would be a hundred times worse.' 'People down here call the Fountain "the cage". Go back into your hamster cage!' I asked about recent confrontations that had been taking place. 'For the last two weeks it's all kicked off again – for just one simple reason. The loyalists have been out on the walls, waving the Union Jack, shouting abuse. People down here go, "Ah, you bastards, fuck you!"' 'There'll be petrol bombs.' 'And before you know it, the police are arriving.' How do they feel about the Apprentice Boys' marches? 'When the Apprentice Boys are down, it's tense.' 'The cops know something's going to be happening. They're coming round the area, searching for petrol bombs and weapons.' 'And the Apprentice Boys, after the march, they've been partying up in the Hall, there's groups of them come down here, breaking windows, throwing paint bombs.' How do people in the Bogside react to that? 'Just go straight back, paintballing their murals, putting their windows through, just giving it back.' 'Aye, if loyalists come down here in the night, more than likely some people will go up and attack the Fountain.'

Do they want peace? '*Deep down*, we want peace. Peace would be brilliant. But I want a united Ireland before I want peace. You see, people keep saying on the news, "We thought times had changed. We thought the trouble was all in the past." It's not in the past!' 'Ireland is still under British rule, and there's always going to be people who want to pick up guns and fight!' 'When you think Martin McGuinness is trying to tell you to support the police, the people that killed your people! You just can't do it like that!' 'Our families have brought him in when he was out shooting the Brits! They brought him in, fed him, before he went back out with all his Volunteers.' 'He's a hypocrite!' 'The police was in the *Derry Journal* a month ago, saying that the Bogside's five years away from accepting the police. They said if they drive through the Creggan, Ballymagroarty, Hazelbank, they don't get attacked any more, but when they come into the Bog they get attacked. But they're not five years away – they'll *never* be accepted here!' 'They'll not be welcome in this area, full stop!'

Why does the Bogside feel more passionately than other areas? ''Cos it's the heartland. It's the heart of the Troubles in Derry.' 'The Battle of the Bogside in '69, Bloody Sunday in '72. That's what triggered it off.' 'It was a no-go area.' Could it ever be a no-go area again? 'I think it's heading that way. We've had two Brits and a cop shot dead …' What would set the Troubles off again? 'If the IRA were trying to ambush a police patrol, and if the police got word of it and killed a few of the IRA men. That would make people angry and want to join up.' Are there local people who haven't joined but who would if the circumstances changed? 'Aye.

If things went back to the way they were, there would be just as many.' 'Sinn Féin's saying, all the time, "Do not get involved in these groups!" but it was all right in the Seventies when they *wanted* people to get involved!' 'See, the peace process … nothing's happened. It's not really the way the news crews make it out to be. There's still punishment shootings, still attacks every two weeks. They mightn't be successful, but they're still tagging, and this country's far from peace.' So what's going to happen in the future? 'I personally think it will get worse. The Real IRA or the Continuity IRA will bomb England eventually. It's gonna fall back the way it was. It's never really changed, anyway.'

In what way hasn't it changed? 'The loyalists are just gonna be part of the cops like they always have been.' 'And now Martin McGuinness wants us to support that force!' What about the things that are obviously changing? For example, the many new people who have arrived in Northern Ireland. 'There's Polish getting attacked left, right, and centre by the loyalists – 'cos that's the scum the loyalists are. I don't mind the Polish coming over, because the Irish went to Scotland and America, and were accepted.'

Would these young men be willing to take part in a cross-community project? 'Tried it before, and it just doesn't work.' 'They just pick a row. I was on a bus where it was half Gaelic and half Protestant, and we were going to Bundoran, which is down south. Fair enough, we were taking a lot of stick from them. They were wearing their Rangers tops under their jackets, wearing Rangers rings, and shouting, "I'll put this in your face, you Fenian bastards!" We said to each other, "All right, we'll sit back and take it from them," and we just sat. As soon as we got off the bus in Bundoran we started shouting, "They're loyalist bastards!" and they never got on a bus as quick in their lives.' 'Everybody round here comes into confrontation with loyalists at some stage.' Can they think of a situation where Catholics and Protestants get on? Holidays? 'If you go on holiday and see someone wearing a Rangers top, you just go, "Nah, doesn't matter."'

I asked whether they wanted to ask me anything. 'No. I'm grand. We just want people to know the truth.' 'It all boils down to the Brits being in Ireland. You wouldn't see the French going into Luxembourg and taking over their country and shooting fourteen people dead!' I pointed out that France has a long and brutal colonial past. 'But the French realized, we're getting ourselves into a lot of shit here, and we're going to get our own people hurt if we don't stop hurting other people!' 'Our heroes are people like Patrick Pearse and James Connolly who rose up against the British.' And Michael Collins? 'He was shot dead for more or less agreeing to twenty-six counties under British rule.' 'It was a bad decision. I wouldn't have took twenty-six.' 'If Britain came tomorrow, and said, "You can have five counties, but Derry will remain British," I would say, "No chance!"' 'It's all or nothing.' 'Aye, it's all or nothing. That's the way it has been – and always will be.'

The two Seans switched off the lights in the youth centre and we went outside. I asked them if they knew why Dominic Bonner hadn't shown up. They said they didn't, and then one of them said that I should phone Bonner up and tell him that they'd kidnapped me. I felt I ought to join in the joke, so I suggested that *they* phone him, while I scream in the background. We laughed, then I walked briskly to my car and drove a little too fast out of the Bogside.

The Bogside Seans brought my Northern Ireland journey to an end. Over the course of two frames of pool (won one, lost one) and an intense but reasonably friendly conversation, the young men had left me in little doubt that they believed fervently in the ongoing struggle against British rule. I thought about the man who had told me that there was no truth in Northern Ireland. He had warned me that I would be bombarded by many 'true versions', sincerely believed, based on subjective experience, and he was right. It is clear that the old identities will die very hard, but I had encountered many others who were striving to create new identities, who, like the city of Belfast itself, were looking to create new ways of existing.

One of these pathfinders is Peter Sheridan, the ex-Assistant Chief Constable of the Police Service of Northern Ireland, who retired from the force in 2008 to become the Chief Executive of Co-Operation Ireland, a charity whose aim is to promote understanding between the two communities in the north and between the people of Northern Ireland and the Republic. Sheridan's policing experience has armed him with a practical and unsentimental approach, and he acknowledges the limitations of the Good Friday Agreement's push for peace without a concurrent push to eliminate prejudice. 'Sometimes,' he says, 'I feel we don't really have a peace process. All we have is a process of violence reduction.' He points out that with eighty-eight peace walls still in place in Belfast, the cold war is still in progress and relationships still can't be classed as normal.

I asked Sheridan to suggest a solution. 'It's not about taking down the walls. It's about taking down the barriers in people's minds about the person on the other side of the wall. And that won't happen just by letting things happen – or else in fifty years' time we'll still be living on either side of that wall.' In other words, the government should be taking more hands-on policy decisions. Just as legislation was introduced in 2001 to ensure that 50 per cent of police recruits would in future be Catholic, so Sheridan believes that legislation is needed to encourage integration in housing and schooling. 'For example,' he says, 'newly built houses could be sold on a fifty/fity basis. Or at the very least, incentives should be offered.' He is critical of the fact that the government has moved off the stage too quickly. 'The Good Friday Agreement has to be underpinned at grass-roots level – and sometimes the best way is to get a group of independent people to look at some of the "big pillars". The reason why Sinn Féin and the SDLP felt that they could sign up to policing was because of the Independent Commission for Policing in Northern Ireland.'

Sheridan believes that language can be important. It is time, he thinks, to stop talking about 'dissident republicans' and refer instead to 'criminal gangs'. 'We need a strategic decision that says we're going to stop using these labels. After all, Americans don't know the difference between the Provisional IRA and the Real IRA, between the dissident republicans and republicans.' He feels that young people should be educated about the dangers of gang culture. 'Young people are getting sucked into that gang mentality. There's an excitement to that life. Let's take these kids to the Bronx in New York and do a programme with them about gang culture – and link it back to here. Let's get them jobs, get them out of that system. We need a strategy.'

Ultimately he believes that people have to stop thinking in terms of their own rights and start to recognize the rights of others. 'There's still no tolerance and no respect. Real human rights is about *me* protecting *your* rights. So if I'm in the Orange Order, how can I protect your rights as a Catholic and a nationalist? And if I'm a nationalist, how can I protect your right to march? But maybe we need to go through this cold-war stage before we get to the stage where people can ask each other to "tell me *my* story in *your* words".' So far as the prospect of a united Ireland is concerned, Sheridan tells me that he has spent the past thirty years trying to unite people, not territory. Whether Ireland is united or not, it doesn't really matter to him. 'As the widow of Stephen Carroll [the policeman shot dead in March 2009 by the Continuity IRA] said, in the quest for a united Ireland, her husband got six feet of it. And that really helps the world, doesn't it?'

My time in Northern Ireland/the six counties/Ulster/the north of Ireland/Norn Iron was at an end. I flew back from Derry to Liverpool on a Friday afternoon, and I found myself sitting in the middle of a large hen party. One girl was wearing a veil on her head and an L plate around her neck, and she and her friends were wearing matching T-shirts proclaiming, 'If found please return to the pub.' I resisted the temptation to whip out my tape recorder and start asking them probing questions about the future of Northern Ireland, but as they drank and shouted to one another about the Liverpool clubs they would visit, it was difficult to imagine them concerned about the colour of the postboxes in Derry or the devolution of criminal justice powers to Stormont. I felt as though I might be flying out of the province in the company of its apathetic – but peaceful – future.

I met plenty of people on my journey who *were* concerned about these things, and most of them seemed aware – at some level – that times are changing, and that Northern Ireland will be forced to adapt its relationship with both Britain and the Irish Republic. The increase in business and investment, the vested interests of those who were once excluded from influence, fading memories of violence, the changing nature of European politics, the ambivalent attitude of Britain and the Republic towards the province, all of these factors will encourage an atmosphere of pragmatism, which ought to have knock-on effects: the vice-like identities of those who once considered themselves British or Irish ought to weaken, integration ought to increase, self-importance ought to diminish, and the old discourses ought to lose their relevance.

Ought to. Not *will.* Because these things aren't certain. It is clear that some of them are happening already, but I also witnessed contrary signs. I spoke to those who argue that so long as a veil remains over the past, true reconciliation cannot take place, and a better society cannot hope to evolve. I spoke to people who believe that identities will not weaken unless the government forces the pace. I spoke to those, like Joe Graham, who believe that that the fighting is destined to return: 'Most likely,' says Graham, 'it won't start again in my lifetime. But we're a Celtic people. That's a deep thing. Bobby Sands, Fergal O'Hanlon, Tom Williams, War of Independence, 1916, Fenian Brotherhood … it's almost spiritual. It's too dismissive to say that people are weary, that the war is finished. Who says? There's nothing sorted!' And I spoke to a few who fear that, in the shorter term, dissident republicans could spark a return to the Troubles. In September 2009 a six hundred pound bomb, intended to destroy a police convoy, was defused in South Armagh. For much of the Troubles the security forces used helicopters to transport troops and supplies around South Armagh; such was the strength of the Provisional IRA in the area that the roads were considered too dangerous for army vehicles. The intention of the 2009 attack was, presumably, to push the security forces off the roads once again, and to provoke repressive security measures that would alienate potential dissident sympathizers. This bomb was defused, but others may not be. For all the hopes and good intentions of so many people, the future is not yet secure.

Northern Ireland has confounded my expectations at every turn. It has been unpredictable and contradictory. A notorious region of bloody conflict, it is one of the most hospitable places I have ever visited. Whoever said, 'If you understand Northern Ireland, you don't understand Northern Ireland' might be the wisest man in all six counties. During my journey I went along to watch two marches, and together they underlined the futility of bothering with preconceptions in this place. The first march was the Lundy Day parade of the Apprentice Boys of Derry. Given the history of the city, given the passions aroused by the Siege of Derry, given that the Battle of the Bogside exploded after an Apprentice Boys' parade, I expected an angry spectacle – or a defiant one at least. What I witnessed was a loud, colourful, and good-natured celebration. At the time I was renting a house from Peter and Joan Pyne in London Street, staying there with my girlfriend. We were upstairs, getting ready to go out, when the sudden thump of Lambeg drums startled us. They sounded alarmingly close, as though the Battle of the Boyne had broken out in the downstairs toilet. In fact the parade began outside the house, and we ran out to watch bands of marchers file past, some in suits with sashes, others in leisure tops, some looking like Sergeant Pepper. They were playing flutes, twirling batons, trying to march in time, laughing, calling to friends by the side of the road, generally having a good time. It was clear that this was not a cross-community event. I would be surprised if more than a handful of Catholics stood in the watching crowd. Nevertheless, my girlfriend and I found ourselves smiling at the exuberance of the scene. Could these parades, one day, become viewed as celebrations of a shared history, rather than as antagonistic displays of triumphalism?

The second march took place in Belfast as the Royal Irish Regiment returned from its tour of duty in Afghanistan. I stood in the middle of a large loyalist crowd, anticipating a warmly appreciative atmosphere as the brave boys marched home from war. Instead I found myself part of a vitriolic mob. Sinn Féin had arranged its own small march in protest at the event; Gerry Adams had declared, 'This is an Irish town and for the British army to host a march at this time is totally and utterly reprehensible.' When the loyalist crowd caught sight of the Sinn Féin protesters, separated from them by rows of shielded and helmeted policemen, they erupted into seething, surging frenzy. I was knocked over, as were a few others around me. A very fat man was briefly sitting on my face. I got up and pushed my way to the front of the crowd, where I found a livid man with a shaved head waving banknotes in the face of a policeman, screaming, 'Take the British money! Take the British money!' These are the people whose wagons are drawn in a circle in the Shankill, who revere the Queen but feel betrayed by her government, and now by her police force. And whatever Sinn Féin would like to believe, as Eamonn McCann pointed out in the *Belfast Telegraph*, Belfast is *not* an Irish town. By signing up to the Good Friday Agreement, Sinn Féin acknowledged that Belfast will remain a UK town until a majority in the north agrees to an end to partition. Anger and resentment are never far away in Northern Ireland, and nor are irreconcilable versions of a single political reality.

If the two sides cannot agree on the meaning of a document that they have both signed, then a single shared history would appear a long way off – but I experienced something close to a shared history during a visit to the wonderful Ulster Folk Museum in Cultra. The Museum is an entire town of original buildings, reassembled on a single site, where I spent an afternoon wandering from a Presbyterian church to a Catholic church to an Anglican church to a parochial house. Dozens of schoolchildren were doing the same thing; I hoped with all my heart that they were learning some *very* important lessons, at the same time as they were giggling at actors dressed as old-time bank clerks and cheese makers.

All the way through my journey I tried not to forget the memory of the bombing of the bandstand in Regent's Park. I did not want to lose sight of one of my intentions: to discover the aims and beliefs of those who had caused suffering. Having spent time with them, I was sure that G. K. Chesterton's rhyme was a red herring. These were not people that God made mad. At least no more mad than he made my own friends and family. But my friends had not been raised to uphold a fervent cause in an atmosphere of grievance. My family had not been born in a land where guns and bombs were a part of life. The occasional envy that I felt of people whose lives had been simplified by passionate belief was put into perspective by a number of things: first, the reality that some had placed principle above human life; second, the fact that the divide, for all of its history and passion, can often seem little more than a manifestation of bewildering prejudice; and third, the obvious difficulties that some now face as the old certainties break down around them, and the world becomes a more complex place.

Those certainties have broken down around the two Seans in the Bogside. As a result I sensed a kind of envy from them; envy of those who had been volunteers in simpler days of right and wrong; envy of those like Martin McGuinness who had lived the life and were now telling them that it was time to put the guns away. The Seans would still swear by the lyrics of Dominic Behan's 'The Patriot Game': 'For the love of one's country is a terrible thing, it banishes fear with the speed of a flame, and it makes us all part of the Patriot Game.' The song remains a republican standard, but its black-and-white certainty, for so long the bedrock of republicanism, can no longer be said to reflect Sinn Féin thinking. The psychiatrist Dr Raman Kapur speaks about Northern Ireland finally 'growing up' as the 'infantile dependence' on Britain and the Irish Republic weakens and the province gains a sense of itself. Yet for some on both sides, growing up will mean a loss of self-esteem, a loss of what Joe Graham calls 'the moral right' and David Johnston calls 'cheap dreams', and a future without the purpose that a struggle once provided.

Yet for the youngsters from the WAVE Trauma Centre, for the thousands who gathered for peace in the wake of the March 2009 killings, for those whom Seamus Heaney had marked out for a 'little destiny', for the people who have never been tempted to sever the Red Hand, such a future represents the return of hope. Almost a stranger after so many years away, its return was welcomed by the Derry-born songwriter Neil Hannon. His beautiful 1998 serenade to peace, 'Sunrise', builds to a towering crescendo: 'From the corner of my eye, a hint of blue in the black sky, a ray of hope, a beam of light, an end to thirty years of night, the church bells ring, the children sing, what is this strange and beautiful thing? It's the Sunrise!' And it's not as though very many British soldiers who served in Northern Ireland during the Troubles look back on their time in the province with fondness. One soldier told me that he has stayed in touch with a lot of his old comrades. I asked him how they remember their time in the province. 'To be honest,' he said, 'we just talk about how fucking miserable it was.'

So as Northern Ireland grows up and puts away childish things – *if* indeed it is growing up – what is the legacy of passionate identity, self-belief, submission to the cause, and focus on the past? One could say that the ultimate legacy has been peace. But the Troubles would probably not have occurred had Terence O'Neill's reforms taken hold, and an almost identical peace could have been achieved had the 1973 Sunningdale Agreement not been so vigorously resisted. Viewed more realistically, the legacy has been more than 3,700 dead over the course of the conflict. In terms of the percentage of population killed, that would be equivalent to about 125,000 deaths in the United Kingdom – more than the population of Oxford, or around 600,000 victims in the United States – the population of that most Irish of American cities, Boston. But numbers of dead, as Stalin once observed, are only a statistic. They can never tell the story. A more personal legacy can be found in a poem written by Caitlin, the young woman who attends the WAVE Trauma Centre in Belfast, and whose father died for no reason that she can understand. Hers is the story of Northern Ireland:

> *I feel stupid*
> *I don't know*
> *Do I have to do it*
> *I like creating stuff*
> *Will the group see this?*
> *Will they like it?*
> *I don't think so*
> *I just want to change*
> *That's all.*

POSTSCRIPT

There are sex scandals and then there are sex scandals. One sort isn't all that unexpected – whether it's the England football captain caught with a team mate's ex-girlfriend, or the brilliant golfer who suffers from a 'sex addiction'. Another sort is rather more unexpected, and it was one of these that took Northern Ireland by surprise in early 2010. Iris Robinson, a 60-year-old MP and wife of First Minister Peter Robinson, was revealed to have had an affair with a 19-year-old-boy whom she was supposed to be looking after following the death of his father. In the province, the news was a sensation. More than a week after the story broke, a Sunday tabloid had printed on its banner: *'The Robinson Scandal – Turn to pages 2,3,4,5,6,7,8,9,10,11&20'*. The paper also included a report of the Haiti earthquake – on page 30.

There were a number of elements that added prurient interest to the Iris Robinson story. She announced that she had been suffering from severe depression at the time of the affair, and had attempted suicide in its aftermath. It was claimed by a BBC investigation that she had arranged for payments to be made by donors to her young lover, Kirk McCambley, in order to set him up in business, and that she had subsequently asked him for some of the money in cash and for some to be paid by cheque to her church. No payments were ever declared to the Northern

Ireland Assembly. It appears that when her husband became aware of the affair and the payments, he told her to return the money to the donors – but he did not report her to the authorities. Technically, this could put him in breach of the Ministerial Code but, according to Northern Ireland Secretary of State Shaun Woodward, 'He is an outstanding politician … I think he has cleared his name.' At the height of the scandal, as allegations flew, Robinson and deputy First Minister Martin McGuinness met privately. McGuinness offered his sympathy to Robinson, and the two men shook hands. This may not sound like much – but it was the *first time* that a member of the DUP and a member of Sinn Féin had ever shaken hands.

For many, notwithstanding speculation about Iris Robinson's mental state, it was the gulf between her words and her actions that inspired amazement. She is a strict Presbyterian whose morality has been very clearly inspired by the Book of Leviticus. 'Homosexuality, like all sin, is an abomination,' she declared to the Assembly in June 2008 – at the very time that she was having her affair. She seems to have been cherry-picking her verses. 18:22 certainly condemns homosexuality as an 'abomination' – but 20:10 goes on to advocate the execution of adulterers.

As a result of the scandal, Peter Robinson stood down temporarily from his position as First Minister – although he was reinstated before very long. While he was away, the DUP and Sinn Féin began talks aimed at reaching a deal on the devolution of policing and justice powers from Westminster to Stormont – described in 2008 by the Irish Taoiseach, Brian Cowen, as 'the final piece of the jigsaw of the peace process'. It is a contentious issue. For years, republicans considered the police to be a tool of enemy oppression, and the Provisional IRA considered them a legitimate target. Nationalists may not have advocated the use of violence against the police, but many have felt badly served by them. Sinn Féin only dropped its opposition to the police on the basis that policing powers would soon be devolved – but unionists and loyalists have been wary about the prospect of ex-IRA men assuming any sort of control over policing and the justice system. Yet if the intentions of the Good Friday Agreement are ever to be fully realised, then control of policing and justice must pass from Westminster to Stormont.

The talks themselves were tortuous and lasted for ten days. Had they failed, what might the consequences have been? An end to Stormont? The imposition of direct rule – perhaps with a Dublin element? A return to the Troubles? Gordon Brown stepped in to stress that if the parties failed to agree, he would call fresh assembly elections. There was a hold-up while fourteen DUP MLAs refused to approve a draft agreement, but in the end an agreement was reached. In reality there was very little doubt that it would be. Not only do the politicians want to maintain their power, but they are genuinely in favour of peace and progress. Rather like most 'normal' citizens, they don't want to see future generations consigned to misery. And aware as they are of history, they don't want to be remembered as the villains who screwed it all up.

Over the course of the negotiations some of Northern Ireland's foibles showed themselves. Early on in the talks, Gordon Brown and Brian Cowen hurried to Hillsborough Castle to oversee the proceedings, despite having pressing – arguably *more pressing* – work to do at home. It is very tempting to view the Ulster politicians as squabbling children, unable to agree, still dependent on the parents to come over and sort things out for them. David Ford, the leader of the Alliance Party, said as much, suggesting that intervention was necessary because 'politicians here are not grown up enough to take their own decisions'. But it is worth noting that the eventual agreement came out of talks between the parties in the absence of the prime ministers. It would be nice to be able to put this down to increasing maturity. Once the deal was agreed, Martin McGuinness said, 'This might just be the day when the political process in the north came of age.' And maybe the politicians too?

So why were the negotiations so long and tortuous? Partly because the parties involved are (or were until recently) at the extremes of their traditions. They still represent people who break out in hives at the thought of offering concessions, and they cannot be seen to give in limply – or to agree too easily. They must appear strong. For some disaffected loyalists – such as Jim Allister, barrister and founder of the Traditional Unionist Voice (TUV) party – the devolution of policing represents a staging post on the blasted road to a united Ireland. For some disaffected republicans, it stands as conclusive evidence that the Sinn Féin quislings are content for the union to remain in place. Most DUP and Sinn Féin supporters, however, have been persuaded to stay loyal to the party line.

Even without the need to keep hardliners loyal, agreement could hardly be straightforward given each side's contradictory interpretations of the Good Friday Agreement. It cannot be an easy thing to weld two different versions of reality together into one detailed and workable plan. Nevertheless, it has been agreed that a justice ministry will come into being, subject to a vote. The justice minister will come from a party other than Sinn Féin and the DUP. Agreement has also been reached on the issue of parading; a new body will be implemented to formulate a framework for 'parade management procedures' and the executive will transfer responsibilities for parading legislation from Westminster.

While some from both sides are claiming that the agreement represents a unilateral victory, there is nowadays a general acceptance that an agreement ought really to benefit *everybody*. In the wake of the deal, Peter Robinson said, 'No future generation would forgive us for squandering the peace that has been so long fought for,' while Martin McGuinness spoke of the need to 'confront all kinds of hatred'. If one is looking for examples of Ulster contradictions, then an analysis of either of these men's changing attitudes down the years might prove fertile territory.

It goes without saying that what they stand for today is not what they stood for in the past – even if they won't admit it. But the people know it – and they are willing to overlook it. This is the implied contract behind the veil of obscurity. *We are not judging your past – because you are promising us a future!* But as these men debated for endless days and nights, as power sharing threatened to collapse, as the grown-ups flew home to London and Dublin, many of the people who tolerate the veil grew exasperated. They wanted an agreement. They were not concerned about the betrayals of old ideologies, or even about the details of the current negotiations. They were not listening to Jim Allister's unrelenting voice, a scary throwback, as he stressed the perils of doing business with 'Sinn Féin/IRA'. They did not seem overly concerned with the problems of parades or the propagation of the Irish language. Agreement was all. Perhaps, in the end, nothing is more important than a peaceful future on almost any terms. After so many years of pain, people have simply had enough. They want life to be bearable, and they are willing to accept compromise. And that, surely, is what growing up is all about.

Appendix

VICTIMS OF THE TROUBLES

On 6 December 1982 the Irish National Liberation Army (INLA) planted a bomb in the Droppin Well pub in Ballykelly, County Londonderry. It was a small device, but it had been placed by a supporting pillar in a room where a disco was taking place. The explosion brought the roof down. Seventeen people were killed, eleven of them British soldiers. Major Bob Stewart, officer commanding 'A' Company, 1st Battalion, Cheshire Regiment, was on the scene within minutes.

'I was at home, about half a mile away, and I heard the bomb go off. I went straight there. I was a major, a sort of duty field officer. I rang the guardroom and asked where the bomb had gone off, and I was told somewhere between us and the Droppin Well. So I jumped in my own car, went straight there, and saw the result. I became the instant, de facto commander for the next seven hours. It was really horrendous.

'I went straight to the bomb site. I had a torch. The first person I met was a lance corporal who was only about 18. He was a very intelligent soldier. In fact my wife was going to teach him Russian. He was lying up against the remains of a fence and he had his stomach out. It was huge like a pregnant woman, and he was complaining and he said he was in agony. I said, "You're going to be OK. You'll live. You'll live." What I didn't know was that he'd broken his back. He became a paraplegic.

'I went into the thing and I knew it was my guys because they had their night off and it was a "white" area – it wasn't an area where we were under threat. Eventually, someone said to me that my clerk was underneath the concrete. I could hear his wife; she was beside her husband, who was dead. And then I found an 18-year-old girl, a local Irish girl, very pretty. Sad, really. I looked down and her boyfriend was trying to look after her and jumped up and said, "Are you a doctor?" I looked like a doctor because I had a jacket and a Barbour on. I said, "I'm not." But I shone my torch and saw her face and she was so young. He said, "I've got to get a doctor!" and that left me with her and I knelt down beside her and I was trying not to be sick because she'd lost two legs and an arm. They were just mangled, and there was blood going everywhere.

'I said to her, "Are you all right?" She said, "I think so." I said, "Are you in pain?" She said, "No. What's happened?" "There's been a bomb." She said, "Oh dear." Then she said, "Am I all right?" I said, "No, not really." She said, "Am I going to die?" I said, "Yes." She was such a brave girl. She said, "Will you hold me while I die?" I just held her. There was nothing I could do. The blood was everywhere and she died in about thirty seconds. I was severely affected by that. I could do nothing more. I was crying too much. To see a beautiful girl actually extinguished. For about thirty minutes I was *hors de combat* before I went back in. I could do nothing.

'Most people, when they're faced with something like that, if they don't weep they should be locked up. When we started taking the bodies out, it was like overdone roast beef. It was the worst. I found four other of my soldiers. Three of them had died and the fourth, we tried to cut his legs off. He was lying on three bodies and I said to him, "We're going to cut your legs off, kid." And he said, "Fuck of a way to get out of the cross-country run, isn't it?"

'I finished the night and felt it was my duty to go and see the wife of my clerk, whom I'd promoted that day to lance corporal. And that's why he was out celebrating at the disco with his wife, because he'd been promoted *by me*, and indeed I'd just finished playing squash with this boy at eight-thirty that night and then he'd gone to the disco and he'd died. So it was pretty horrendous. I walked into her hospital room at five-thirty that morning and she was conscious. I said, "You know what I've come to tell you, don't you?" She said, "Yes. He's dead, isn't he?" I said, "Yes. I'm so sorry." I said, "You can come and live with us, move into our house." Well, she didn't want that because her mother turned up pretty rapidly from England.

'The whole thing was probably the worst experience of my life in terms of what happened and very seminal in convincing me that an officer's duty is to look after the people he's responsible for. I went home that morning and got into a bath at about seven-thirty. I felt filthy and I lay there weeping. Then my wife came in and said, "The commanding officer wants to speak to you on the phone." I said, "Tell him to piss off. I've had enough." But she said, "He insists," and he said, "I need you to go down to the morgue at the Altnagelvin Hospital to identify the six soldiers we think are dead in your company." I said, "Oh for God's sake, can't you get someone else to do that? I've been on this all night." "Well, I would," he said, "if you had any officers that knew the soldiers like you do. All your platoon commanders are brand-new and your second in command is on leave, and it's got to be an officer to identify them. So, who else to identify them?" I said, "I can't believe you're asking me to do this!" But of course I understood it had to be me, so I drove down, and by about a quarter to nine I was at the Altnagelvin morgue, where there were about seventeen bodies around this room, just lying on the floor. It was extremely difficult.

'My clerk was the worst of the lot because he seemed to be unhurt but his hair had changed colour, and it didn't seem at all like him. He was the last person I'd identified. It took me until about one o'clock to identify six soldiers that I knew. I was in there for a long time. I met the brigade commander, who said, "Are you all right?" "No! I'm bloody not! I've been here four hours and I'm puking up because I can't take much more." I was expecting the commanding officer to say, "Don't worry, Bob, I'll take over." He didn't. He passed on.

'I said, "All the coffins are to be sealed." So that the parents didn't see what had happened to their kids. Also there was another reason. I wasn't sure that I'd identified everyone exactly. They were dead – because they weren't there – but it's a bit difficult when you've only got half a head, eyes out – horrendous. It's not easy. And soldiers are just normal human beings and nothing equips you for that sort of thing. Just horrendous. The people that do the post-mortems, they came out with coffee and they were eating their sandwiches, but to me it was horrendous.

'After that, my company was reduced from about a hundred and thirty people to seventy. I had to write letters to relatives. It took me ages and I suppose I went over the top, really. I had to write six letters, and I couldn't really hack it. It took me ages. I did them all by hand, in script. I even drew the "A" Company in longhand. When I've visited families I've found that in the corner of the room they have a sort of memorial. They always have his hat, they have his medal, the regimental badge, and they're as likely as not to have the letter of condolence. That's what a mum and dad have. So it struck me that I had to be really careful. It wasn't, "I'm sorry to report that your son is missing in action." Second World War. But I think I did it wrong. "A" Company had a leaping horse, and I drew that badge for each one of them, and it was probably too formal. But the words were the most important thing. I said that all of them died without feeling a thing.

'That was a terribly traumatic event in my life that affected me deeply. They gave me some commendation for it that I've thrown in the bin because it's not something I'm proud of. In my company, I had six killed and thirty-five wounded. That is a Great War casualty rate, if you think about it.'

Sean is a Belfast man in his mid-forties. When he was 11 years old his brother was killed by loyalists.

'Thirty-five years ago my brother was killed. I was 11, so I was, but I remember it as if it was yesterday. Two women came round to my mum's door, and said, "I think your son is lying there dead." I was in my pyjamas, and my mum jumped up, got on her coat, and we ran outside.

'What had happened was that my brother was standing on the Ormeau Road asking a girl for a cigarette. While he was talking to the girl, a car came up the road and hit the two of them. She went one way and he went straight up in the air. Then the car reversed back over him, drove over him, and crashed while trying to get away. It was random – they weren't looking for anybody particular. They just saw a Catholic and they drove at him.

'My mum and me ran outside. Two guys tried to grab me, but I shoved them aside. My brother was lying at the side of the kerb with blood pissing out of his head. On the other side of the road there was a guy hitting one of the guys who'd knocked down my brother. The next thing, the army had arrived, and one of the soldiers was down by my brother, looking for a pulse. He took off his beret, took off his flak jacket, threw down his rifle, and he put the flak jacket under my brother's head. He must have been a Catholic, because he said the Act of Contrition into my brother's ear. He knew what to do when a Catholic was dying. My brother was still alive but he wasn't conscious. My mother put her hand on his head, and when she took her hand away, part of his brain was in her hand.

'The next thing, the ambulance came, and my brother was put inside. We got to hospital, and he was rushed into theatre. I was sitting in the waiting room, and my mum was in the cubicle. In the next cubicle was one of the drivers of the car. He made a remark. He said, "I hope the Fenian bastard dies!" About five minutes later the doctors said to my mum, "I'm sorry. Your son is dead. There's nothing we can do." As soon as they said this, the guy jumped out of the next cubicle. I can still picture his face. He physically laughed in my mum's face, and shouted, "The Fenian bastard's dead!" My cousin was there by then. He stood up, gripped the guy, and started really punching him hard. An RUC man grabbed my cousin, but a soldier grabbed the RUC man and shook him to make him let go of my cousin. The soldier said, "Let him take him outside and give him the same death that young lad was given!" The whole thing was panic and chaos. The doctors grabbed my cousin, and the cunt just stood there and continued to laugh.

'You know, fair play to my mum, she says she forgave them. I don't know how she could forgive them. I don't have hatred against Protestants, but I will never in my life forget that guy's face when he laughed in my mum's face. You know, at one stage, I thought I should join one of these organizations and get revenge – but why? What for? Someone killed my brother, so I was going to get revenge and kill someone else's brother. Was that the right way to go? No.'

On 24 October 1990 Patsy Gillespie, a civilian worker at the Fort George army base in Derry, was taken from his home by armed men, and forced to drive a van to the Coshquin army checkpoint on the border with the Irish Republic. As he arrived at the checkpoint a device on board the van was detonated. The explosion killed Gillespie, the first of the IRA's 'human bombs', as well as five British soldiers who were manning the checkpoint. One of these soldiers was 30-year-old Stephen Burrows. I went to Blackpool to meet his father, Ralph.

'I had two sons in the army, both in the King's Regiment. Stephen was the first to join up. I didn't have a problem with it. We were living in Nelson, Lancashire, at the time and there wasn't much work, and young lads get to 18 and they think life's an adventure, and it's a steady job, so they joined the army. I didn't think much about him going to Ireland, until he actually was sent there when he were 19, and then we got the shits. I was worried about him being there.

'I remember the first time he came home on leave, I took him down to the club to meet my friends. We were walking down the street and he was looking up at all the houses. I said, "What are you doing?" He said, "I'm sorry, Dad, it's a habit." He were watching for snipers. He did two or three tours of Ireland, and he was always the same when he came on leave, watching out for everything.

'When his younger brother joined, the two of them always said, "We're in no danger, Dad, because we're good. We'll look out for each other." When there was an incident, when there was soldiers killed, they'd be queuing up for the telephone, to phone home and say, "I'm OK."

'Stephen, in particular, he said the Irish people were magic, wonderful, great. And he used to say what surprised him was the fact that these people could just go about their daily lives as if everything were normal. Any trouble that occurred, they just seemed to accept it and get on with things. He respected them. Several times he said, "If they sort things out in Ireland, I'd love to go back."

'Well, Stephen had got married and the last tour he did was twelve months. He lived in accommodation with his wife and his son, and he was very happy with that. He was a nice, easygoing lad, very popular, a pleasant bloke. Apparently he was a good soldier – but he never got anywhere. He'd gain a stripe and then he'd lose it. He was what they call "one of the lads".

'I remember the day. It were a strange day. My wife, Barbara, and I both worked at Pontin's Holiday Camp. It were a summer season job. I was a porter, shifting stuff, looking after campers, and she cleaned the chalets. I got up in the morning to go to work and it come on the news that some soldiers had been blown up in Ireland. There was no regiment mentioned – and this is a very strange thing. I'd worry myself sick every time my son was over in Ireland, and yet at that time he'd been there twelve months in married quarters with his wife and his son and we'd all got relaxed. He'd done twelve years, and given his notice, and he was coming home at Christmas. He was out, finished with the army. I'd just had my fiftieth birthday, and he'd phoned me up and said, "I can't be there but I'm with you in spirit" and he said, "I'll be seeing you at Christmas and I'll be out of the army. I'll be seeing more of you."

'Those were his last words on the phone and when we heard the news that soldiers were killed, it never entered my head. I must have been blasé, you know. Oh, Stephen's OK, he's coming out in two months. I didn't realize I'd stopped worrying, but I had.

'As we got to work somebody said, "We heard it was the Irish Rangers." Now, as it happens, there *was* one Irish Ranger killed – because there was an incident somewhere else at the same time. It was all coordinated and planned. At work we were all talking, "Oh, isn't it awful?", that sort of thing. We got home about five o'clock. There was a cottage at the back where the landlord lived, and there was a note on our door and it said, "Come and see me in the cottage." I went round and the land-lord said, "There's been a phone call for you. You've got to phone this number in Preston." And I knew then.

'I didn't really feel anything, It was beyond me, you know? I phoned this number and I remember saying, "Is it my son? Is my son dead?" 'I can't say anything, Mr Burrows, there's a man coming round, there's a man coming round …'

'So we just sat in the flat waiting – and then when the knock came, Barbara went to the door. I had the tension, like. I knew what were coming but I didn't feel anything. Nothing. And the man said, "Mr Burrows, I'm sorry to inform you …' All the formal words. When he finished, I said, "Sit down." Barbara were shaking her head, she were crying, and I went to make three cups of tea, and I said to the man, "Horrible thing you have to do. That must be awful for you." He said, 'It is. I've never done it before and I hope I don't do it again." And then he went.

'My daughter lived a few doors down and I said to Barbara, "How are we going to tell Debbie?" So we went out, walked out of the house and there were a shout from my son, Martin. He jumped off the bus. He'd been out the army twelve months then, he'd done nine years. He said, "Is it true, is it true about Stephen?" I said, "Yeah," so we all went to my daughter's and knocked on the door. My daughter came and opened the door and I think my words were, "The bastards have killed Stephen." She put her arms round me and started crying, and then I started. The landlord said afterwards he thought there were a bloody pack of wolves outside. It never hit me until then. I was just numb, and my daughter's there, and I was screaming, just howling, howling. That's how it come out that day.

'I just remember little things about the funeral. It was just a sort of blur. My daughter was pregnant, she was due any time, and I remember mentioning it to the guy who was looking after the next of kin. He said, "Bloody hell, I'm glad you told me that," and he rushed to the telephone, and they put an ambulance on at the back in case she went into shock birth.

'I remember lowering the coffin. It were a nasty rainy day, and there were soldiers round the coffin, they were lowering him into the ground, and one of the soldiers started sliding in the mud. I'm staring at this guy's boots thinking he's going to fall into the grave, and I don't know what my face was like but there was a hand on my shoulder. It was Captain Meredith, who said, "Stay calm now, stay calm." I said, "Did you think I was going to throw myself onto the coffin?" He said, "Well, yes, something like that."

'After the funeral we went to the local Territorial Army place and there were drinks all round, and this one bloke was on his knees, crying. "It should have been me," he was saying. He'd been taken ill on the day and Stephen had taken his place. I put my arms on him and said, "No, you've got to make the best of your life." I'm not religious at all but I was saying to him, "There are plans for you, these things are meant to be."

'A couple of weeks later I decided to go to Nelson, where Stephen was born and brought up. That was an incredible experience. It was Armistice Day and I marched, laid a wreath, and went into the local British Legion. I were in there, talking to somebody, and someone came up and said, "Oh, I'm sorry about your son," and then word got round and everybody were coming up. Barbara was with me and there were drinks all over the table, everyone was buying me pints, and I remember a big Irish man that I'd known for donkey's years crying and hugging me. He said, "I'm ashamed to be Irish." I was saying, "Oh no, don't be ashamed, you're a good Irishman." You comfort other people, it's a strange thing.

'After a while I went to sign on for work and I was sat in the Job Centre, and they said, "Why did you leave your last job?" Well, I was gone again, totally gone, and my wife's explaining to this girl, "He can't work, he's got to go and see a doctor." That was it. I was signed on sick, and was on the sick for a long time. I had a breakdown, I suffered depression. It was a really bad, bad time for six years. The years were going by, I couldn't work. I was incapable, I had lost concentration. It was life-changing. It changed me. His wife started courting and got married again. Life goes on for widows. It doesn't for fathers, I can tell you. I had been a very easygoing, laid-back guy, no worries, and I used to love it when we were all together and the boys came on leave, and we all went out. You know that song "You'll Never Walk

Alone"? We'd say it was the Burrows' national anthem. I hate that song now, it hurts me.

'I had nobody to talk to back home. People were saying, "Oh, I'm sorry about your son," and that was it. If I tried to talk about it, people – even my mates – would say, 'Oh, don't get upset, have another drink,' and I could never speak to anybody. I was down in this deep, deep well that I couldn't get out of, and I remember my wife saying to me one time, "You're speaking to me then? You haven't spoken to me for two days." I had no recollection of two days, just gone. And I had no confidence in anything. Sometimes, when I was talking to people, I'd see that glazed look come over them and they'd be thinking, oh shit, he's off, so I'd stop talking. I hated it all. I wanted justice, but I thought, they'll never get them, so I wanted revenge. I was bitter, full of hatred.

'I just hated the Irish, the sound of the Irish. When I went over to Nelson, where I come from, I'd go and have a few beers. Once I remember somebody had said something, and I said, "You want to come and talk to me about the IRA, come here, you fucking bastard!' I were just ranting. "Anybody else sympathizing with the IRA, come here!" And someone I knew come up to me, put his arm round me. "Ralph, come on," he said, "we're Irish." So I said, "I'll kill all the Irish!" but then I realized what I was saying, and I said, "I don't mean you."

'At the time, the IRA were putting incendiaries in litterbins, and I found myself walking up to bins and looking in them. "What are you doing?" Barbara said, and I went, "Oh, nothing."

'The regiment was very good. The other families were local to each other, and they were in touch with each other all the time. It was nice when I went to see them and we had these little meetings, and I could tell them what I were going through, and they would say, "Yeah, yeah, I'm like that." We had meetings at the regimental headquarters in Liverpool, and we formed the Friends of the Regiment, and we had meetings every three months.

'There's a do in Liverpool every year round about 24 October. They've got a big plaque there, and a big black book with all the names in it. The ex-soldiers, who were Stephen's friends, had got in touch with the families, and they held a service and then got lathered – as they do. I was out of touch when it started, but now I go every year. When I went the first time, it surprised me that young serving soldiers came as well, and I can remember hearing, "Bugsy's dad's here!" This one young soldier came up to me. "Mr Burrows," he said, shaking my hand, "obviously I didn't know your son, but I know all about him." Stephen is remembered not just as a casualty but actually as a human being.

'I didn't go to the Remembrance last year because I was in Ireland, in Derry. Where the bomb went off is just a road now, but I went there to lay some flowers. There's a plaque there to Patsy Gillespie, the Irishman who was killed, the man who was made to drive the car. There was nothing left of him. When I first met Mrs Gillespie, his wife, she said, "I feel awful for you," and I said, "No, no, your husband couldn't help it – any man would have done the same for his wife and kids." He had said to her he'd be home soon, but he would've known he was going to die. They tied him in, fastened him into the car. My son knew him as Patsy from the kitchens. I imagine my son was on the telephone, standing by the car window, and he'd have looked inside the car and seen Patsy. That would be the last thing he'd know.

'In 2000 I was invited to the Glencree Centre for Peace and Reconciliation in Wicklow. It improved my life. I started meeting and speaking to people – really talking to them. When I first went there it was just the English people, then we met a group of Irish people, and it was only after that we met the combatants. The first meetings I went to, for a long time, I still had this great hatred and bitterness, this need for revenge.

'When I first met the Irish group they were all on edge because some of their relatives had been killed by British soldiers, but we all became friends, because we listened to each other. That was what changed me. It came my turn to talk. I told them what happened to my son. I was shitting myself, I didn't want to talk – they're all strangers – but somebody else had just told a story, and I found myself thinking, God, that's awful. So I went through the thing, and I thought, thank God I've got it over with, and then I listened to others. I listened to a woman – her daughter had been shot by a rubber bullet, by a British soldier – and she kept saying that the British army killed her daughter. I went over to her afterwards. She jumped up, she was looking at me as I walked towards her, and she said, "Sorry about your son," and I said, "Yeah, your daughter. Oh God, isn't it awful?" All we had at first was sympathy for each other, but later I said to her, "It wasn't the British *army* that killed your daughter. Think about it. A British *soldier* shot your daughter. It could have been an accident, it could have been a stray bullet, or it could have been deliberate from a right nasty bastard. It wouldn't be the British army saying, 'Let's go out and shoot 15-year-old girls.'" She went, "Well, no." Three months later we had another meeting and this lady came over to me and she said that her family had talked about it, and she said, "All the family are saying they understand what you mean. I was telling them about you, what a nice chap you are, *and your boy was a soldier …*" Because, of course, they hated the British army.

'I hadn't changed up to then, but that was the start of it. I thought to myself, something I've said has changed somebody's attitude. I started thinking, maybe it's not all black and white. I started hearing about the history of the thing. The first person who talked about it was a good man. He was a facilitator at one of the meetings and he was telling me what it was like for him, growing up as a Catholic boy. He told me how he was picked on because he were Catholic, how he didn't have certain rights, how in some places Catholics couldn't get jobs. In England we never knew that. Nobody I spoke to ever knew that. We just knew them as mad bastards. But there's still a big leap from that to violence.

If you look at Martin Luther King in America, that was a non-violent movement that more or less achieved its goals. And there *was* a civil rights movement in Northern Ireland.

'But the bitterness, the hatred that I was feeling, the need to go out and kill somebody else – it's what the Irish have been doing for generations – and all it was doing to me was eating me up inside. I can remember saying this at one meeting and then I said, "I don't feel that bitterness any more," and it was like a release. I couldn't get revenge, I couldn't do anything at all, but without feeling this bitterness, I felt more at ease. What was in my head then was peace in Ireland. And I thought, great. Rest in peace, son.

'I started meeting ex-prisoners that had done bad things, men who got up to sixteen years for incidents. When we first met it was very fraught, you know, but now … I actually have friends amongst them … because their attitude isn't the same any more. I've heard stories about what it were like for them, stories of why they joined the IRA. But I wanted to know what actually leads you to kill someone. How do you get yourself into a state where you can actually do that? That's what I wanted to talk about – and it was very difficult because you didn't know if they were going to tell the truth or make things up. The first time we met, there were six of them, and they weren't saying, "I wish I hadn't done what I did, I was wrong." Nobody said that. The only thing I got was a big fella who put his arm around my shoulder, and said, "You're a good man. I'm really sorry about your son." Well, that was something, you know, the nearest thing I got to "We shouldn't have done it". Nobody's ever said that.

'I didn't have any clever words to say. I weren't like someone in the movies, where the guy says something and they all go, "By Jove, he's right, he said something brilliant!" I just said, "Talking is the only way you'll get together and have peace in Ireland." I say this over, and over, and over.

'A lot of people say, "How can Martin McGuinness run the country? It's totally out of order. It's totally wrong." But somebody has to be in charge. Somebody has to be in government. I don't have a problem with it being ex-combatants, provided they're fair to all sides in their new capacity. For goodness sake, Ian Paisley and Martin McGuinness, number one and number two! I mean I walked into a room at Glencree and I saw it on the television, these two sat together, and I was totally stunned. There was hope. I said to the IRA men, "I'm glad to see that Paisley and McGuinness have been listening to me!" There was total silence for a second, and everybody started laughing. Because if them two can talk to each other, then the Catholics can talk to the Protestants across the road.

'I've thought a lot about forgiveness, and the first thing I say straight out is – I'll never forgive. It's not for me to forgive, it's for my son. I can never forgive. I'm never going to have somebody come up to me and say I'm really sorry for what I did. When I've asked the IRA chappies, some of them have said, "We want the peace, we want the Good Friday Agreement, we don't want to do this ever again, but at the time we thought we were right. It was the only right thing to do." They can't go beyond that. They say they wouldn't join in now if it came back – but they say that, at the time, it was the only way. I've said to them that they murdered my son, and they've said, "Don't use that word!" It gets their backs up, they start to argue that it wasn't murder, but that's not the discussion I want. I want to move forward. I said to one man, "Have you achieved your end, what you were after?" He said, "No." We're searching, all of us, we're still on the journey. You can't forget the past. I'll never forget that these people killed my son.

'The whole concept of equal compensation for all the victims of the Troubles is ridiculous. I go and plant a bomb, it goes wrong, it blows me up, and somebody gets twelve thousand quid – how bloody stupid is that? The hierarchy of victimhood, it comes up over and over again in our discussions. The guy that's done sixteen years for planting a bomb isn't a victim like I am.

They made the choice to do what they did, but I'm an innocent victim. If I had been brought up a Catholic in Northern Ireland, being harassed, and my life was awful, my front door was being kicked in by soldiers, what would I have done? Good question. We were all thinking about this, and I said I couldn't see me killing people. But then a lady said to me, "You said you could kill the person who killed your son!" I'd said that before I got rid of all the bitterness, when the anger was still there. It's a thin line. But I think there *is* a difference.

'The worst is the tit-for-tat thing. My friend Hugh, he was semi-crippled for years, with five bullets in him. He was a Catholic. Some loyalists had been killed, so they went round to kill Catholics, just saw him and went boom, boom, boom, boom, boom. He was a lovely fella, a very brave chap. He was in pain for years, and last year he died. He wasn't involved at all – and that is murder pure and simple. I cannot understand the mentality of someone who can walk into a pub, kill total strangers, and then walk out. Both sides have done it. Now, OK, I can understand that the IRA wants to get rid of the Brits, they want to get the soldiers out of their country. It's not right, but I understand it. But to do that indiscriminate killing – I cannot understand it. If somebody said to me that he'd done that, I'd say, "You're a fucking animal." That's not human. Someone who's done that can't be a victim. He's a murderer.'

Joe Graham, writer, historian, civil rights veteran, and republican, describes breaking horrible news to the parents of a young man:

'There was an 18-year-old boy going with a girl in Ardoyne, and there was a wee bit of action one night and the Brits opened up and hit your man on the side of the head and blew part of it off. I was in a car, and I was told I couldn't go up to him, because the Brits would open up, but I drove up, grabbed him, pulled him across my knee, backed down the road to a house, and called an ambulance. He was dead, near enough. They rushed him to hospital, and I was amazed to see he lived over on Springfield Road. So I sat in my motor and I shot across – and my thinking was, imagine having a lad of 18 and being in bed when he was dying and not getting a chance to see him. I shot on, and banged on the door of his house and a man came down, a very tall man in bare feet, just his trousers on. "Hello," I said. "You've got a son?" He said, "Do you know where he is?" I said, "I've got some very bad news for you. If I left this to the cops, you wouldn't hear about this till six o'clock tomorrow night. Your son's very seriously wounded. He's been shot." The man drained white. "How is he? How is he?" I said, "I'm going to tell you honestly, there's very little chance. I'd say none." "Oh my God." So he went back to the stairs, and started to go up to tell his wife, and he turned round to me, and said, "What will I tell her?" The dilemma that man was in – to have to go and say to his wife, "Our child is dead." He went up the stairs and went to the bedroom door, went in, and closed it behind him. And then a *caoin* went up. Do you know that word? It's an Irish word, it means the wailing of a mother on the death of a child. Well, a *caoin* went up. And it was frightening.'

On 22 September 1972, the Royal Ulster Constabulary in Crossmaglen, South Armagh, received a telephone call that a claymore mine (an anti-personnel mine that fires shrapnel on detonation) had been spotted on the road at Drumuckaval. A party of soldiers was dispatched to the scene. As they investigated the claim a machine-gun opened up from the southern side of the border, killing a Second Lieutenant of the Argyll and Sutherland Highlanders. In response to this ambush two officers of the Royal Ulster Constabulary made their way to the scene, to recover the army equipment that had been left behind. As they returned to their *police station they drove into another IRA ambush. One of the police officers, Sam Malcolmson, was shot repeatedly.*

'When the opportunity came to join the RUC in 1969, I jumped at it. I served in an area in South Down, in Newcastle. The station that I served in, there were seven or eight young lads, all 19, 20 years of age, and we did get up to mischief. We had a little bit of respect for authority, but we didn't believe authority was always right.

'When I went to South Armagh I served in Crossmaglen. In the early days I could go into the shops. I was doing malicious-injury claims for the people, going around making sure they got their compensation when the IRA detonated a bomb. I was doing normal police work. I can remember in the early days, sitting in Camlough village in full uniform, drinking my pint of milk, eating a KitKat, early in the morning, and there was not a threat. However, that situation changed quite suddenly. Crossmaglen did open up a new, more vicious world to me. One incident that always sticks in my memory was going out the Dundalk Road, down to Richardson's Cross. A Saracen, one of the heavy army vehicles, had been blown up, and a young soldier was trapped under the vehicle. When we arrived at the scene we had just drove over that bomb a few hours earlier, and we were in a small car. Our car would not have shown above the high hedge, but obviously the army vehicle did. It was blown up, and the young soldier was trapped underneath.

'That guy was burning to death, and I suppose this will always stick in my mind. It would have been a kindness for someone to have shot him at that stage. I remember some people standing near Richardson's Cross, and they were jeering and laughing and shouting at what was going on. I wonder, to this day, if they had been brought down to watch that body burning underneath that Saracen, would it have changed their minds?

'I can remember photographing that group of people, and in that photograph is possibly the person who shot me some weeks later when I was attending the scene of another ambush, where a young soldier had been shot dead.

'I have often wondered about the person who shot me. In some ways I feel I would like to talk to him. I can understand that he went out, he shot me, I was part of the establishment. He treated me as just game. But the following day, when he read in the paper that my mother dropped dead at the side of my bed, after she had rushed over to the hospital, what went through his mind? Did he think, good! I've got two for the price of one? Or did he show some remorse, and think, well, I'm sorry, that shouldn't have happened – I didn't mean his mother to die as a result of what I done?

'He is out there somewhere today. He is living a life. Is it normal? Does he still justify what he done? Does he think back, and say to himself, how did it help the cause of republicanism by doing what I done?

'It's still a very confusing part of my life. I can remember being taken in the ambulance to Newry Hospital. The rest of it is a blank. I was transferred to the Royal Victoria Hospital. I was unconscious for some time. It's something I cannot even come to terms with. I can't sit down and talk to my father about it. It's just too emotional. It wouldn't do any of us any good to relive it.

'I am asked often about forgiveness – but I could never forgive. The people who done that, they have to earn my forgiveness, or if there is a God up there, he will tell me if it is right to forgive or not, but personally I will not forgive or forget what happened, how this family was broken up in those early days. My memories are of leaving the house to go back to Crossmaglen, of leaving my mother and having a joke, and saying to her, "I'll see you in a couple of weeks." Little did I realise that it would be a year later before I could even visit her grave, and try to get on with a normal life.

'I spent over nine months in hospital. The first five or six months was spent lying still. I wasn't allowed to be moved. I had to lie on a special bed because of severe spinal injuries. This was so that the bone and the spinal column could be given time to heal, or for new bone to grow. In those early days I was in and out of consciousness. I was on drugs, and it was a very confusing time in my life.

'I was left with complete paralysis of my left leg, and chronic pain. I still have two bullets embedded in my spine. Those cannot be removed. I am left in a situation at the moment where I take morphine daily, to kill the pain. I still think of having my paralysed leg amputated. My leg is useless without the calliper. I have met another person who was in a similar situation, and he had his leg amputated at the knee, so that he could wear one of these new artificial limbs which are designed to give you more spring in your walking action. It's not a decision that you could take lightly, and I don't think doctors could advise on it.

'I was maybe a two-minute headline on the news. If you are dead, you get a few more days, your funeral is covered, and you're in the spotlight a little longer, but if you've been injured the general public just assume, OK, they've been injured, but they're alive. However, being alive can mean surviving without limbs.

'Recently one of our members, who is badly disabled and sits in a wheelchair, said, "Could death be all that bad?" and that made me wonder. It made me think of just how frustrating it must be for him to sit in that wheelchair. He has got a highly active mind. He must be frustrated at not being able to do things that other people are doing, and for him to question whether death is so bad – that summed it up for me.

'I was injured in 1972 and from then until the formation of the Disabled Police Officers' Association, I was out on my own. So some of us got together, and in late 1982 we decided right, why not? Let's form the Disabled Police Officers' Association, so we had a few meetings. We decided, in the early days, to have a couple of barbecues and a Christmas dinner, and when we met we suddenly realized that there were problems that people had not even thought about. Problems with disabled living, problems with DHSS benefits: one lad who had lost two legs wasn't entitled to mobility allowance. All these things came to the fore, and suddenly we had these problems to deal with.

'In the early days I would have gone into someone's house unannounced, just simply rapped on the door, and I was either admitted, or told, "Sorry, he's in bed," or "He's not in the mood to see you." That was seeing a disabled person in the true light. Grown-up men sitting in the corner crying, maybe hadn't shaved for a week, had just lost interest in life. I would have little sympathy. Sympathy is no good. There's too many people around who'll pat you on the head and patronize you, or who'll tell you how good you are at coping with disability.

'It annoys me greatly that, at this present time, politicians can stand up and admit mistakes were made in relation to the old boys who survived the First and Second World Wars. I don't want to be remembered in fifty years' time. I don't want some politician standing up and saying, "Yes, the victims of the Troubles should not have been forgotten about." If they want to do something for us, let them do it now, when we can appreciate it, not when we are dead and gone.'

On 23 October 1993 two members of the IRA, dressed in white coats, entered Frizzell's fish shop on the Shankill Road, carrying a bomb. The Ulster Defence Association's Shankill headquarters was in offices above the shop, and the IRA wrongly believed that the UDA leadership was upstairs, holding a meeting. One of the IRA men, 23-year-old Thomas 'Bootsy' Begley, placed the bomb on the shop's counter. The intention was to order the customers out at gunpoint, and to set the device to detonate once the shop was empty. The plan failed. As Begley primed the bomb, it exploded prematurely. The building collapsed. Nine innocent Protestants, including two people who were walking past the shop, were killed. Begley died instantly. Sean Kelly, the other bomber, survived. The UDA's retaliation was predictable and brutal. On the night before Halloween two masked gunmen wearing boilersuits entered the Rising Sun bar in Greysteel, a quiet village on the banks of Lough Foyle. One of the gunmen shouted, "Trick or treat!" before opening fire. Forty-five shots were fired. Seven Catholics, aged between 19 and 81, were killed. In the course of that week twenty-three people were killed in Northern Ireland.

Alan McBride's wife, Sharon, a 29-year-old mother, was killed by the Shankill bomb. She was the daughter of Desmond Frizzell, the owner of the fish shop. I met Alan at the WAVE Trauma Centre in Belfast, where he now works as manager.

'The twenty-third of October 1993 was a beautiful day, so it was. I'd got up, and it was my wife's turn to work in her father's fish shop, and I was going to go along the Lagan on my bike, cycling with my daughter. At about two o'clock a friend called round to say that there'd been a bomb on the Shankill, and did I want to come down and see if Sharon was OK?

'Growing up in Belfast, bombs, shootings, and killings were happening all the time, and I suppose you just never thought that it was going to be anybody belonging to you, so I went down there more to pacify him than myself. The shop – where it had been – just wasn't there. It was a pile of rubble. People were picking through rubble looking for bodies and stuff. Sharon and her father were killed that day. I was asked later on whether I recognized items that were taken from their bodies, and of course I did. Just telling Zoe that her mother had died was difficult, and not being able to go near a church, because I felt that angry with God. I just didn't know why – *why us?*

'For the first couple of years I was chasing Gerry Adams round Dublin Airport, Washington, and Boston. There's old footage on TV archives of me confronting these people. I was writing letters to Sinn Féin, taking a very public stance against what they were doing. I mean, Gerry Adams carried the coffin of Thomas Begley, the person who planted the bomb that killed my wife.

'So for me it was a very personal thing. I had been thinking about that big question – why? – and thinking about my own upbringing, and thinking about sectarianism. About two years on, I came to the conclusion – and this was a big breakthrough for me – that the young people that murdered my wife, they were young, they were only 19 years old at the time, if they had lived elsewhere and not been part of this environment, they probably wouldn't have done the things they did. It was very convenient sometimes for us to just blame the paramilitaries for all the trouble.

'Now, in saying that, I think that they have to share their responsibilities. I grew up in the Westland, a segregated Protestant community, but I didn't go out and kill anybody. So I think the people that did the killing should absolutely be in jail, but it's just too easy to escape the bigger question for me which is around the society that was created. You have to look at the fact that since the Unionists took power in the 1920s, they abused that power, and they created a situation which was highly discriminatory.

'I was speaking at a hunger-strike commemoration a few years back with another unionist, and somebody asked him whether, if the majority of the people wanted a united Ireland, would he as a democrat, live with it? The guy said it would depend on what jurisdiction you were talking about. If the majority of the people of *Northern Ireland* wanted a united Ireland, then, yes, he would live with that, because Northern Ireland was his country. But if the majority of people on *the island of Ireland* wanted to unite, then he would have problems with that, because that's not the country that he lives in. Well, I thought that this was like playing with loaded dice, because he knows the answer to his question. It's going to take some years, if it ever happens, for the Catholics to be in the majority in the north of Ireland. It will never happen, in fact. That's why the state of Northern Ireland was created – to produce a permanent Protestant majority. It's easy to be a democrat when you know the outcome of an election.

'When I was growing up I never ever thought about discrimination. As a young lad I was going, "Frigging right! Give them as little as we can. If you go into our public spaces and look for anything remotely connected with Irishness in terms of statues and memorials, you'll find that everything's very British Imperialistic. Anything that the republicans or nationalists have wanted, like protection for the Irish language, or the Interpretative Centre at the Maze Prison, things which actually tell their own history, have always been opposed by the unionists, who've been dominant. They're still dominant.

'I've done a lot of work with Catholic and Protestant kids and we talk through this whole issue around identity. Catholics, by and large, could write down ten things off the top of their heads about what's good to be Irish. They'll talk about the language, the music, the culture, the various traditions, the Gaelic Athletic Association … You do the same activity with the young Protestants, and ask them, "What does it mean to be British?" And they haven't a notion. They don't know what it means to be British. They don't know. Then you ask them, "What's good about being a loyalist?" and they'll talk about 12 July, the eleventh night, two days in the year. They can tell you what they're not – they're not Catholics, they're against that. My dad would say that it's about being loyal to the Queen, but even that, what's it about?

'My dad was a member of the UDA. I don't know that he ever killed anybody. He has certainly never told me that he did. He was in the UDA when they were a legal organisation, and they were involved in vigilantism, bus runs for old people, stuff like that. My father joined an organisation that patrolled the streets, checked driving licences, stopped people coming into the area. They looked almost like a police force. Some of the people who joined up in those days, progressed into the ranks of the UFF, and ended up killing. You see, these things go through small stages. They don't go straight from A to D. The UDA came onto the streets in the early 1970s, stopping people with road blocks, but that gathered momentum and, by the late Seventies, they were going out murdering Catholics.

'At one time they were rational people – but as the conflict grew and developed, sectarian killings started to happen. It became 'tit for tat' killings – a Catholic killed one night, a Protestant the next. On quite a number of occasions, it was actually their Catholic neighbours or their Protestant work mates that set them up to be killed. You always had to watch what you said, even if you were just a normal civilian. If you didn't know someone, there was no way that you would have told them what your father worked at. And even now, you still sort of say to yourself, "Who can I trust?"

'I can honestly say that in the Protestant community, I don't remember any occasion, if an innocent Catholic was killed, that there was widespread rejoicing in the community. I never remember that happening. But there was no deep sense of remorse either. I think it was just, "So what? That's the way it goes, they got one of ours, we got one of theirs." And the politicians, of course, were stoking up the fires. The Shankill bomb, and then what happened at Greysteel the week after, was a watershed. I mean, obviously, I lost my wife in that bomb, and people who lost their loved ones in other atrocities would say that theirs was the line in the sand, but the Shankill bomb and Greysteel were two of the last high-profile attacks before the first IRA ceasefire. We were at the beginning of the end when that happened. I think that people had just come to say, "Enough's enough." It wasn't going anywhere. The British weren't winning, the IRA weren't winning, and what we came up with was the Belfast Agreement which has produced where we're at the moment.

'Within republicanism, I think they have gone down the road of rewriting history almost, whether it be through truth commissions or other processes, trying to undo the fact that in the eyes of many, many people, they were sectarian themselves. They're trying to put more of the blame onto the British government's policies in Ireland. I think that's fair, in that it's all part of conflict resolution to try to claim some merit in what you were doing. That said, Jackie McMullan [ex-IRA prisoner and hunger striker] wrote a remarkable piece for *An Phoblacht* [Sinn Féin's official newspaper] a couple of years back where he was basically asking the IRA to own up to the fact that it wasn't a clean war, it was a dirty war, and that a lot of the things that the IRA did were not good. There was no glory in them. I think that was a very honest appraisal, because when you talk to many republicans, you would think that they never did anything wrong in the conflict. You would think that the only problem here was the British, and that the only people they ever killed were soldiers and policemen. And nowadays, if you talk to Irish republicans in America who left here a few years ago, they have a romantic take on what it was like.

'But there are all sorts of hierarchies that exist; there has been a lot of talk of a recognition payment of £12,000 to be given to all the victims of the Troubles in Northern Ireland. But for me the issue is very simple – guilt and innocence. If you take the Shankill bomb as an example; my wife and Thomas Begley, who was the bomber, both died. At one level me and Mrs Begley have both lost someone in the conflict, so our pain, I imagine, is comparable. But her son murdered my wife, so to put them on the same page, in terms of their guilt or innocence, is offensive to me.

'But there are also hierarchies around high-profile killings and ones which were less high-profile. I think this is a hierarchy which we need to combat and to stand against, because it's not fair. People always remember the Shankill bomb and Greysteel, but they often forget the fact that there were two council workers killed in Kennedy Way, two brothers killed in County

Armagh, and two others also killed, that same week. It was a very bad week in Northern Ireland. Their families, of course, will always remember those people, but in terms of media attention, they are seldom remembered.

'Media attention is a double-edged sword, to be honest with you. At one level the atrocity that killed my wife will never be forgotten. In fact her family name will never be forgotten, because the bomb was in her father's shop. And there is some comfort in that for me. But at the same time there is something healthy about trying to forget. I don't mean as in not remembering, but in allowing yourself to move on. And when these atrocities are continually brought up, even like what you are doing now with this book, it does sort of regurgitate the whole thing. I mean, when I got remarried, ten or eleven years after the bomb, the front page of a newspaper had "Shankill Widower Married". That's what people know me from, d'you know, so there is a kind of disempowerment.

'But the answer is not to say, "Well, we were all hurt and we were all involved," because that's nonsense. There's people who come in here that were hurt very severely. I work with a wee injured group, and one of them said, "Look, we're all victims!" "How can you say that?" I asked. I sit in the room here with people with no legs, people with no arms, people who have mental disorders, people who have lost loved ones. How can you compare them with the person who had to spend a few extra hours getting to work because of a bomb scare? All of our experiences are not comparable, so this idea that we have *all* suffered and we are *all* victims isn't right.

'Of course, I recognize that had we all grown up and lived elsewhere in the United Kingdom, then we probably would have been OK. But it rings very hollow to me when people try to dismiss other people's pain by saying that we're all hurting, we're all victims. Apart from anything else, there have been people who have made quite a bit of money out of the Troubles. People who have no vested interest in ever seeing it come to an end; people in the security services, in the prison services, or in insurance companies. So it's not as simple as just saying that we are all in the same place.

'If somebody phones us up, here at WAVE, and says, "Look, my husband was killed in … and I would love to speak to his killer," then we would go to one of the political representatives of the paramilitary organisations, and say, "Look, this person has requested … would they meet?" More often than not, the perpetrator is willing to come in and sit down and discuss things. They are usually in a very different place from wherever they carried out that murder – but that can be hard for the families. Because they think they are coming in with a demon, a real devil, and then they see someone who could be living next door to them, who, in another life, they probably could have been friends with. It's that ordinariness that sometimes the families find difficult. It might be easier if the person is just a monster.

'Of the killers I've met, most of them would regret the fact that they killed for their cause. But they would also argue that there was no other way. I would challenge that – and I *have* challenged it – but it doesn't mean to say you can't have a relationship of sorts with these people. When I look back now on Gerry Adams's decision to carry the coffin of Thomas Begley, I see it was a very difficult call. If he hadn't done it, it would have looked as though he was blaming Sean Kelly and Thomas Begley for the Troubles. In a sense he was trying to show solidarity for these people, whilst saying publicly that the Shankill bomb was a mistake. But, of course, he said that because there was innocent people killed. It's very different from saying that he's sorry for it. In a sense it was a sort of suicide bomb – only the person that carried it didn't realize that he was a suicide bomber.'

ACKNOWLEDGEMENTS

I have a lot of people to thank. They include people who made me feel welcome in a strange place (strange as in unfamiliar ...), people who put me in touch with others, people who agreed to be interviewed, people who attempted to clear up my considerable confusion, people who read through passages of text, people who assisted me with transcription, the list goes on. I am nervous about forgetting anybody, and if I do, I hope I'll be forgiven ...

So – my thanks to the following: Vicky Thomas, Christine Foley, E-quip Business Solutions, David and Judy Lindsay, Katie Lindsay, Bobbie Hanvey, Ronan McNamara, Carol Lynn Toland, Menachem and Ruth Brackman, Ronnie and Shoshanna Appleton, Chris Shaw, Trisha McGee, Louise Dean, Andrea Catherwood, Peter and Joan Pyne, Matthew McCreary, Gerry Foster, Adrian Callan, Alan McBride, Andy Park, Billy Moore, Brendan Duddy, Dominic Bonner, Patrick Magee, Dr. Raman Kapur, Alistair Little, Jo Berry, Joe Graham, John Kelly, Ken Bloomfield, Peter Sheridan, Ralph Burrows, William McKee, Anna Lo, Bob Stewart, David Johnston, Denys Rowan Hamilton, Jim Campbell, Gordon Corrigan, Jim Wells, Mark McCrum, the late Richard Ferguson, Peter Hart, Nick Perry, Andy Tyrie, Tony Henderson, John and Nancy Yates, Jonathan Munby, Antoinette Herron, Anne Faul, Michael Cooper, Carrie Twomey, Paddy

Piper, Kevin Carson, Fra McCann, Ken McGilloway, Max Arthur, Meekal Hashmi and Mishal Husain, Bill Emlyn Jones, Lionel Levine, Judy Levine, Kim Levine, Duncan Neale, Mike Wood, Suzy Klein, Simon Frumkin, Dorothy Sahm, Harry Mount, Osian Barnes, Bridget Fallon, Malcolm Rushton, Michael Sparkes, Charles Malpass, Orlando Wells. I am grateful to others who have declined to be identified. And I would like to thank Claire Price for her support and enthusiasm over many, many months.

On the publishing side, I would like to thank Louise Stanley, Kirstie Addis, Steven Burdett, Craig Adams, Iain MacGregor and Hannah MacDonald at Collins. Thanks also to Jim Gill at United Agents. I have received assistance from a number of libraries and research institutions. In Belfast, the Linen Hall Library and the Irish Republican History Museum. In Dublin, the Military Library at the Cathal Brugha Barracks. In Derry, the Apprentice Boys Memorial Hall and the Museum of Free Derry. In London, the British Library, the London Library, the Sound Archive at the Imperial War Museum, and the Department of Research and Information Services at the Royal Air Force Museum.

This book has been a pleasure to research and write. One of my aims has been to steer as objective a course as possible through a world of subjective passions and emotions. I hope I have succeeded. Any errors and omissions are, of course, my responsibility and nobody else's.

Finally, I have just learned of the passing of John Beresford-Ash. John and his wife Agnès showed me great kindness and hospitality during the writing of this book. I was very lucky to meet him.

Joshua Levine
April 2010

INDEX